Aging and the Environment

M. Powell Lawton is Director of Behavioral Research at the Philadelphia Geriatric Center. He is an environmental and clinical psychologist whose research has evaluated a number of issues in housing, institutional care, and neighborhood problems of the aged.

Paul G. Windley is Professor in the Department of Architecture at Kansas State University. He was an original organizer of the conference that produced these chapters. His research has dealt with the environmental aspects of aging and mental health in small-town and rural areas.

Thomas O. Byerts is Director of the University of Illinois Gerontology Center and Associate Professor of Architecture, Chicago Circle Campus. He directed the Gerontological Society's research-stimulation and information-dissemination program on housing and environment and is now studying congregate housing and barrier-free design.

Contributors

John Archea
Architecture Department
Georgia Institute of Technology
Atlanta, Georgia

Alton De Long, Ph.D.
School of Architecture
University of Tennessee
Knoxville, Tennessee

William Ittelson, Ph.D.
Department of Psychology
University of Arizona
Tucson, Arizona

Eva Kahana, Ph.D.
Department of Sociology
Wayne State University
Detroit, Michigan

Leon A. Pastalan, Ph.D.
School of Architecture and Design
University of Michigan
Ann Arbor, Michigan

Amos Rapoport, A. M.
School of Architecture
University of Wisconsin
Milwaukee, Wisconsin

Kermit Schooler, Ph.D.
Dean, School of Social Work
Syracuse University
Syracuse, New York

Jerry Weisman, Ph.D.
Division of Man-Environment
  Relations
Pennsylvania State University
University Park, Pennsylvania

Aging and the Environment
Theoretical Approaches

Gerontological Monograph Number 7 of the Gerontological Society

M. Powell Lawton, Ph.D.
Paul G. Windley, Arch.D.
Thomas O. Byerts, A.I.A., M.Arch.

Editors

SPRINGER PUBLISHING COMPANY
NEW YORK

Springer Publishing Company, Inc.
200 Park Avenue South
New York, New York 10003

82 83 84 85 86 / 10 9 8 7 6 5 4 3 2 1

Library of Congress Cataloging in Publication Data

Main entry under title:

Aging and the environment.

   (Gerontological monograph no. 7 of the Gerontologi-
cal Society)
   Includes bibliographical references and index.
   1. Gerontology — Addresses, essays, lectures.
2. Man — Influence of environment — Addresses, essays,
lectures.   3. Human ecology — Addresses, essays,
lectures.   I. Lawton, M. Powell (Mortimer Powell).
II. Windley, Paul G.   III. Byerts, Thomas O.
IV. Series: Gerontological monograph . . . of the
Gerontological Society ; no. 7.
HQ1061.A4572   305.2′6   81-21236
ISBN 0-8261-3760-1   AACR2
ISBN 0-8261-3761-X (pbk.)

Printed in the United States of America

CONTENTS

PREFACE

This book is intended for two major audiences: those interested in person-environment interactions and gerontologists. A wide variety of disciplines make their contributions under these rubrics, including environmental psychology, social psychology, sociology, architecture, planning, public administration, and others. The content of this volume deals with environments inhabited by older people; the person side of the behavioral system is represented by the older person. Because of the inevitable changes in sensory acuity, psychomotor speed, mobility, and social roles with age, the older person becomes more reliant on the physical environment. In many instances, however, the environment on which the older person depends is dysfunctional. For both the researcher and the designer, the instances of environmental match and mismatch, if examined within a more general theoretical framework, are highly instructive and pave the way toward improving the environment for people of all ages.

Therefore, the reader should not feel that the book is only about older people. Perhaps to a greater extent than has been true in other content areas, gerontologists have been among the pioneers in advancing the general study of person-environment relations. This book focuses on theory, thus, by definition, it establishes a far wider base than one targeted population group. The authors have used the older person as an example rather than as purely a target group. Thus it seems clear that environmentalists with interests as diverse as designing for children, designing for people in rural areas, designing for transportation systems, doing research, or developing theory in any of these areas, should find highly relevant material in this volume.

The beginnings of this volume were inspired by the perceptiveness of Carl Eisdorfer, now President, Montefiore Hospital and Medical Center, New York, and Jessie Gertman, then at the Administration on Aging, U.S. Department of Health, Education, and Welfare. In 1971, with Dr. Eisdorfer as Principal Investigator and Mrs. Gertman as Project Officer, the Gerontological Society began to conduct a series of two project grants lasting seven years on Environments and Aging.

The purpose of this project was to mobilize interest in both research on and the design of the environments primarily inhabited by older people. The project endeavored to mobilize the interests of the broad interdisciplinary constituencies mentioned above in identifying and disseminating relevant research knowledge, encouraging its use in design practice, and in stimulating further research. Practitioners in both the design and service areas were major targets of the project, as well as educators concerned with training future personnel in these areas. Policymakers also figured prominently in all the project's activities.

One type of activity was the convening of a number of conferences and workshops for the multidisciplinary discussion and critique of relevant areas. Some of these topics included national housing policy, the rural aged, human engineering and product design, urban planning and the aged, and architectural education.

The present collection of chapters grew out of one such conference. It was originally organized by Paul G. Windley, Thomas O. Byerts, and Gene Ernst, and it dealt with theory development in environment and aging. This conference, sponsored by the Gerontological Society project and co-sponsored by Kansas State University, was the first concerned with theory as such. Therefore, in addition to bringing together gerontologists with an interest in theory, a number of eminent investigators in the more general field of person-environment relations were invited to prepare papers relating their own orientations to the core theoretical issues. This effort had the dual purpose of exposing aging and environment theory to the mainstream of environment and behavior and the converse.

Following the meeting, a lengthy cycle of critiques, revisions, and further elaborations occurred. Some of the material contained in this volume was included in a sourcebook of concepts in environment and aging that was used and tested in a number of architectural school curricula throughout the country. Another cycle of critical feedback occurred prior to the final revisions of the chapters that appear in this volume.

Throughout the first six years of this two-phase project of the Gerontological Society, Thomas O. Byerts, an editor of this volume, was its Director. During the final year, when design school curricula were the focus of the project's effort, Paul Taylor served as Project Director for the Gerontological Society. Carl Eisdorfer not only initiated the project but served as Chair of the Steering Committee for the first five years. His creative inspiration was embedded at all phases and has in some way influenced every chapter in this volume. The original Steering Committee also included Sandra C. Howell, Leon A. Pastalan, M. Powell Lawton, and Rosalind Lindheim. The succeeding Steering Committee was composed of Leon A. Pastalan (Chair), Michael Bednar, Sandra C. Howell, Joseph A. Koncelik, Victor Regnier, and Paul G. Windley.

The steady support of both the Administration on Aging and the Gerontological Society was essential to the success of the project and to the completion of this book. Special acknowledgement must be given to Stephen Cutler, Editor for Behavioral and Social Sciences of *Gerontological Monographs*, for his work in behalf of this publication.

M.P.L.
P.G.W.
T.O.B.

Introduction

M. POWELL LAWTON
PAUL G. WINDLEY
THOMAS O. BYERTS

AN ORIENTATION TO THEORY
IN ENVIRONMENT AND AGING

This first published collection of chapters dealing with theory in man-environment relations[1] and aging begs two major questions: Where has theory led us thus far? and Where should it take us now? Answering the first question requires us to look at the discipline of man-environment relations (MER) as a whole, rather than to its application to the elderly alone, because theoretical advances in the mainstream of MER will usually be applicable to gerontology. MER is a relatively new science (modern MER being considerably younger than gerontology, for example), and one must search extensively to find material that genuinely qualifies as theory. It seemed extremely important, therefore, to anchor the application to gerontology within the larger MER arena. To that end this volume begins with Ittelson's discussion of some of the value judgments implied by a theory of person and environment (Chapter 2). An example of a specific theoretical orientation is offered in De Long's view of environment as communication (Chapter 3). While it would have been desirable to include similar treatments of a number of other systematic approaches to MER, space limitations precluded that alternative. In place of such extended treatment of many theories, the two chapters that conclude this book take a sweeping view of a variety of approaches to organizing knowledge regarding the way in which people interact with their environments. Both Rapoport (Chapter 9) and Archea (Chapter 10) have contributed a great deal over a period of years to the growth of MER, and their chapters, in different ways, complete the process of sketching some of the major bases for theories of MER. Their chapters not only fill in the holes left by the necessary omission of general treatments

---

[1]The phrase "man-environment" and corresponding masculine pronouns have been used throughout this volume as a stylistic convention. It is hoped that this usage will be considered gender-neutral by the reader.

1

of a number of theoretical approaches, but more importantly, they begin the process of telling where gerontological MER theory has been and where it needs to go. Thus, these two final chapters perform an integrating function for both general and gerontological MER theory.

AN ORIENTATION TO THEORY IN MER

The chapters comprising the first section of this volume may be viewed in the perspective of other theoretical work in MER. While considerable elaboration has occurred since the publication of Preiser's (1973) collection of essays on the theory of man-environment relations, it still remains one of the best introductions to this area. In one of these essays Altman (1973) set the stage by calling our attention to three directions in which the "psyches" of MER types might be oriented.

1. An orientation to the design process, where progressive steps in the process include programming, design, construction, use, and post-construction evaluation. Clearly, this orientation is toward a product and the production requires the synthesis of knowledge from a wide variety of sources (for example, climatology, land use, engineering, human needs, interior decorating, and so on). Evaluating the product and feeding this information back into the stream of the design process for later products thus uses the new knowledge produced.

2. An orientation to place, where psychological and behavioral processes are incidentally studied as they may relate to the outcomes of, behavior in, or adjustment to places such as cities, neighborhoods, hospitals, homes, and so on. The applied researcher is the major actor in the place-oriented arena, concerned as he is with maximizing the quality of the outcome, whether it be civic pride, neighborhood satisfaction, security in one's dwelling, or whatever. The knowledge produced is thus used directly to improve quality of life for people in similar places.

3. An orientation toward environmental processes, for example environmental cognition, territorial behavior, crowding, etc. The basic MER researcher, Altman suggests, is more interested in these processes, in testing out the effect of independent variables on behavior (or psychological processes) of any kind. Understanding of the general effects of these processes, independent of the places where they occur, is sought. This approach is basically an analytic task, as opposed to the synthetic approach associated with the design process.

In considering this very useful tripartite division of approaches to MER, it seems to us that the pursuit of knowledge characterizes all three approaches, no one more than any other. The designer's product may be judged in terms of the extent to which it meets the stated or implicit goals of the program. Knowledge of the quality outcomes associated with the properties of places is fed back into the reconstruction or new design of other places. Environmental processes have determinable general or specific effects on places or products as well as having predictive value for the understanding of behavior without regard to application.

In contrast, the relevance of the three approaches to theory moves in the order from the product (least relevant), to place, to environmental process (most relevant). The function of theory is weakest in the phase of description (design phase), moderately strong in explanation (place), and strongest in prediction (environmental process).

The present volume, by its explicit focus on theory, largely ignores design. Place, on the other hand, is rather important in a number of the chapters. Lawton (Chapter 3) adopts primarily the place perspective in much of his research, though the elements of his model tend toward the environmental process. Three of the gerontological theory chapters deal extensively with places, at least as the exemplars of their more generalized analyses of environmental processes: Kahana uses the institution (Chapter 7), Schooler (Chapter 6) the dwelling unit in the ordinary community, and Pastalan (Chapter 8) treats relocation and adaptation to the institutional and residential environment. Thus, only three of the substantive chapters (Rapoport's and Archea's being considered integrative) deal relatively purely with environmental processes: De Long's on environment as communication (Chapter 2), Windley's on environmental ability as an intrapersonal mediator of transactional processes (Chapter 4), and Weisman's on environmental perception and cognition (Chapter 5).

The study of MER has developed as an intensely multidisciplinary effort, and the group of people presently involved in advancing its further development is still small enough to allow the continuation of intensive dialogue that creatively mixes the elements of design, place, and process. Thus, in other theoretical treatments from the Preiser (1973) symposium, Altman's (1973) social systems ecological model, Esser's (1973) neurobehavioral model, Studer's (1973) technological interventionist position, Willems' (1973) psychological ecology model, and Wohlwill's (1973) psychophysical parallelism, one can easily detect the same blend of design, place, and process that is presented in this volume.

GERONTOLOGY AND ENVIRONMENTAL PROCESSES

MER as applied to later life is slightly younger than MER in general, and the development of theory in gerontology or lifespan development is still relatively primitive. Looking, for example, at most of the chapters in the predecessor to this volume (Byerts, Pastalan, and Howell, 1979) or at the first textbook in environment and aging (Lawton, 1980), the emphasis is strongly on place (cities, rural areas, housing projects, institutions, and so on), with design being as yet only marginally integrated and process being relatively absent.

An explanation for place predominance is easy to find. Whether we are concerned citizens or researchers, it is those older people who are in trouble in particular places who strike our attention: the isolated, lonely live-alone; the inner-city resident afraid to walk in her neighborhood; the suburban elderly, grown old in a location with few goods and services; the poor rural resident without emergency resources; the resident of the substandard nursing home; the involuntarily evicted renter in an old neighborhood experiencing regentrification; and so on, at great length.

For these people in need, the applied social researcher has been very valuable in producing hard knowledge relevant to the betterment of their lifestyles. And the best applied research has often been directed by a strong theoretical orientation (Lowenthal, 1964; Rosow, 1967; Bengtson, 1975). However, Pastalan (Chapter 8) advances the idea that theory should be incidental or secondary as compared to the more important mission orientation of social research. Thus, Pastalan offers an alternative to theory which is right in the mainstream of much gerontological research: Having chosen a specialized, location-specific, and often deprived target population for study, it is entirely understandable how the gerontological researcher may view the mission aspect of his work as primary. Nonetheless, the thrust of the entire book conveys the message that better theory will, in fact, lead both to better missions and better design. At present, the void is greater in theory than in design and the place-related mission. Let us pause for a moment over the examples that Altman (1973) gives of environmental processes: privacy, territory, personal space, and crowding. Similarly, among a series of issues that Rapoport (1973) named as requiring consideration by any theory were the nature and meaning of space, complexity, crowding, density, privacy, and environment as communication. As one looks at later works on MER, one might add that most of the books dealing with the behavioral aspects of environment also maintain this emphasis on process (Altman, 1975; Mehrabian & Russell, 1974; Moore & Golledge, 1976; Wapner, Cohen, & Kaplan, 1976). Others have broadened the scope to include concerns with the effects of places and processes that are less strictly psychological (Holahan, 1978; Mehrabian, 1976).

One is immediately struck with how MER research in gerontology has avoided most of these issues. A handful of reports have appeared on privacy (Lawton & Bader, 1970; Kiyak, Kahana, & Fairchild, 1977), territoriality (Lipman, 1968; De Long, 1970), communication (De Long, 1974), personal space (Watson & Maxwell, 1977), cognitive mapping (Regnier, 1976), and complexity (Sterns, 1971), while virtually nothing has appeared in the literature on crowding. The most general aspects of environmental cognition have been addressed by descriptive, design- or place-oriented research (Carp, 1976; Lawton & Nahemow, 1979) and occasionally in the terms of connotative meaning (Jirovec, 1977). However, these scattered studies are merely tesserae in the larger mosaic; if these issues constitute the true "stuff" of environment and behavior theory, then gerontology is indeed lacking.

Rapoport's (1973) list of issues to be grappled with does contain others than those quoted above: how people use space; environmental preference; evaluation of environments; the effects of the environment on people generally; and analyses of specific environments. This second list of Rapoport thus brings us back into the familiar arena where most gerontological MER research has been concentrated — issues that, to be sure, are relevant to and must be squared with any particular theory, but nonetheless issues whose relevance to design and to place is more immediately evident than their relevance to theory.

Returning to the gerontological chapters in this book, some of the basic processes are discussed by Weisman (Chapter 5 on environmental cognition, cognitive mapping), Lawton (Chapter 3 on complexity, environmental cognition, information processing), Schooler (Chapter 6 on environmental cognition), and Kahana (Chapter 7 on privacy, complexity, territoriality), but it is clear that these issues are for the most part either insufficiently analyzed and integrated into the larger theoretical model or are simply utilized in the models without benefit of empirical testing in tandem with other components of the model. This observation leads us to two alternative conclusions. First, that the fragmented nature of these current efforts is due to the early state of development of theory building rather than to the lack of relevance of these issues to the elderly. Or, second, that these issues are really less salient to the elderly. Pursuing the latter point, one could, perhaps, make some supporting assertions. For example, perhaps the external (objective) environment is so depriving or threatening to the older person that this threatening quality overshadows the possible effect of idiosyncratic cognitive constructions of that environment. Perhaps decreased sensory acuity leads to higher thresholds for privacy or crowding, so that these spatial concerns go unnoticed by the elderly.

One could go on, but in the absence of positively supporting data for these assertions (of which there are none) and in the presence of the general observation that people do, after all, continue to be people even after age 65, it hardly seems worth our while to suggest that the alternative conclusion has any validity. It is clear that the intrapersonal and microenvironmental processes suggested by Rapoport (Chapter 9) and Altman (1973) deserve our attention if theory in this area is to become more precise and predictive.

While Rapoport scours the theoretical orientations of the six gerontological chapters for the basic models implied by each and finds them grossly lacking in the sociocultural and symbolic models, Archea (Chapter 10) provides a fitting cap for the book as a whole. That is, he first gives a perspective different from that of Rapoport on some underlying models of the environment-behavior interaction, linking each to the mechanisms by which the interaction occurs. He then mines the subject of the relationship between theory and method, making explicit a variety of assumptions in each conceptual approach. The greater part of his effort provides a fitting conclusion to the entire volume. While beginning as a commentary on Pastalan's chapter, Archea carries this topic forward to indicate how the goals of basic and applied research, mission and theory, are interwoven and are not in any way mutually contradictory.

The sweeping panoramas portrayed by both Rapoport and Archea are thus useful in giving us the larger view of where we have been in theory development. Far more important, however, is the armature they have provided for the forms of theories of the future. Their synthesis exposes how little there is now, but gives clear signposts as to how we should proceed.

REFERENCES

Altman, I. Some perspectives on the study of man-environment phenomena. In W. F. E. Preiser (Ed.), *Environmental design research*, Volume 2. Stroudsburg, PA.: Dowden, Hutchinson, and Ross, 1973.

_____. *The environment and social behavior.* Monterey, CA.: Brooks-Cole, 1975.

Bengtson, V. T. Generation and family effects in value socialization. *American Sociological Review*, 1975, *40*, 358–371.

Byerts, T. O., Pastalan, L. A., and Howell, S. C. (Eds.). *The environmental context of aging.* New York: Garland Publishing, 1979.

Carp, F. M. User evaluation of housing for the elderly. *Gerontologist*, 1976, *16*, 102–111.

De Long, A. J. The microspatial structure of the older person. In L. A. Pastalan and D. H. Carson (Eds.), *Spatial behavior of older people.* Ann Arbor: University of Michigan Institute of Gerontology, 1970.

_____. Environments for the elderly. *Journal of Communication*, 1974, *24*, 101–112.

Esser, A. H. Structures of man-environment relations. In W. F. E. Preiser (Ed.), *Environmental design research*. Volume 2. Stroudsburg, PA.: Dowden, Hutchinson, Ross, 1973.

Holahan, C. J. *Environment and behavior: A dynamic perspective.* New York: Plenum Publishing Corporation, 1978.

Jirovec, R. L. Optimal residential environments across the lifespan. Paper presented at the annual meeting of the Gerontological Society, San Francisco, November 1977.

Kiyak, A., Kahana, B., and Fairchild, T. Privacy as a salient aspect of person-environment fit. Paper presented at the annual meeting of the Gerontological Society, San Francisco, November 1977.

Lawton, M. P. *Environment and aging.* Monterey, CA.: Brooks-Cole, 1980.

Lawton, M. P. and Nahemow, L. Social science methods for evaluating the quality of housing for the elderly. *Journal of Architectural Research*, 1979, *7*, 5–11.

Lawton, M. P. and Bader, J. Wish for privacy among young and old. *Journal of Gerontology*, 1970, *25*, 48–54.

Lipman, A. A socio-architectural view of life in three homes for old people. *Gerontologia Clinica*, 1968, *10*, 88–101.

Lowenthal, M. *Lives in distress*. New York: Basic Books, 1964.

Mehrabian, A. *Public places and private spaces*. New York: Basic Books, 1976.

Mehrabian, A. and Russell, J. A. *An approach to environmental psychology*. Cambridge, MA.: MIT Press, 1974.

Moore, G. T. and Golledge, R. G. (Eds.). *Environmental knowing*. Stroudsburg, PA.: Dowden, Hutchinson, and Ross, 1976.

Preiser, W. F. E. *Environmental design research*. Volume 2. Stroudsburg, PA.: Dowden, Hutchinson, and Ross, 1973.

Rapoport, A. An approach to the construction of man-environment theory. In W. F. E. Preiser (Ed.), *Environmental design research*, Volume 2. Stroudsburg, PA.: Dowden, Hutchinson, and Ross, 1973.

Regnier, V. A. Neighborhoods as service systems. In M. P. Lawton, R. J. Newcomer, and T. O. Byerts (Eds.), *Planning for an aging society*. Stroudsburg, PA.: Dowden, Hutchinson, and Ross, 1976.

Rosow, I. *Social integration of the aged*. New York: Free Press, 1967.

Sterns, H. L. The relation of age to experience, mode of evaluation and complexity in visual preference. Unpublished Ph.D. dissertation. Morgantown: West Virginia University, 1971.

Studer, R. G. Man-environment relations: Discovery or design. In W. F. E. Preiser (Ed.), *Environmental design research*, Volume 2. Stroudsburg, PA.: Dowden, Hutchinson, and Ross, 1973.

Wapner, S., Cohen, S. B., and Kaplan, B. (Eds.). *Experiencing the environment*. New York: Plenum Publishing Corporation, 1976.

Watson, W. H. and Maxwell, R. J. *Human aging and dying: A study in cultural gerontology*. New York: St. Martin's Press, 1977.

Willems, E. P. Behavioral ecology as a perspective for man-environment research. In W. F. E. Preiser (Ed.), *Environmental design research*, Volume 2. Stroudsburg, PA.: Dowden, Hutchinson, and Ross, 1973.

Wohlwill, J. F. The environment is not in the head. In W. F. E. Preiser (Ed.), *Environmental design research*, Volume 2. Stroudsburg, PA.: Dowden, Hutchinson, and Ross, 1973.

1

Some Issues Facing
A Theory of Environment and
Behavior

WILLIAM H. ITTELSON

This volume is addressed to theory development, underlining a belief shared by many of us that our most difficult problems stem from the rather inadequate and shaky theoretical base from which we operate and that an adequate theory will quickly lead to the resolution of major issues both methodological and substantive. This chapter will endeavor to discuss some basic issues in environment and behavior. This volume deals explicitly with environments and aging. I shall take this to be a special case of the larger question of environments and behavior and will address my remarks to that context, leaving the explication of specific implications for aging in the able hands of the other authors represented in this volume.

MAN AND ENVIRONMENT — A DICHOTOMY?

Each of us lives and carries out our life's activities in a world that we experience as being separate from us and as having an existence independent of us, although we are in constant interaction with it. The phenomenological separation of self and environment is not an immediate given but is rather an achievement of some magnitude. To students of human development, the attainment of a fully autonomous sense of self is one of the significant features of at least the early stages of development. The mature adult sees himself as being separate from, although interdependent with, a surrounding world.

This dichotomous view of self and environment, so essential for the effective functioning of the individual, becomes a problem when it is uncritically

Source: *Environmental Psychology*, Second Edition, edited by Harold Proshansky, Leanne Rivlin, and William H. Ittelson. Copyright © 1970 by Holt, Rinehart and Winston, Inc. Copyright © 1976 by Holt, Rinehart and Winston. Reprinted by permission of Holt, Rinehart and Winston.

accepted as a premise upon which scientific theories may be erected. Nevertheless, man-environment dichotomy has permeated most of Western thinking about social and scientific problems. It certainly underlies the history of thinking in the behavioral sciences where the primary emphasis has been on the effect of environmental variables on behavior. In psychology both the person and the environment have been conceptualized in a variety of ways, although historically, psychology has tended to stress environmental variables, and the charge of excessive environmentalism is frequently made. Of course, the environment most commonly referred to is not the full-scale environment with which we are here concerned. Most commonly in psychology, at least until quite recently, environment has meant one of three things: It is either the social and interpersonal environment, with scant attention to the physical or the environment as internally represented, or it is a set of discrete external stimuli. All of these aspects may be part of, but are not coextensive with, the full-scale environment toward which studies in environment and behavior are directed. In that context the environment has variously been looked upon as a source of information, as a set of limits or constraints, as a set of behavioral opportunities, as a setting within which behavior occurs, and in a variety of other ways.

My interest at this point is not in the various types of definitions and conceptualizations of the environment, but rather in the underlying assumption that behavior is a product of a complex function of variables related to the individual on the one hand and variables related to the environment on the other hand. This is expressed in a variety of ways, sometimes verbally, sometimes symbolically. However, there is always an implied directionality, often explicitly represented with an arrow, that says that person and environment lead to behavior, and no other combination of the variables is acceptable.

DIFFERING THEORIES ON THE MAN-ENVIRONMENT EQUATION

Exactly how this equation is solved, of course, varies with the period and the investigator. At one extreme, for example, we find complete environmental determinism which grew out of the work of a number of scientists, in particular, geographers and economists in the 1920's who held that a wide range of human behavior is directly and entirely determined by the environmental circumstances within which the behavior occurs. In effect, the person was ruled out of the equation, the environment became the sole determinant, and considerable supporting evidence was assembled. Partly in reaction to extreme environmental determinism, an equally extreme but diametrically opposed position developed, one that claimed that the environment makes absolutely no difference in human behavior and that man's apparently infinite adaptability to circumstances is all one needs to consider. There is probably at least as much plausibility to this position as there is to strict environmental determinism. One can cite masterpieces painted in garrets and treatises written in jail to convince oneself that, while other creatures may be subservient to their environments, man rises above it. But neither of these positions has in fact been acceptable to the majority of the investigators, and today one is much more likely to encounter a presumably more sophisticated approach dedicated to a careful analysis of the parameters, both personal and environmental, as they are encountered in the actual situation.

This brief survey of some of the ways in which environment has been seen as entering into the behavioral equation illustrates the fact that a single underlying assumption runs through them all. Whether one considers the environment to be a set of lifted weights in the psychology laboratories of late nineteenth century Germany or a set of complex environmental displays used in some late twentieth century laboratories, man and environment are seen as being separate, and behavior is the result of some complex relationship involving the two.

There is, however, another direction in which this process quite obviously operates, one that is of particular interest to architecture and the design professions, for example. While it may be true that environments produce behavior, it is certainly true that behaviors produce environments. Conceptions of man, the builder, are equally rooted in the assumption of a man-environment dichotomy, but they look at the process in terms of a different direction — at man's effect on his environment. In so doing they may be touching upon a characteristic that distinguishes man from all his fellow creatures of the earth. Man is, of course, not the only tool-making and tool-using animal, but the way he goes about doing it is qualitatively and quantitatively so different that it has frequently been suggested as one of the specifically defining characteristics of man. Since earliest times, dimly seen through the lens of archeology and paleontology, man has always been the builder. The transformation of man the builder into man the maker of environments has come with such dramatic suddenness in our own time that most of us remain stunned, unable to grasp its significance or cope with its implications.

This bi-directionality of man and environment, then, brings me to the first issue deserving attention. The necessary sense of an autonomous self translated into a world view that dichotomizes man and environment has been re-internalized as a dichotomous man, man the responder to environments on the one hand and man the creator of environments on the other; both of them stand separate from an external environment, which itself is split into aspects that are sources of responses and those that are products of human activity. Two rather different ways of thinking and talking have grown up around these two viewpoints. Man the responder and the environment to which he responds have been treated in what can loosely be labeled the scientific domain of thought, while man the builder and the environment that he builds are encompassed in the general approach of design and technology.

Bridging the Gaps

There have, of course, been attempts to bridge these gaps and to bring dichotomous man back into unity both with himself and with his environment. Thus, those concerned with man the maker of environments have conscientiously tried to make their technology more scientific, both by demanding and using more and better findings from the behavioral sciences and by directing themselves internally toward a more basic analysis of their problems. Bridging theories of great importance have emerged from technological considerations — information theory and systems theory, for example, as well as practices such as technology assessment, which hope also to provide bridges into the presumed scientific study of man.

On the other side, from the behavioral sciences, bridging attempts have stemmed from a variety of directions. The most straightforward has been a simple assertion by definition that man and environment are inseparable. Indulging oneself in holistic definitions of this sort is a favorite pastime of soft-headed psychologists such as myself and frequently calls forth the scorn of our more hard-headed colleagues. Along theoretical lines, bridging attempts most frequently take the form of turning the directional arrow back on itself. This view accepts the premise that person and environment lead to behavior, but then adds that behavior produces new person-environment situations which in turn lead to new behaviors. In this way it develops a feedback model that accounts for both directions of effect.

The study of environment and behavior represents the most recent and ambitious attempt to conceptually and empirically link the two halves of dichotomous man. It involves the joint efforts of behavioral scientists and environmental designers to forge out a new field of study. However, as I have already suggested, the two groups approach this task implicitly accepting the assumption of dichotomous man, and each tries to provide bridging concepts that grow out of ways of thinking which are, in fact, incompatible with each other. The second issue of interest is that this effort is bound for failure, or at best partial and limited success, unless and until the two groups — behavioral scientists and environmental designers — develop ways of thinking about their common problems that embrace both approaches and that are acceptable to both groups.

It would, of course, be comforting to think that this can be accomplished by simply adding the theories and concepts of the two, or perhaps putting them into a blender and coming out with a smooth amalgam which will cover all contingencies. Unfortunately, the behavioral sciences and the design professions will have to face up to the hard fact that such a solution is not available, that in very fundamental ways their modes of thinking about problems are incommensurable. This is certainly not the place to elaborate in detail the relationships and conflicts between science and technology, or even in more limited terms, between behavioral science and environmental design. The scope of the problem can, however, be suggested by simply looking at contrasting criteria for acceptance of the solution to a problem.

In the sciences it is generally agreed that an issue is resolved when an adequate theory is developed. This is no less true in the behavioral sciences, although the theories may be less general and less elegant than in other areas. In short, and skipping all questions of definition and precision, knowledge is expressed in terms of a theory that encompasses the phenomena in question. In contrast, in the design professions and in technology in general, function is the ultimate criterion. If it works it is successful, and successful working is taken as evidence that the designer possessed the requisite knowledge. In the same vein, progress in science, insofar as it can be defined at all, is usually seen in terms of theory replacing theory, that is, a better theory replacing a lesser. Progress in the design field is defined by practice replacing practice, that is, better practice replaces poorer practice. I raise these issues only to suggest that the problem of theory development in our area is considerably more complex than simply learning to talk to each other; indeed, it touches upon some very basic philosophical issues.

Let me illustrate how deep some of these issues run by noting the traditional stance that both science and technology take toward the social uses to which their works are put. This is, of course, the very issue toward which the broader area of environment and aging is directed. It is the supreme paradox of our time that science at the very peak of its power, achievement, and success may well turn out to be the most unsuccessful of all human endeavors. From an evolutionary point of view, it is hard to imagine any other human activity that offers so clear and present a danger to the survival of the species as does contemporary science and its concomitant technology. While making life far better for some individuals, science is clearly raising the possibility of making life impossible for all humans and perhaps for all organisms of any kind. The threat, of course, lies not in a danger to individuals, but in the danger of producing an environment within which life cannot exist. Parenthetically, it is an interesting though rather futile exercise of the imagination to note that, if science does indeed accomplish this result, the fact will never be capable of scientific demonstration, nor indeed will it be a fact at all in any useful sense of the term.

We all know the familiar answer to this implied indictment of science and technology. First of all, the argument runs, one cannot charge science with its good or evil consequences, for science itself is value-free—it is neither good nor bad. It deals only with the search for immutable truths, and if one must assign value to it, it will have to be the same value as truth itself which most people agree is good. In any event, this charge is irrelevant, because the indictment should be aimed not at science, but at technology; technology is separate from science in the sense that science, though dependent on technology, does not produce technology. But, the argument continues, technology is also value-free; technology in itself is neither good nor evil. There may be poor technology in the value sense. Only the human uses in technology result in value effects for better or for worse. The capstone of the argument asserts that the human uses of technology are outside the realm of science or technology. They lie in the areas of politics, of statesmanship, perhaps even of religion. But wherever human uses lie, if people choose to use technology for worse rather than for better, the responsibility is neither that of science nor of technology. Some such argument in essentially this form is subscribed to by both the scientific and design and technological communities. It is also subscribed to by the great majority of statesmen in decision-making positions.

These conclusions, attractive though they may be, are based on the false premise that we in fact know how to accomplish whatever we want to; the plain truth is that we do not. Even the relatively simple problem of choosing among alternative existing technologies frequently proves insurmountable. And the choice of what among possible alternative technologies should be developed in the future is made in almost complete ignorance as to the probable consequences of the various alternatives, except perhaps in the most limited and extreme cases. Of course, choices are made, decisions are taken, but in the absence of adequate knowledge they are inevitably based on short-term economic or political gain. All the changes in social priorities, all the decisions of what we want to accomplish are meaningless if we do not know how to produce environments that will have the desired consequences for human behavior. And, therefore, the issue goes far beyond the question of deciding what to do and reorganizing social priorities in order to accomplish it. For example, social priorities have to a certain extent been altered, and society has given at least a limited mandate to develop adequate environments for the aging. And even in such a relatively restricted area as this we simply do not know how to do it, although we are rapidly learning. With respect to larger-scale issues we are barely scratching the surface. I think we all accept the proposition that a great deal more knowledge is necessary before we are minimally able to design environments that will, within reasonable limits, produce anticipated behavioral consequences, and that one of the necessary components of the subject matter for such study will be the very social, political and moral uses to which environmental design and technology can be applied. The third issue of interest is that we, as students of environment and behavior, push our investigation to its logical limit; we find that we are committing ourselves to a study that neither our scientific and professional colleagues nor our political and economic leaders want us to undertake. It is in fact a revolutionary undertaking in the scientific and perhaps ultimately in the political sense. Since most of us are not revolutionaries, I see a danger that our field of study will not be pushed to its limits and may unfortunately settle for something far short of its potential.

TOWARD A NEW THEORY

One of the major arguments running throughout my remarks to this point is that current difficulties in the study of environment and behavior essentially reduce to questions of theory rather than of method or substance. An adequate theory will replace the concept of dichotomous man rather than simply attempt to bridge the chasm. Such a theory will take as its starting point the inseparability of man and environment and will recognize that neither man nor environment is ever encountered, nor can either be defined independent of the other. Such a theory will inevitably contain elements which are inimical to current approaches both in behavioral science and in the design fields.

I do not mean to suggest that there are no current attempts at such theories. Indeed there are. One can list without any elaboration: ecological theory, systems theory, structural theory, and transactional theory — each has as one of its central assumptions the essential unitary nature of its subject matter. However, I do not believe that any one of these or a combination thereof is as yet adequately worked out for direct application to environment/behavior problems, although my own prejudice is that transactional theory most closely approximates this. Nevertheless, I believe that none of these adequately deals with the fact already referred to that man has become the maker, the creator of his own environment, both on the individual level and on the social level. Recognition that the environment is a human creation, that the environment is artifact, is perhaps the major significant step needed for the development of an adequate theory. To say this, however, is not to imply a nature-versus-artifact dichotomy. To be sure, the environment seen as artifact seems to stand in sharp distinction to the natural world, but as soon as this is said, the internal contradiction becomes apparent. If man and all his products, if technology and its artifacts, are not part of nature, what are they part of? The city may be inhuman, but it cannot be unnatural. Design and technology as human process and building and artifact as human product are part of the natural subject matter for study. They have no other place to go. To say that environment is artifact is tantamount to saying that environment is natural; man and his products are as much a part of nature as are the birds and their nests or the bees and their hives. To recognize man's environment as artifact is, therefore, simultaneously to deny the existence of a natural-versus-manmade dichotomy, and at the same time, to point out the particular directions that the study of human environment must take.

I will not attempt to elaborate the details of a theory approached from this point of view. It is clear, however, that considered as a subject matter for scientific study, the environment as artifact is a rather strange creature. Against the vast and unlimited reaches of nature, the supply of human environment is obviously definitely limited, a concept which has been popularized by the notion of Spaceship Earth. Not only is it limited, but the human environment is also transient and constantly undergoing fundamental change. The subject matter that we study today is not the same as that we studied yesterday. We have long recognized that one never puts one's foot twice in the same stream. The constant change in the human environment raises a much more fundamental issue. There are no functionally equivalent replicas of yesterday's environment for today's study — the grandeur that was Rome, the peasant villages of Vietnam, the beauty of Glen Canyon — all are gone, never to return. The causes of these changes are many and complex, but within the context of this discussion we can note that much of the change is brought about by the very fact that the environment is being studied and understood. In a very basic sense we cannot know the environment without changing it. The traditional subject matter of scientific study is natural, unlimited, unchanging and remote. In place of this the student of environment and behavior faces a subject matter that is man-made, limited, transient, and close enough to be changed by the very process of studying it.

This final characteristic is perhaps the most significant and carries the greatest implications for our study. In contrast to traditional science searching for fixed and immutable laws underlying an eternal and unchanging nature, we are trying to understand a subject matter that is changed through the very process of our studying and knowing it. From the very outset, then, we are faced with a paradox — the more we learn about environment and behavior, the more we change it, and the less we know. Much has been said about the concept of the self-fulfilling prophesy within the behavioral sciences. In the present context, however, it may be profitable to consider a more difficult but potentially more powerful notion that might be called the "self-falsifying hypothesis." To the extent that any hypothesis about the nature of environment and behavior contains elements of validity, it will also contain within it the possibility — indeed, the inevitability — of changing the environment in ways that will ultimately deny the applicability of the original insight. In a fully worked out study of environment and behavior the ultimate test of the validity of a hypothesis may well be its falsification. The hypothesis which is eventually falsified by events contingent upon the existence of that hypothesis was in fact correct.

The reasons for this peculiar state of affairs follow from the fact that in trying to understand environment and behavior we are dealing with contingent rather than lawful relationships, with things that did not have to be the way they are and with future states that cannot be predicted from present conditions. This is not to say that prediction is impossible but to open for study the question of what kinds of predictions can be made. For example, prediction of future states is probably not possible in principle. Knowledge about environment and behavior cannot be achieved independently of human action, and the very knowledge thus obtained is itself contingent on the human activity it engenders.

Environment and Behavior: A Study of Change

The study of environment and behavior, then, is the study of choice, of action, and of change. As illustrations, I will briefly mention two of the many types of choices which can be informed through this study. All environmental changes are probably at least in part irreversible. Some are undoubtedly completely irreversible. At the present state of our knowledge we do not have the information necessary to tell us to what extent we are choosing chains of action that will lead to irreversible changes, except perhaps in the most extreme cases. As our study progresses we will hopefully be able to make finer and finer discriminations of those choices that are forever irreversible from those that are at least potentially modifiable.

Environmental changes also have an impact on the range of possible future choices. Every change both expands and restricts future options. Again, we do not yet know how to tell those changes that result in a sharply restricted range of future possibilities from those that maximize future options. When we can do this it will, at least in principle, be possible to develop a social model that will at regular intervals assess its current situation and redirect change by making choices that will predict the greatest range of alternatives at the end of the next assessment period, and so forth. Whether this or some other model will turn out to be the optimum arrangement, of course, would be one of the subjects of the study itself.

I have suggested that among other things the study of environment and behavior will enable us to tell reversible from irreversible choices and to distinguish actions that will expand future options from those that will restrict them. These considerations lead us to the next issue. What the body politic will choose to do will, of course, not be determined by our study. However, as our knowledge grows, it increasingly becomes our responsibility to inform decision makers of the probable consequences of specific solutions to problems as well as to emphasize the importance of considering as wide a range as possible of alternative solutions. In this way we can bring into active consideration the long-term consequences of optional courses of action, as well as making known the nature and limits of those predictions that can be made and the areas in which long-term prediction is not possible. Our study will thus ensure that those individuals and groups who normally take action through social and political processes will be informed of the probable consequences of their choices in ways that go far beyond current concepts and may alter the very concept of social responsibility.

The study of environment and behavior, then, is the study of change, change not imposed by some external and autonomous force, but change growing out of the natural process within which mankind plays a central role. Man alone of all the many faces of nature on this planet can deliberately and self-consciously choose and direct the process of environmental change. Most of what I have written, and indeed the main thrust of most studies of environment and behavior, is aimed at making those choices more informed and that direction more effective. We already have the capacity for self-destruction. The struggle to acquire the capacity to survive contains within it the necessity of developing new standards for decision, perhaps what Hardin (1972) has called the "new ethics for survival." The ancient dilemma that the individual ethic may not serve the collective good and that the social ethic may violate individual canons of conduct has now been complicated by the recognition that neither may be conducive to global survival. The elaboration of an environment ethic is a pressing need of our time. We in the field of environment and behavior cannot develop the details of such a system of ethics, but we can be aware of the major ethical implications of our work. This, then, is the final issue to which I would draw your attention. A system of ethics implies, indeed demands, knowledge of the consequences of behavior. The work that we do, however small each piece of it may seem, will over time cumulatively provide the knowledge base requisite for the development of an informed environmental ethic, and it must be our hope and faith that such an ethic can exist harmoniously with the individual and social ethics to which we all so deeply subscribe.

SUMMARY AND CONCLUSIONS

To the man-environment dichotomy, so directly derivable from phenomenal experience, has been added a dichotomous view of man, separating man the responder to environments from man the creator of environments. Around each of these views has developed a system of thought and action roughly paralleling the scientific and the technological that is inherited by the student of environment and behavior. Attempts to straddle these dichotomies by providing a variety of bridging concepts and theories offer an immediate and important first step but do not provide an adequate long-range solution; a theory is needed that reunites these two diverse elements of human activity. However, if we pursue this direction to its logical conclusion, we find that we are undertaking a task which in general our fellow citizens have not asked for and do not want. A fully adequate theory of environment and behavior will inevitably contain elements contrary to the prevailing views of the intellectual community. The implications of such a theory both in terms of subject matter and of understanding move into areas presently considered more clearly political in the broad sense of that term. And finally, as knowledge of environment and behavior grows, we recognize the inevitability of developing an environmental ethic that at least potentially may come into conflict with already established ethical systems.

Perhaps these issues really add up to one: The need for knowledge of environment and behavior is clear and pressing. If we in this field do not meet that need future generations may no longer have the opportunity.

REFERENCE

Hardin, G. *Exploring new ethics for survival.* New York: Viking, 1972.

2
Synthesis and Synergy: Developing Models in Man-Environment Relations

ALTON J. De LONG

REDEFINITION VERSUS REDISCOVERY

In writing on metatechnology, William M. Austin, the late linguist, related prediction, technology, and change to two types of modification strategies: linear and perpendicular (Austin, 1969). In the linear form the spear became modified from a sharpened stick to a stick with a stone tip, then a stick with a metal tip, and eventually to an all-metal stick with a metal point which became unwieldly and ineffective as a weapon. Were it not for perpendicular innovation, weaponry might have become so cumbersome as to have become virtually useless. Perpendicular strategies of innovation, according to Austin, involve miniaturization and a synthesis of existing properties that lead to a unique reformulation of circumstances. Thus, at some point, it was realized that the arm and the spear could be reduced into the more efficient bow and arrow. The bow and arrow similarly underwent linear modification until it was manifested as the extremely powerful but equally cumbersome cross-bow which demanded the considerable strength of two men. Once again a miniaturization and synthesis led to a perpendicular transformation that drastically increased the efficiency of weaponry: the gun and the bullet.

Although the perpendicular transformations of which Austin spoke are far from clearly understood (we can neither predict nor elucidate the creative process), they do appear to possess several recurring properties. They involve a synthesis and integration of extant phenomena leading to a productive yet different and basically unanticipated set of implications. Perpendicular transformations involve aspects of the past, the present, and the future.

With respect to developing models for man-environment relations, it has

been clear for some time that traditionally employed paradigmatic empha-
ses are often cumbersome and inefficient. Considering the man-environment relationship a mutual–causal transaction, to take but one example,
suggests a need for a paradigm that places more emphasis on the contextual
matrix of behavior (De Long, 1972a; Hall, 1976; Tibbetts & Esser, 1973)
and less on cause and effect.

While it seems tacitly acceptable to state that man-environment relations require a paradigmatic shift, and that the shift must be perpendicular
in Austin's terms, it does not follow that previous models from more traditional concerns can be considered obsolescent and totally discarded. If
Austin's analysis of technological (and conceptual) change is valid, the essence of a new paradigm is already present. What is lacking is the synthesis
and conceptual synergy to create a fundamentally different interpretation
of existing models that will have productive, though perhaps unanticipated, implications.

A serious pitfall in this process is the tendency to be trapped by the "rediscovery syndrome." The logic underlying this syndrome is indeed tempting, because if a genuinely innovative paradigm is needed, arguments for
abandoning inefficient precursors can be profoundly persuasive. Yet it is
difficult to imagine the emergence of the bow and arrow if the relationship
between the inefficient arm and the cumbersome metal spear are totally
discarded. What seems more likely to emerge under such circumstances is
the rediscovery of the spear and the time-consuming process of searching
through its linear implications.

The perpendicular transformations of Austin are in every sense conceptual revolutions, akin to the conceptual revolutions derived from the theoretical formulations of Calhoun (1971). What both formulations have in
common is that when existing structures or models (either technological or
conceptual) become too inefficient and cumbersome to deal with existing
information or situations, a basic reformulation involving existing relationships occurs leading to a synthesis and reduction of complexity and yielding
a model capable of incorporating substantially more information.

BASIC REQUIREMENTS FOR A MODEL
OF MAN-ENVIRONMENT RELATIONS

While it may be premature to specify all requisite components necessary for
a satisfactory paradigm in man-environment relations, it is possible to enu-
merate several requirements that appear mandatory. A tentative listing
would minimally include the following:

1. Any serious model in the field of man-environment relations must be
   able to simultaneously account for both synthetic and analytic orien-

tations (that is, it must apply with equal facility to the processes of scientific investigation and creative design).

2. A model of man-environment relations must be based upon principles of complementarity rather than those of competition (that is, it should be inclusive rather than exclusive).

3. A model of man-environment relations must be able to account satisfactorily for the role of context in the execution and interpretation of behavior (that is, it must elucidate the role of context during processes of encoding, synthesis, and design as well as during those of decoding, analysis, and investigation).

4. A model of man-environment relations must be able to identify invariant relationships based upon the continual variation present in behavior and the environment (that is, it must be able to move from the continuous to the discrete).

5. A model of man-environment relations must be able to handle fundamental relationships between time and space (that is, the temporal dimension must be accounted for as effectively as the spatial dimensions).

6. A model of man-environment relations must be generic and still possess the specificity required for productive application at a wide variety of research and design levels.

It is certainly tempting, given the legitimacy of these requirements, to say that it is extremely doubtful that the social and behavioral sciences presently contain a methodological paradigm capable of satisfying these demands. It is, therefore, tempting to set out to derive one. Yet, to do so would be to set in motion the "rediscovery syndrome." The situation is analagous to the pre-Columbus Indians who moved heavy materials on their backs while their children played with toy carts with wheels. Such a paradigm does exist, although its users and outside observers have never seriously considered its potential generality. The remainder of this chapter will deal with outlining its contours in terms of the above-mentioned criteria.

CONGRUENT CONCERNS AND DIVERSE MODELS

The model to be examined is that of coding behavior. The generality of the model has been extrapolated from the specific paradigm developed by American structural linguistics and is theoretically consistent with models developed in a wide variety of disciplines (De Long, 1972a). The communication process, for example, as a generic model for man-environment relations and its pertinence to other paradigms was elaborated in 1972. More recently, other theorists in environmental perception (Saarinen, 1976) and man-environment relations (Rapoport, 1977) have advocated a communications approach.

American structural linguistics is heir to a long and intense intellectual tradition (Waterman, 1963) and precursor to transformational linguistics (Dinneen, 1967). Before dealing with specific issues it might be instructive to briefly point out where there is a generic congruence between the concerns of the linguist and the concerns of the man-environment researcher, since the congruence may not be intuitively obvious. The points of overlap can be summarized as follows:

1. Both are concerned with physical phenomena external to man, but which require internal representation.

2. Both are concerned with the manner in which a complex medium is simplified so that behavior can proceed within a reasonable timeframe.

3. Both are ultimately concerned with the properties of perceived physical form.

4. Both are concerned with socially shared and socially defined phenomena. (For discussion of why the environment is necessarily socially defined see von Foerster, 1962.)

5. Both are concerned with analysis (unit identification) and with design, that is, the creation of meaningful statements that may be unique (never before experienced).

6. Both are concerned with a medium of human communication.

ON CONSTRUCTING A REALITY

The notion that man constructs models or internal representations of his environment, and that such models constrain his perception of and behavior within his environment is gaining wider acceptance (Anderson, 1975; Downs & Stea, 1973; Sonnenfeld, 1974). Such a position, however, is hardly a recent revelation. Indeed, linguistics has been deeply concerned with an identical proposition for well over a century. In Europe the linguistic relativity hypothesis was elaborated, debated intensely and with considerable sophistication during the 1800s under the rubric of "Humboldtian ethnolinguistics" (Miller, 1968). In this country during the 1930s, 1940s and 1950s it re-emerged as the Sapir-Whorf hypothesis (Whorf, 1956) and underwent similarly intense debate and investigation leaving in its wake hundreds of experiments, papers, and numerous symposia and books.

The essence of the notion of linguistic relativity is simply that the grammatical and lexical categories of a language determinably influence the perception, patterns of thought, and habitual behavior of its speakers. In other words, the conceptual and cognitive mold of a language forces onto its speakers the boundaries of reality. Phenomena lying outside the structural boundaries of the linguistic system, by definition, do not exist since the speaker has no way of encountering them. Thus, people construct a reality congruent with the categories presented to them by the language they learn to speak.

While the linguistic relativity hypothesis seems clearcut and intuitively obvious, the past century of debate has made it abundantly clear that the issue is superficially transparent. A conclusion as acceptable as any other seems to be that as long as one remains totally unaware of the structural categories that segment reality, the influence tends to pervade, but awareness alters the issue considerably, and increasing awareness appears to be the evolutionary prerogative of man. It would seem that the understandable excitement and enthusiasm among the cognitivists with respect to the influences of cognitive models on perception and behavior in the environment could be judiciously tempered by a careful inspection of the century-long record of an identical issue mirrored through the medium of language.

ON CONSTRUCTING THE CONSTRUCTION OF REALITY

If man, as well as other animals, constructs his reality, the most crucial issue with regard to the theory of man-environment relations lies in the process of constructing the construction [see von Foerster (1973) for the neurophysiological arguments]. It is at this point that the linguistic model has an invaluable contribution to make to any concern for cognition and man-environment relations.

There is a general consensus among linguists and anthropologists alike that the cognitive categories, structural classes, or more generically, the codes that people employ, vary from linguistic system to linguistic system or from culture to culture. To this extent, one can say they are arbitrary. It was generally assumed for some time that the categories of experience imposed upon the world by various languages and cultures were substantially determined by specific needs within the context of a given environment in order to facilitate survival. Thus, the enormous elaboration of distinctions and resulting categories pertaining to the various states of snow among Eskimos was attributed to the importance of their interpretation of snow to their ultimate survival. The intuitive clarity of this proposition was considerably weakened, however, by Levi-Strauss' (1966) classic study *The Savage Mind* in which he concluded that various ethnoclassification schemata seem less related to the vagaries of specific habitat than to the *need to classify for the sake of classifying.* The real value of classification, Levi-Strauss argued, was to insure that everything in the environment was ordered and had its place. Still, if classification is to be remotely adaptive, it cannot be completely arbitrary and without some significant relationship to the surrounding environment, for that would reduce classification to nothing more than fantasy.

Linguistics is very helpful on this point because, in knowing that they were dealing with arbitrary and relative systems, linguists were forced to discover a discovery-procedure that would accurately and reliably permit them to identify the structural classes and units of a system about which they knew nothing. In other words, the linguist who had successfully analyzed Hindi did not by virtue of that experience gain any insight into the structure and functioning of Navajo: He had to begin all over again. The linguist, then, was forced to discover how to enter a strange, totally foreign system and, through the application of methodology, discover the structure of the categories of experience of the users of the system. He had to develop a methodology for identifying the code. It is not surprising that in order to do so, the linguist began speaking of the environment.

The identification of code units is methodologically ingenious and revolves around the interaction of the organism with its environment. It involves the application of criteria of similarity (organism) and event distribution or context (environment) such that if a_1, a_2, a_3 (distinct events which are in some way similar) are always found to be distributed in unique, non-overlapping contexts, that is:

$$a_1(C_1), a_2(C_2), a_3(C_3) \text{ then, } a_1 = a_2 = a_3.$$

[A] then becomes a class (a category of experience) consisting of variants $/a_1/$, $/a_2/$ and $/a_3/$ whose differences are nonfunctional because their variation is uniquely allocated across different environments or contexts.

An alternative way of illustrating the distributional and relational principles involved is to take a design problem; namely, can we so allocate the events /1/, /2/, and /3/ in the environment such that we can functionally nullify their uniqueness and thereby transform them into functional equivalents? Yes, quite simply: 1/2, 2/4, and 3/6. We have one relational class [1/2] consisting of three variants which are functionally equivalent once we specify certain nonoverlapping contexts.

Another way of highlighting the essence of the relational discovery procedure based upon complementarity is to consider the most powerful tool of science: the experiment. Under ideal experimental conditions the scientist attempts to control the entire environmental context so that he can observe the introduction of systematic variation (say a_1, a_2, and a_3). The reason for so doing is obvious: He wants to focus on the differences between the events he manipulates. If he introduces a_1 under one set of circumstances (say C_1), a_2 under another (C_2) and a_3 under still another (C_3), the uniqueness of the events he varies will be extremely difficult to pinpoint and will be lost both perceptually and functionally. In other words, the scientific experiment implicitly recognizes the relational and distributional nature of cognition and makes an explicit attempt to avoid its customary mode of operation by establishing a constant frame within which to carry out the experiment. The act of cognition, insofar as it is concerned with constructing a model of reality, operates principally by searching for similarities between diverse events and is of necessity a simplifying process. The scientific experiment operates principally by highlighting differences and tends to complexify the world. At the point of overload (too much data), science resimplifies through the use of theories and models, but in so doing it changes the character of reality. While every man can be described as a scientist, the mode of operation of normal cognition seems more akin to that of the designer than that of the scientist; hence we continually create and recreate the world we inhabit. It is this aspect of science that Hall (1976) refers to when he points out that traditionally science has avoided the role of context.

Returning to our initial point — how do we customarily construct our constructions of the environment — we can now say several things. The cognitive construction of reality is achieved through the transactional relationship between the organism and the environment; each provides an indispensible ingredient. The organism supplies criterial judgements of similarity between events, and the environment provides the distributional relationships between the events to be categorized. Both are essential for cognition. The environment, therefore, cannot be deterministic; nor can the organism be deemed completely free. Both extremes, however, are approached as, for example: when the role of the environment increases, which apparently happens with the elderly and the infirm (see Lawton's environmental "Docility Hypothesis," 1970), or when the organism is unable to efficiently compute criteria for similarity (for example, over-sensitive discrimination in some types of schizophrenia).

Evolution has, then, provided us with a mechanism organized in such a way that it requires input from both the organism and the environment to determine the cognitive construction of reality. The importance of this lies in the fact that there is a virtual guarantee that the organism's internal representation of reality will bear some systematic relationship to the physical reality of the environment in which he exists. The often repeated observation that man is literally determining what he shall become through his technology and his design decisions is not idle speculation.

Additionally, we have the easily derived proposition that the code is cognition. It is through codes and coding behavior that we come to know what it is we know about our environment — social and physical (De Long, 1970a, 1972a,b). It is through coding behavior that we acquire knowledge and discover its implications through manipulation. Further, since coding behavior is more basic than communication, we can suggest that each organism (excluding the precocial species that are principally programmed genetically) in a very real way discovers reality for itself. In communication coding is a socially-shared phenomenon, and it might initially seem that coding is inextricably related to communication behavior. It is quite possible, however, to engage in coding behavior without concomitant social communication. A realistic example lies in certain types of schizophrenia. We know from a variety of empirical studies that the schizophrenic codes his reality (Laing, 1966), and that his behavior is precise, systematic and predictable (Condon & Ogston, 1967). His systematization is not shared, however, and does not constitute social communication. Experiental space requires only an observer and the observed. Social space requires two observers and the observed so that consensual validation of the object can occur (see De Long, 1977b; von Foerster, 1973). This point is entirely consistent with the interesting and unique conclusions and implications of Maturana (1970) concerning the "biology of cognition." The socially-shared attributes of coding within the context of communication can be seen to accrue despite individual discovery through the learning mechanism of the operant whose characteristics are clearly implicated in cultural behavior (Jones, 1971; Hall, 1959).

That this model possesses the capability of simultaneously dealing with processes of synthesis and analysis as well as the creation of redundancy (or structure) and information can be made clear through simple illustration. Assigning numeric values of $a_1 = 1$, $a_2 = 2$, $C_1 = 2$, $C_2 = 4$; and treating events a_1 and a_2 as behavior (numerator); and C_1 and C_2 as context (denominator); and keeping in mind that behavior can be the context for still other behavior, we can show the following:

$$a_1C_1 \neq a_2C_1 \text{ i.e., } (1/2 \neq 2/2) \tag{1}$$

$$a_1C_1 = a_2C_2 \text{ i.e., } (1/2 = 2/4) \tag{2}$$

$$a_1C_1 \neq a_1C_2 \text{ i.e., } (1/2 \neq 1/4) \tag{3}$$

The first formula can be considered a generic representation of scientific investigation, holding context constant. The second formula, which creates an invariant relationship by allocating variability in behavior uniquely across variability in the environment, can be considered a generic representation of design, or synthesis. Finally, the third formula can be considered a generic representation of magic, an endeavor that Levi-Strauss (1966) has argued is a mode of acquiring knowledge which parallels science. Formulas

1 and 3 both generate information (differences) by holding either the behavior or the context constant. Formula 2 generates redundancy by systematically varying both behavior and context (for a more detailed discussion of these properties, see De Long, 1978a). Structure and redundancy, as well as information, then, can be seen to be natural complements arising from the very nature of the relationship of the organism to its environment within the framework of this paradigm. Further, the operation of these three formulas can be shown to apply not only to a wide variety of phenomena including visual illusions, language and proxemic behavior, but to systems with hierarchical levels of complexity as well (De Long, 1978b).

This brief discussion should indicate that it is not simply adequate to invoke cognition and the notion that man creates categories in order to negotiate his environment. This much has been clear for some time. What has not been made clear from the cognitive literature is a simple, coherent mechanism that integrally relates the organism to its environment and accounts for how the organism constructs its construction of reality. Attention and serious examination of this model both in terms of theory and method would seem useful in avoiding the need to set in motion once again the rediscovery syndrome.

TIME-SPACE RELATIONSHIPS: EVOLUTION AND THE SURVIVAL VALUE OF COGNITION

An understanding of the evolutionary heritage of man as a temporal, contextual factor is a central ingredient for a serious model of man-environment relations. The evolution of man is, after all, a temporal accounting of the relationship between man and his environment. We shall briefly turn to a consideration of several neurophysiological and neuropsychological models that illustrate the evolutionary, adaptive value of the cognitive process and suggest that the expression of emotion plays a central role in how we construct our models of reality.

MacLean's (1963, 1969, 1975) model of the triune brain indicates that man's central nervous system consists of three chemically and anatomically distinct substrates that evolved at different points in time and process information in characteristically different ways (Esser, 1972).

The substrate of most importance for the current discussion is the paleo-mammalian cortex (the limbic system), the common denominator of all mammals. The limbic system is responsible for emotional behavior. Mac-Lean has identified pathways connecting the hypothalamus with the septum and the amygdala that are intimately related to behavior conducive to the preservation of the species and the preservation of the individual, respectively. Stimulation of the septal area, for example, gives rise to behavior of sociation, whereas stimulation of the amygdala gives rise to aggressive behavior or eating. The emergence of this substrate with the appearance of group-living mammals is instructive, because if group living is to have survival value, animals must be kept together, must be social, and must be able to recognize other members of the group. Emotion is what effectively holds members of a small group together. Not only does MacLean find that stimulation of the septum gives rise to behavior of sociation, but such stimulation is also innately pleasurable. Precisely how emotional behavior can hold members of a group together and facilitate mutual recognition can be seen by looking at another model from neuropsychology.

Pribram (1963, 1971) argues that the emotional process is related to a continual matching process between an internal component and the external environment. When internalized expectations are not congruent with what the animal encounters in the external environment, the animal's ongoing behavior is effectively shut down until it either determines the discrepancy to be irrelevant or until it can bring about a congruence through a change in the external component or its internalized schema. This is essentially equivalent to the concepts of accommodation and assimilation as employed by Piaget and Inhelder (1970). It is this stopping of the ongoing behavior that Pribram argues is the function of the emotional mechanism. It is a protective and highly adaptive mechanism which insures that the animal who finds itself in a situation genuinely disparate with its expectations will be behaviorally shut down in order to assess the unfamiliar context.

These two models can be shown to be congruent with the general process of cognition if we point out several characteristics of coding behavior within the context of communication systems. Communication involves tremendous sharing behaviorally, whether we think of kinesic, linguistic, proxemic, or cultural communication. In fact, such sharing kinesically involves a precise microsynchrony that is present within 24 hours after birth (Condon, personal communication), as well as classes of movement that occur very predictably (De Long, 1974a). Coding behavior involves two aspects that lead to behavioral predictability and redundancy: classification and order. Within any given communication system, then, the users predictably employ certain behavioral classes and certain patterns of ordering. Codes, then, can be seen to function to behaviorally mark group membership (De Long, 1972a). Further, the animal has two warning mechanisms which behaviorally tell it when it is encountering an outsider. First, if behavioral classes are emitted in a deviant pattern, the animal has a preliminary indication that things may not be quite right. This is the adumbrative function of which Hall (1964) speaks. Second, if the wrong classes of behavior are emitted, the animal is neurologically led into the test-operate-test-exit sequence in order to make an appropriate evaluation.

If motivation can be viewed as the "go" mechanism and emotion as the "stop" mechanism (Pribam, 1971), then codes can be viewed as the mechanism that mediates between the two states, telling the animal, in effect, "it is safe to proceed." It should be obvious that coding behavior resulting from the transaction between the organism and his environment is closely related to emotional behavior, and is effective in behaviorally marking group members as well as in delineating the familiar from the unfamiliar.

TIME-SPACE RELATIONSHIPS: RELATIVITY IN BEHAVIORAL AND CONCEPTUAL SYSTEMS

The contextual matrix for behavior-environment relationships previously discussed is typically considered only from a spatial point of view. That is, principal emphasis is usually given to the places where behavior manifests itself: Certain behavioral variants, for example, are matched with behavioral settings. While time is acknowledged as being important and is occasionally considered central to analysis and design (for example, scheduling within shared territories, etc.), for the most part time is treated as a constant backdrop against which the more salient characteristics of behavior emerge. Yet the perception of time, like the perception of space, is fundamentally contextual, and, depending upon the spatial situation, time itself can undergo radical alterations.

Time and space in behavioral and conceptual systems appear to be characterized by the same type of relativity as that defined by Einstein such that if the spatial scale of an environment is changed with respect to an observer, the perception of time by the observer is appropriately altered (De Long, 1977a, b, c). Studies conducted thus far clearly indicate that if the scale of an observer's environment is compressed (reduced), the perceived temporal units of the observer are compressed in the same proportion as the environmental reduction. If the scale of the observed environment is 1/12 full size, the perception of 60 minutes will occur in 5 minutes of elapsed, clock time. If, however, the observed environment is increased in scale with respect to the observer, the perception of temporal units is expanded. Thus, if the scale of an environment is twice its normal size for an observer, during an elapsed, clock interval of 60 minutes the observer will perceive 30 perceptual minutes as passing.

These studies, based upon several hundred subjects, indicate that the perception of time is a function of spatial scale, and, further, from a theoretical point of view, they suggest that there should be a connection between perceived time and information processing in the nervous system. Although experiments of this type are still being planned, the work of Ornstein (1975) shows a clear relationship between perceived time, information processing, and coding behavior. To study the relationships between the perception of temporal duration and cognitive processing, Ornstein developed a series of ingenious experiments involving visual and auditory stimulation. Ornstein found that as the number of stimuli in a given interval increased, or as the complexity of stimuli within the interval increased, the perception of duration also increased; in other words, a given temporal interval was felt to be longer. Additionally, Ornstein found that if methods of coding stimuli within the intervals were used that reduced the relative complexity, the temporal interval was perceived as being shorter in duration. Finally, if coding schemes were developed that permitted various levels of access to the information contained within each interval, those methods that promoted greater awareness or access to information generated a lengthened experience of interval duration. His findings are summarized as follows:

> These . . . studies make a cognitive, information-processing approach to the experience of duration necessary. . . . (They) show that by directly increasing cognitive processing the experience of duration is lengthened. (p. 82)

Within the framework of developing models in man-environment relations it is becoming increasingly apparent that time can no longer be considered merely a constant, background variable. The emerging relationships between space, time, information processing, and coding behavior appear so fundamental that the explication of any one of them may well require the contextual specification of the others. The role of coding behavior would indeed appear to be central, mediating as it does between information (perceived complexity), structure (redundancy and familiarity), and cognitive as well as emotional processing; and permitting an examination of the basic links between the experience of time and space.

CONCLUSIONS

Models can be constructed to deal with any of a wide variety of levels of specificity or generality. At one extreme, the level of specificity can be so narrowly focused that it becomes virtually impossible for the model to process any information from related areas. At the other extreme, of course, the generality can be so great that the model can process all information and yet tell you nothing. Productive models are those that can effectively and meaningfully focus on a given level of specificity and can also intelligibly organize the next level of generality.

The model of coding behavior outlined in this chapter and suggested as an appropriate starting point for man-environment relations has been productively applied to microkinesic communication in children (De Long, 1974a, 1977d); to the static-structural and dynamic-processual properties of small group organization (De Long, 1971); and to proxemic spacing behavior (De Long, 1978b); as well as to the design of the environment (De Long, 1975). With respect to gerontological research, coding behavior has been employed in identifying patterns of proxemic transactions among the elderly (De Long, 1970b) and for providing an organizing conceptual framework for current areas of research in the field dealing with environmental press, environmental dispositions, congruence and stress (De Long, 1974b).

The purpose of this chapter has been to suggest that a perpendicular transformation yielding a conceptual model and paradigm appropriate for the field of man-environment relations has already occurred; and that the resulting model displays a rather remarkable facility for synthesizing and incorporating existing patterns of findings derived from extremely diverse orientations. The model suggested, it is important to note, is based upon both analysis and synthesis as complements. Hence, it is a model emphasizing inclusiveness and synergy. Models based upon analysis alone tend to be competitive, and, rather than being inclusive, they exhibit signs of censorship and territoriality. Competitive models view the recurrence of 4^3 (64) in the *I Ching* (Wilhelm, 1967) and the genetic code as random coincidence, while complementary models view the recurrence of 4^3 in such disparate levels of complexity as an indication of how man structures his relationship to his environment.

REFERENCES

Anderson, B. F. *Cognitive psychology*. New York: Academic Press, 1975.

Austin, W. M. Technology and prediction. *Technology and Human Affairs*, 1969, *1*, 14–15.

Calhoun, J. B. Space and the strategy of life. In A. H. Esser (Ed.), *Behavior and environment: The use of space by animals and men*. New York: Plenum, 1971.

Condon, W. S. and Ogston, W. D. A segmentation of behavior. *Journal of Psychiatric Research*, 1967, 5, 221–235.

De Long, A. J. Coding behavior and levels of cultural integration: Synchronic and diachronic adaptive mechanisms in human organization. In J. Archea and C. Eastman (Eds.), *EDRA II*. Pittsburgh: Environmental Design Research Association, 1970a.

_____. The microspatial structure of the older person. In L. A. Pastalan and D. Carson (Eds.), *The spatial behavior of older people*. Ann Arbor: Wayne State University–University of Michigan Institute of Gerontology, 1970b.

_____. Dominance-territorial criteria and small group structure. *Comparative Group Studies*, 1971, 2, 235–266.

_____. The communication process: A generic model for man-environment relation. *Man-Environment Systems*, 1972a, 2, 263–313.

_____. Environment as code. Paper presented at the annual meeting of the American Association for the Advancement of Science, Washington, D.C., 1972b.

_____. Kinesic signals at utterance boundaries in preschool children. *Semiotica*, 1974a, *11*, 43–73.

_____. Environments for the elderly. *Journal of Communication*, 1974b, Autumn, 101–112.

_____. Coding the environment. In W. F. E. Preiser (Ed.), *Psyche and design*. New York: ASMER, 1975.

_____. Conceptual evolution and design: The potential manipulation of spatial scale and time-frames. *Evolutionary Environments*, 1977a, 4, 2–8.

_____. Time, space and geometry. *Portfolio*, 1977b, *1*, 25–30.

————. Design as metaprocess: Time-space relationships in environments. *Journal of Interior Design*, 1977c, *3*, 3–18.

————. Yielding the floor: The kinesic signals. *Journal of Communication*, 1977d, *27*, 98–103.

————. Context, structures and relationships. In A. H. Esser and B. Greenbie (Eds.), *Communality and privacy*. New York: Plenum Press, 1978a.

————. Proxemics and context: An empirical analysis. Unpublished manuscript, Knoxville: University of Tennessee Architecture Department, 1978b.

Dinneen, F. *An introduction to general linguistics*. New York: Holt, Rinehart & Winston, 1967.

Downs, R. and Stea, D. *Image and environment: Cognitive mapping and spatial behavior*. Chicago: Aldine, 1973.

Esser, A. H. Evolving neurologic substrates of essentic forms. *General Systems Yearbook*, 1972, *17*, 33–41.

Hall, E. T. *The silent language*. Garden City: Doubleday and Co., 1959.

————. Adumbration as a feature of intercultural communication. *American Anthropologist*, 1964, *66*, 154–163.

————. *Beyond culture*. Garden City, New York: Doubleday, 1976.

Jones, J. Operant psychology and the study of culture. *Current Anthropology*, 1971, *12*, 171–189.

Laing, R. D. *The divided self*. Baltimore: Penguin, 1966.

Lawton, M. P. Ecology and aging. In L. A. Pastalan and D. H. Carson (Eds.), *Spatial behavior of older people*. Ann Arbor: University of Michigan Institute of Gerontology, 1970.

Levi-Strauss, C. *The savage mind*. Chicago: The University of Chicago Press, 1966.

MacLean, P. Phylogenesis. In P. H. Knapp (Ed.), *Expression of the emotions in man*. New York: International Universities Press, 1963.

————. The internal-external bonds of the memory process. *Journal of Nervous and Mental Disease*, 1969, *149*, 40–47.

————. On the evolution of three mentalities. *Man-Environment Systems*, 1975, 5, 213–224.

Maturana, H. The biology of cognition. Urbana, IL.: University of Illinois, Biological Computer Laboratories Monograph, 1970.

Miller, R. L. *The linguistic relativity hypothesis and Humboldtian ethnolinguistics*. The Hague: Mouton, 1968.

Ornstein, R. E. *On the experience of time*. New York: Pelican Books, 1975.

Piaget, J. and Inhelder, B. *The psychology of the child*. New York: Basic Books, 1970.

Pribram, K. A. neuropsychological model: Some observations on the structure of psychological processes. In P. H. Knapp (Ed.), *Expression of the emotions in man*. New York: International Universities Press, 1963.

————. *Language of the brain*. Englewood Cliffs, NJ.: Prentice-Hall, 1971.

Rapoport, A. *Human aspects of urban form*. New York: Pergamon Press, 1977.

Saarinen, T. F. *Environmental planning: Perception and behavior*. Boston: Houghton-Mifflin, 1976.

Sonnenfeld, J. Environmental perception personality and behavior: The Texas system. *Man-Environment Systems*, 1974, *4*, 119–125.

Tibbetts, P. and Esser, A. Transactional structures in man-environment relations. *Man-Environment Systems*, 1973, *3*, 441–468.

von Foerster, H. Logical structure of environment and its internal representation. In R. E. Eckerstrom (Ed.), *International Design Conference Aspen 1962*. Zeeland, MI.: Herman Miller, Inc. 1962.

————. On constructing a reality. In W. F. E. Preiser (Ed.), *Environmental design research*, Vol. 2. Stroudsburg, PA.: Dowden, Hutchinson & Ross, 1973.

Waterman, J. T. *Perspectives in linguistics*. Chicago: University of Chicago Press, 1963.

Whorf, B. L. *Language, thought, and reality*. New York: The Technology Press of M.I.T. and John Wiley, 1956.

Wilhelm, R. *The I Ching or book of changes*. Princeton, NJ.: Princeton University Press, 1967.

3
Competence, Environmental Press, and the Adaptation of Older People

M. POWELL LAWTON

The beginnings of the environmental psychology of aging have, for the most part, been empirically oriented. It was natural that early concern should have been directed toward housing (Carp, 1966; Rosow, 1967), the relocation mortality effect (Aldrich & Mendkoff, 1963), or the effects of institutionalization (Beattie & Bullock, 1963; Lieberman, 1969), since these areas represent dramatic environmental changes whose effects are, to some degree, observable even without the aid of the microscopic eye of formal research. However, as in the general behavioral sciences, the development of theories to give direction to such research has been slow. This presentation will incorporate earlier first attempts at theorizing (Lawton, 1970; Lawton & Nahemow, 1973; Lawton & Simon, 1968; Nahemow & Lawton, 1973) and expand these expressions into a more comprehensive effort to link the physical environment to the behaving older person.

In one sense, all behavioral science may be seen as an effort to link behavior with the environment. While all behavior occurs in an environmental context, this context — particularly the physical environment — has been typically ignored or at best implicitly assumed. The incomplete incorporation of the physical environment into the mainstream of behavioral science has several origins.

1. The explicit definition of behavioral science as being concerned with variations in behavior explainable in terms over and above those relating to the physical environment. That is, the physical environment can, with some reason, be thought of as relatively constant in some experimental laboratory situations. When the individual is the focus of study, the researcher has a natural readiness to hold constant anything he can so as to be able to focus on differences among individuals.

2. The limiting of the definition of "environment" to mean other individuals or groups of individuals, rather than the physical environment. Developmental and personality theorists, such as Freud (1959), Allport

(1937), and Murphy (1947), have frequently meant interpersonal relationships when they spoke of environment. The influences of parents, siblings, the total family constellation, peers, teachers, or work supervisors are frequently lumped together as environmental influences. Similarly, organizational theorists and sociologists have variously referred to group processes, milieux, norms, and cultural pressures as environment, without specifying to what extent these stimuli are composed of multi-individual influences as contrasted with aspects of the physical environment. It is of interest to note that little attempt was made to differentiate the personal, social, and physical aspects of these conceptions of environment, in spite of the prominent place given to the environment by people like the urban ecologists (Lewin, 1935; Murray, 1938; Park, Burgess & McKenzie, 1925).

3. The tendency of many theorists to transform environmental stimuli into internal representations of the environment. Lewin's (1935) concept of "life space," while implying a physical environmental referent, was in fact developed almost wholly as a phenomenological concept, as were many other theoretical attempts to introduce meaning as an intervening variable between stimulus and response. Such a tendency is very strong today, as evidenced by the preoccupation of man-environment researchers with environmental cognition; this stream threatens to deemphasize the physical environment as completely as do the theories that simply ignore it (Wohlwill, 1973).

A comprehensive theory of the ecology of aging must incorporate both non-physical, extra-individual stimuli and intra-individual environmental representations into its framework. However, as Wohlwill (1973) has persuasively argued, unless consensual reality — "the environment out there" — is utilized as a standard, there will be no basis for interpreting individual differences in cognition of the environment. Furthermore, the broadly social (as contrasted to physical) environment is not only an aspect of the situation external to the behaving individual, but its stimulus value is determined by intertwining physical dimensions such as distance, modes of communication, density, and territory.

Rapoport (1973) has grouped existing models for man-environment interaction into 12 categories, which are clearly overlapping and based variously on philosophical, contentual, and methodological differences (see Chapter 9 in this volume). Lucille Nahemow and this author have worked on an approach that is related to Rapoport's competence and ecological models. Our statements have been based on general knowledge from the field of gerontology and have heretofore not linked the theory with specific research findings other than a few studies of social interaction as a function of spatial and personal characteristics. This presentation will recapitulate our theoretical work and attempt a more comprehensive linkage to research knowledge from a number of areas of gerontology.

AN ECOLOGICAL MODEL OF AGING

Much of the research in aging has been essentially descriptive in nature, a necessary step in the development of a science. Adequate documentation is at hand pointing to biological, social, and personal deficits associated with being old. Much recent research has been directed to the unraveling of the possible sources of these deficits (explanatory research), frequently leading to the modification of presumed causal relationships between chronological aging and behavior (Baltes & Labouvie, 1973). Whatever the explanation of the deficit, few older persons may be found who exhibit no deprivation in the biological, psychological, or social spheres.

In any case, the frequency of such deprivations makes it appropriate to seek descriptive terms for them and to work toward a predictive model for the behavior of older people. The major predictive components have been referred to as competence and environmental press. Competence is seen as a characteristic of the individual, for heuristic pruposes conceived of as relatively independent of factors outside the individual. Environmental press were described by Murray (1938) as stimuli possessing some motivating quality to activate a cognate individual need. They are thus environmental characteristics with some demand quality for the individual, whether the demand is objective (alpha press) or one construed by the individual (beta press). The outcome whose prediction is sought through knowledge of competence and environmental press is the behavior of the individual. This is the familiar ecological equation:

$$B = f(P, E)$$

That is, behavior is a function of the person and the environment. The components of this equation will be defined with greater specificity.

COMPETENCE

The term competence represents, to be sure, a limited aspect of all that might be included in the P component of the ecological equation. The term has a clear evaluative connotation, as contrasted with some psychological and social characteristics that are presumed to represent qualitative variations among people, rather than variations ranging from adaptive to nonadaptive. These common nonevaluative personal characteristics are needs, traits, and personal style. Needs have been represented as varying in their positions in the hierarchical structure among individuals (Edwards, 1953; Murray, 1938), but the different hierarchical structures do not necessarily lead to differential levels of psychological adjustment. In Murray's conception, for instance, some individuals may be seen as high in needs for achievement and order and low in needs for nurturance and affiliation. This constellation of needs will lead to a different behavioral outcome than will a different constellation, but no particular hierarchy in itself is any more or less likely than another to lead to an adequate behavioral outcome. The critical determinants of adequacy of outcome are, rather, the degree to which any need constellation is internally consistent (lack of, versus presence of, conflict among needs) or congruent with environmental opportunities for gratification.

Not all conceptions of needs are nonevaluative, however. Sometimes called motives, developmentally-related hierarchies have been posited by Erikson (1963) and Maslow (1964). As the hierarchy ascends, higher levels become more complex and less egocentric, which immediately connotes an evaluative dimension. In addition, the failure of an individual to achieve the normative progression up the hierarchy as he moves through the life cycle is seen as a lower level of maturity, even though there are satisfyingly adaptive states of adjustment for every level of the hierarchy.

Personality traits were seen by Allport (1937) and many others as enduring inner aspects of the individual that are revealed in characteristic behavior. Traits are considered consistent not only over time but also across situations. Clearly, some traits are more likely to lead to need fulfillment than are others, and in this sense traits may be evaluated in terms of their adaptive value. However, many traits are neutral or of unclear adaptive quality, such as orderliness, friendliness, or assertiveness. In addition, much research has been ambiguous regarding the extent to which traits endure over time or vary over situations. The classical experiments on honesty by Hartshorne and May (1928) demonstrated how greatly the behavioral honesty of school children varied with the particular situation presented, while longitudinal developmental studies (Tuddenham, 1959) have found limited support for consistency of traits in the same individuals followed over time. The concept of a trait has enough of a static quality, an ambiguous evaluative reference, and a lack of clarity of assignment to intra-individual as compared to transactional processes to make it unsuitable for inclusion in the model (see also Windley's Chapter 4 in this volume).

A personality style is, on the one hand, difficult to distinguish from a trait, and on the other it is much more closely linked to extra-individual factors than is either need or trait. Style seeks to describe enduring ways of perceiving, cognizing, and responding to the world outside oneself, ways that are relatively independent of specific needs. Research on field dependence, for example, has investigated the tendency of some individuals to focus on external perceptual cues for their spatial orientation, while others rely more on the internal cues offered by the semicircular canals of the inner ear (Witkin et al., 1954).

While such styles have not been empirically shown to be completely independent of adaptive adequacy (field-dependent individuals show some tendency to have lower IQs than do the field-independent, Witkin et al., 1954), there appear to be broad ranges of stylistic preference that cannot be clearly evaluated in terms of their implied competence. Although personality style is not thus seen as an aspect of competence, it is a critical aspect of the person-environment transaction and will be discussed later in terms of an additional interactional term in the ecological equation:

$$B = f(P, E, P \times E)$$

Having eliminated three major sources of individual differences from consideration as aspects of competence for the present, characteristics that do fall into this aspect of the P component will be described. The definition of these categories will, as far as possible, stress those aspects that appear to be least dependent on environmental input. As we shall see, such purity is a myth; nevertheless, the search for a model requires one to try to characterize processes as mainly the person, mainly the environment, or mainly their interaction. The difficulty we face is that all knowledge about people is gained from some kind of behavioral response, whether it be a blood chemistry measurement or the molar behavior of an older person on a shopping errand. The processes that seem to most clearly represent competence are biological health, sensory-perceptual capacity, motor skills, cognitive capacity, and ego strength.

1. Biological health refers to the absence of disease states (as contrasted to functional health which is a behavioral outcome resulting from the interaction of personal and environmental factors) and is commonly indexed by laboratory tests of biological functions, signs, symptoms, and medical diagnoses.

2. Sensory and perceptual capacities include the primary processes of vision, audition, olfaction, gustation, somesthesis, and kinesthesis, as well as the more differentiated aspects of these senses, such as depth perception, flicker fusion, or pain perception. Behavioral responses from the subject are frequently required to measure processes like reporting the relative strength of two stimuli.

3. Motor skills are obviously related to biological health and sensory-motor capacity and are not usually measured for diagnostic purposes separately from either health or more molar complex behavior in a specific environment. However, muscular strength can be measured with a dynamometer and complex coordination with relatively standardized apparatus like a pursuit rotor.

4. Cognitive capacity is what intelligence tests have sought to measure with only partial success — that is, the presumed innate, relatively invariant capacity of the individual to comprehend, process, and cope with the external world. One must acknowledge the many difficulties inherent in

this conception. However, capacity must be distinguished from cognitive performance which is the behavioral outcome of the person-environment transaction, and as such, it is what the intelligence test actually measures. An example of a cognitive capacity would be a vocabulary test (a skill that declines less with age than do others), administered with optimal clarity of presentation to a person with unimpaired senses who was fully conversant in English, and in a situation where there was no time pressure, no competing stimuli, and an expectancy of minimum stress created in the subject.

5. Ego strength is thus far a construct whose measurement is almost totally dependent on behavior-in-context, and therefore is not includable as a variety of competence that can be operationalized in terms of intrapersonal qualities. It is mentioned here merely to indicate the possibility that there may be individual differences in psychological strength that are independent of external events.

These five classes of competence may be seen as falling into an ascending order of complexity, of interdependence with one another, of potential dependence on environmental events; therefore, as the hierarchy ascends from biological health to ego strength, it becomes increasingly difficult to conceptualize the more complex levels of competence as intraindividual, rather than interactional, processes. In an earlier attempt to define competence Lawton (1972) ignored the distinction between intra-individual and interactional competences, suggesting the hierarchy of behavioral competence reproduced in Figure 3.1. While this single hierarchy is more inclusive, the more complex sublevels such as self-maintenance, instrumental self-maintenance, effectance (White, 1959), and social skill vary more with the external situation than do the more limited physical-health, sensory-perceptual, and cognitive processes. Therefore, competence is defined as the theoretical upper limit of capacity of the individual to function in the areas of biological health, sensation-perception, motoric behavior, and cognition. Measurement of competence in these areas is most satisfactory when it filters out the possible influences of contextual factors, as do some medical laboratory tests. Many other varieties of measurement — cognitive tests, for example — are contaminated with environmental effects. Nevertheless, the construct of intrapersonal competence seems worth preserving for its usefulness in constructing a model.

Competence as defined here is intrinsically difficult to measure and operationally impossible to distinguish from behavior in an evaluative context. The difficulties involved in making this assumption of an intra-individual quality called competence are many. In attempting to operationalize competence, the only available approach is to utilize an evaluative concept of behavior at a relatively low level in the hierarchy as a proxy competence variable and behavior at a higher level as the dependent variable representing the outcome of the $P-E$ transaction. For example, if one wishes to examine cognitive performance (B) as the outcome of P and E factors, the P

FIGURE 3.1. Schematic diagram of sublevels of individual organization.

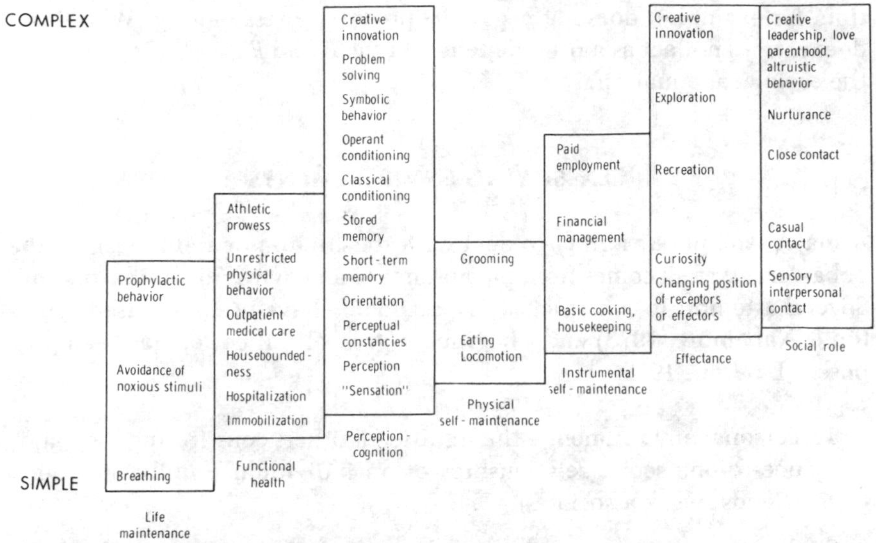

COMPLEX

```
Creative
innovation
Problem
solving
Symbolic
behavior
Operant
conditioning
Classical
conditioning
Stored
memory
Short-term
memory
Orientation
Perceptual
constancies
Perception
"Sensation"
Perception-
cognition

Creative                Creative
innovation              leadership, love
                        parenthood,
                        altruistic
                        behavior
            Exploration
                        Nurturance

Paid
employment  Recreation  Close contact

Financial               Casual
management              contact

            Curiosity
            Changing position   Sensory
            of receptors        interpersonal
            or effectors        contact
Basic cooking,
housekeeping

            Effectance          Social role
Instrumental
self-maintenance

Athletic
prowess

Unrestricted
physical
behavior

Outpatient
medical care

Housebounded-
ness

Hospitalization

Immobilization

Grooming

Eating
Locomotion

Physical
self-maintenance

Prophylactic
behavior

Avoidance of
noxious stimuli

Functional
health

Breathing

Life
maintenance
```

SIMPLE

Source: Lawton, M. P. Assessment, integration, and environments for older people. *The Gerontologist,* 1970, *10,* 38–46, Fig. 1, p. 41. Reprinted with permission.

component of the equation might be represented by less complex levels, for example physical health, autonomic reactivity, or visual acuity. If, on the other hand, an aspect of social behavior is being studied, the same measure of cognitive performance (score on an intelligence test, for example) would become the independent variable representing competence, the P component.

ENVIRONMENTAL PRESS

Murray's (1938) definition of press referred to an environmental force (physical, interpersonal, or social) that tended to activate an intrapersonal need. In the model proposed by Lawton and Nahemow (1973) the concept of need is not utilized. Instead, press are defined in normative terms. That is, an environmental stimulus or context is seen as having potential demand character for any individual if empirical evidence exists to demonstrate its association with a particular behavioral outcome for any group of individuals. For example, Tuckman (1967) found that attendance at a senior center was significantly related to the distance between an individual's residence and the center. Distance may thus be viewed as a possible negative press tending to reduce participation. The fact that distance does not operate as a negative press for a given older individual or for a group of other kinds of people (children going to a school providing bus transportation, for example), does not negate its potential press quality. Whether it does or does not act as a press depends on the P and $P \times E$ components of the ecological equation.

CLASSIFYING ENVIRONMENTS

A major lack in our ability to deal with the environmental aspects of the behavioral system comes from the absence of an environmental taxonomy. Several attempts to construct such a taxonomy have been discussed (Lawton & Nahemow, 1973) and a beginning gross classification has been proposed (Lawton, 1970):

1. Personal environment — the significant others constituting the major one-to-one social relationships of an individual (family members, friends, work associates);

2. Suprapersonal environment — the modal characteristics of all the people in physical proximity to an individual (for example, the predominant race or the mean age of other residents in a person's neighborhood);

3. Social environment — the norms, values, and institutions operating in the individual's subgroup, society, or culture;

4. Physical environment — defined as the nonpersonal, nonsocial aspects of the environment.

A number of man-environment investigators such as Dibner (1973), Hershberger (1972) and Wohlwill (1968) have sought higher order abstractions to contrast environments. Making no attempt to be exhaustive or to trace references to each, some dimensions that have been suggested are:

- Natural versus man-made

- Large versus small

- Crowded versus sparse

- Stable versus unstable

- Patterned versus random

- Homogeneous versus heterogeneous

- Complex versus simple

- Redundant versus limited

- Rich versus impoverished

- Public versus private

- Legible versus illegible

- Controlled versus autonomous

- Habitable versus uninhabitable

- Supportive versus demanding

- Novel versus familiar

It is immediately obvious that many of the above dimensions are not easily translatable into purely environmental terms. They are roughly ordered from clearly physical to clearly interactional. That is, external physical quality is usually a sufficient basis on which to classify an environmental display as natural or man-made, but whether a physical aspect of the environment is novel or familiar depends on the individual to whom it is presented. Thus, there appear to be three levels of environmental definition when one attempts to dimensionalize the environment into higher order abstractions:

1. The phenomenal physical environment — the unique, idiosyncratic experience of a physical object by one individual (for example, novel versus familiar);

2. The consensual physical environment — while the environmental quality must be experienced by the individual, enough individuals experience the quality in a similar way so as to suggest a convergence on the real object (for example, crowded versus sparse);

3. The explicitly physical environment — qualities that may be measured in centimeters, grams, and seconds (for example, natural versus man-made).

Taking as an illustration the quality complexity, simplicity can be defined as phenomenal, consensual, or physical. As an idiosyncratic judgment, each person in a study by Wohlwill (1968) ranked a series of photographs for their perceived complexity. The rankings by all judges were then pooled to construct a consensually ordered series of photographs scaled for complexity. Other investigators have operationalized complexity in such explicit physical terms as varying the numbers and arrangements of dots (see Sterns, 1971; Wohlwill, 1968).

The further development of such small scale taxonomies (or environmental typologies) should include the following: striving to define as many qualities as possible in both explicitly physical and consensually physical terms; expanding the list in the direction of greater inclusiveness; the empirical understanding of the interrelationships among environmental attributes and ultimately the evolution of a functional taxonomy.

A second, empirical, approach to taxonomy has been through factor-analytic techniques, using environmental features as items. Before the correlational analysis is done, however, a conceptual phase is required to specify which potential features are to be included in the environmental item pool. Thus, in a national survey of 4000 older people living in the community, Schooler (1969) decided that the information given by subjects to questions on knowledge and accessibility of resources, the physical characteristics of their dwelling units, and ratings of the quality of the dwelling unit should constitute the items to be correlated. Five factors roughly corresponding to these features were obtained. These factors represent presumed underlying dimensions that account for the intercorrelations among the items making up the factor. If the cluster of items thus defined makes conceptual sense and can be named so as to communicate the higher order meaning, then a useful step has been taken in dimensionalizing the environment.

The factor-analytic technique should be pursued further so as to arrive at the definition of relatively pure empirical dimensions that can be used to characterize a variety of environments through the successive approximations by a number of investigators working in a variety of situations.

Murray's (1938) term "press" has an obvious similarity to the concept of stress. Press, however, may be positive, neutral, or negative, while stress implies only a potentially negative environmental demand. A television set in an older person's dwelling may be considered a positive press — its presence has the potential for eliciting turning-on-and-watching behavior. In contrast, a lack of heating fuel may be a negative press — it may elicit physical exertion, shivering, or risk of illness and death, beyond the point of tolerance of the older person. Both the television set and the empty fuel tank are consensually defined as press because they are known to be behavior-activating to some individuals. However, for other people they may be neutral — for example, if the television set is in the home of a person who cannot comprehend or if the fuel tank is empty in August. In this model the major dimension on which press are classified is their strength — they may vary from low to high demand quality. Their positive or negative quality, in terms of eliciting adaptive or nonadaptive behavior, can be determined only by knowledge of the competence of the individual.

At this point acknowledgment should be made that not everyone would agree that environment can be conceptually differentiated from the person. A hard core transactionalist would point out that as members of the behavioral system, man and environment are indivisible. The behaver's actions, cognitions, and feelings at a given moment incorporate aspects of the environment and the environment is defined only through the use, cognitions, and feelings of individuals and groups. The approach of this presentation is agnostic on this issue, but it is firm in its insistence upon the empirical necessity for not only separating the person from the environment, but upon differentiating subaspects of the environment as discussed above.

BEHAVIOR

The dependent variable or outcome of the ecological equation is behavior. In our conception, behavior may be either outwardly observable motoric behavior or an inner affective response. The inner response is, of course, far more difficult to measure than is motoric behavior. Sustained levels of affective response have been indexed as morale (Kutner et al., 1956) or life satisfaction (Neugarten, Havighurst & Tobin, 1961); responses of more limited duration have been indexed as affect balance (Bradburn, 1969; Moriwaki, 1973); and momentary responses as mood (Culbertson, Pomeroy & Cunningham, 1972; Cameron, 1975). Many overt motoric responses are accompanied by some affective response, but an affective response may occur in the absence of motoric behavior. In the discussion of the ecological model, behavior will usually refer both to the overt and inner affective response, but most empirical knowledge has been derived from the analysis of overt behavior.

The ecological model of aging suggests that behavior is a function of the competence of the individual and the environmental press of the situation, as represented schematically in Figure 3.2 (Lawton & Nahemow, 1973). This scheme is not a mathematical representation but merely an aid to conceptualization. Continua of competence and strength of press form the two axes, and as such they are greatly oversimplified. A behavior (or affective response) is seen as the resultant of a combination of a press of a given magnitude acting on, or perceived by, or utilized by, an individual of a given level of competence. One source of oversimplification is the fact that neither competence nor strength of press is a unitary characteristic. The empty fuel tank is most probably only one element in a total constellation of environmental demands. Similarly, Figure 3.2 demands that we look at an individual as possessing some degree of overall competence. In reality, the best we can do is to hope to characterize an individual in terms of a profile of competences — low in biological competence, high in sensory competence and moderate in cognitive competence, for example — much as vocational psychologists have attempted to do in the case of abilities.

Murray's (1938) need-press system had the great advantage of pairing specific individual needs with specific environmental press that were relevant to these needs. Our conception lacks this specificity, but this lack also

FIGURE 3.2.   Press-competence model.

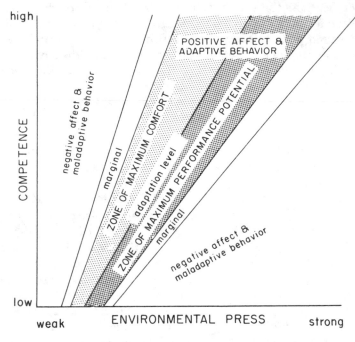

Source: Lawton, M. P. and Nahemow, L. Ecology and the aging process. In C. Eisdorfer and M. P. Lawton, Eds. *The psychology of adult development and aging.* Washington: American Psychological Association, 1973. Copyright 1973 by the American Psychological Association. Reprinted by permission.

seems in greater accord with the complexities of competence and environmental contexts. Finally, the representation of behavior as the point defined by the magnitude of the competence-press combination is also clearly oversimplified. Behavior and affect must be thought of as especially variable over time, since press are never stable, and even competence is fluid with respect to time and across different intra-individual domains.

In any case, in Figure 3.2 behavior is characterized as falling in the range of adaptive through nonadaptive, and the affective response is evaluated as positive or negative from the point of view of the individual himself. The adaptiveness of behavior may be judged by either or both normative and teleological standards (Lawton, 1972), that is, the extent to which it meets society's expectations and/or the individual's standards or requirements for goal fulfillment. Adaptiveness is commonly measured by counting or rating observed behavior, as in measures of self-care ability (Lowenthal, 1964; Lawton & Brody, 1969), use of leisure time (Burgess, Cavan & Havighurst, 1949), and social behavior (Burgess, Cavan &

Havighurst, 1949; Granick & Nahemow, 1961; Lowenthal, 1964). Quality of affect may also be rated by external observers or by the self-report measures of life satisfaction, affect, and mood described above.

Acknowledging the error necessarily involved in dealing with such soft data, the behavior of an individual of any given level of competence, when faced with a given environmental press, may be broadly seen as adaptive or maladaptive, depending on where the coordinates locate his behavior in Figure 3.2. Clearly, the less his competence and the stronger the environmental press, the less likely are behavior and affect to be acceptable, as represented by the areas biased toward the upper left and lower right corners of Figure 3.2. Behavior or affect mapped as falling between the leftmost and rightmost diagonal lines is considered at least minimally adaptive or positive.

The model incorporates another concept, adaptation level (Helson, 1964), which represents a state of balance between the level of external stimulation and the sensitivity of the individual's sensory, perceptual, and cognitive state. That is, the individual tends to adapt to any given level of stimulation in such a way that awareness of the stimulus recedes. A change in the intensity of the stimulation brings the stimulus into greater awareness. A warm bath produces an immediate experience of something new, as registered by temperature, touch, and kinesthetic receptors. After a time, if one remains motionless, the sensations of water touching the body, of warmth, and of body position become less keen, sometimes verging on the point of no sensation at all. As the water cools, or if more hot or cold water is added, the sensations are reexperienced but will gradually move toward a zero or neutral point again. This point at which sensation is minimal is called adaptation level (AL). Stimuli of a broad range of intensity may become adapted to in this way, although as intensity approaches the highest levels, adaptation becomes impossible and pain or other signs of stress may appear (Glass & Singer, 1972). In general, the higher the level of stimulus intensity, the greater the change in intensity required in order for the individual to experience the physical change psychologically. The physical value of the stimulus experienced as neutral (that is, at AL) is not only a function of the current stimulus intensity but also of the individual's earlier experiences with other stimuli in that class. The bath-taker may have had lifelong experience with (and therefore preference for) water of 110°; should the bath initially drawn be only 100°, he may persist in the experience of the water as cool without ever coming to the neutral, AL experience. Finally, the magnitude of stimulus intensity defining AL also varies with other contemporary environmental aspects. It may take a higher water temperature to reach AL for the individual when the air temperature is cool or if snow is visible through the window. An example of the effect of previous experience in determining the frame of reference for judging the noise level of a community was provided by Wohlwill and Kohn (1973) in a study of migrants to a middle-sized city. Migrants who had come from small communities judged the noise level of the middle-sized city as significantly higher than did the migrants from large cities. The AL of the former to noise level was relatively low as compared to the latter, so that the experience of the contrasting middle-sized city was noisy to one group and quiet to the other.

According to the model, not only is there a tendency for every individual experiencing a given environmental press to establish an adaptation level, but the magnitude of that neutral stimulus level is partly determined by the competence of the individual. The dashed line running diagonally through the center of Figure 3.2 represents the hypothetical AL for all combinations of competence and press level (that is, the average person in the average environment). Any individual of a given level of competence, if exposed to a press level that would elicit behavior of a quality indicated by a point on the AL line, would come to experience the press as neutral, meaning that his affect would be neither positive nor negative, that the behavior elicited would be routine and adaptive, and his awareness of his competence level, his environment, and his behavior or affect would be relatively low. This steady state characterizes much of everyday behavior. For the ordinary practiced driver even as complex a skill as handling a car in traffic may be performed at AL under routine conditions.

Figure 3.2 indicates that the lower the competence of the individual, the lower the strength of press must be in order to maintain this steady state of automatic but adaptive behavior and neutral affect. What happens if the press level is too great, that is, the combination of competence and press defines a point somewhere to the right of the AL line? A radical excess of press has been indicated to result in behavior that is maladaptive or affect that is negative. However, for any given level of competence there is a range within which press level may increase before the experience becomes negative. At a moderately high level, the environmental situation comes into greater awareness as a stimulus motivating the person to behave in a nonroutine way or to arouse his affect. This mild-to-moderate environmental demand is likely to elicit striving, socially outgoing behavior, interest, or pleasure. This zone to the right of AL has been labeled the "zone of maximum performance potential" in Figure 3.2. In other words it expresses the folk wisdom that a challenge of the right magnitude for a given individual is likely to be responded to favorably.

The zone to the left of the AL line — a state of lower-than-average stimulation, or weak environmental press — also in the extremely low-press conditions will be associated with maladaptive behavior or negative affect. Short of the extreme state of deprivation is a range of mildly low press level for an individual of a given level of competence where he is underchallenged but maintains behavior at an adaptive level and with relatively positive affect. This has been labeled the "zone of maximum comfort" in Figure 3.2. The person in this area may be aware of the understimulation (the stimulus level is perceptibly below his AL), his behavior may be relatively passive, and his emotional state may possibly be one of boredom, but these negative states are not inappropriate.

An additional concept, the optimization principle (Wohlwill, 1972), aids in understanding the dynamic balance between stimulation level and competence. Wohlwill reviews some evidence primarily from psychophysical studies suggesting that any mild deviation from AL is experienced as affectively pleasant, as in the instance where the person adapted to tepid water enjoys either a mild increase in warmth or in coolness. This suggestion corresponds with the common observation that people sometimes seem to seek change for its own sake, and with much of the growing body of literature on curiosity and arousal (Berlyne & Madsen, 1973).

Figure 3.3 graphically portrays the hypothesized relationship between level of stimulation, AL, and affect. Neutral affect is experienced at AL and again at some point following either a moderate increase or decrease in level of stimulation. Between AL and the neutral points to each side of AL, the perceptible change in stimulation may be experienced as enjoyable; positive affect is optimal in this range. Beyond these points, further increase or decrease in stimulation is likely to be experienced as either deprivation or overload, respectively.

The optimization concept is represented in Figure 3.2 by the zones of maximum comfort and maximum performance potential. The comfort

FIGURE 3.3. Changes in affective response to stimuli as a function of extent of deviation from adaptation level.

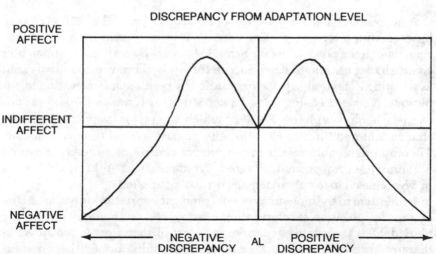

Source: Joachim F. Wohlwill. The physical environment: A problem for a psychology of stimulation. *Journal of Social Issues,* 1966, *22*(4), 29–38. Copyright 1966 by the Society for the Psychological Study of Social Issues. Reprinted by permission.

zone may imply smugness, lassitude, dependency, underachievement. This state can result from successful effort at tension reduction. The maximum performance zone may be associated with activity, mild restlessness, goal-directed behavior, or achievement—behaviors characterizing efforts to create tension. Thus, while the affect associated with both zones may be positive, the two zones differ in the type of behavior they elicit.

The model displayed in Figure 3.2 illustrates the environmental docility hypothesis (Lawton, 1970), which suggests that high competence is associated with relative independence of the individual from the behavioral effects of environmental press, while low competence implies heightened vulnerability to environmental press. This generalization is consistent with the relative freedom that mentally and physically healthy people with adequate incomes have to live satisfying lives in a variety of both favorable and unfavorable environments. In contrast, people of lowered competence in any of these areas have difficulty coping with the demands of marginally adequate environments. In Figure 3.2 the total range of adaptive behavior/positive affect is wider at higher levels of competence than at lower levels. Looked at another way, a small change in press level may make a much greater difference in adequacy of behavioral outcome for the less competent than for the highly competent. In general, the hypothesis suggests that lowered competence increases the proportion of behavioral variance that is associated with environmental, as compared to personal, factors.

THE ECOLOGY OF CHANGE

One purpose of scientific investigation is acquisition of the skills necessary for successful intervention. Competence is by no means a static quality, even though the possibilities for behavior change by way of environmental change have been emphasized. Successful psychotherapy is commonly seen as resulting in favorable behavior change by permanently elevating intrapersonal competence, for example, ego strength. Lindsley (1964) has contrasted therapy with prosthetics, which refers to favorable behavior change achieved through elevating the support level of the environment. Therapy presumably results in permanent change and therefore can be withdrawn as competence is elevated. Prosthesis, on the other hand, results in favorable change only so long as it is being applied.

In addition to the dichotomy of environment versus the individual as the points of application of intervention efforts, intervention may involve the individual as the relatively passive recipient of the intervention (psychotherapy, corrective eyeglasses) or as the active initiator of either environmentally or personally applied intervention. Figure 3.4 indicates some examples of this four-way classification, which has been discussed in greater detail elsewhere (Nahemow & Lawton, 1973).

For the present purpose, the issue of elevating competence through ac-

FIGURE 3.4.   Ecological change model.

Point of application	The Individual's role	
	Respondent	Initiator
The environment	A Social and environmental engineering	B The individual redesigns his environment
The individual	C Rehabilitation, therapy	D Self - therapy growth

Source: Lawton, M. P. and Nahemow, L. Ecology and the aging process. In C. Eisdorfer and M. P. Lawton, Eds. *The psychology of adult development and aging.* Washington: American Psychological Association, 1973. Copyright 1973 by the American Psychological Association. Reprinted by permission.

tive and passive behavior on the part of the individual is of primary concern. The range of increase in press that can be most effectively utilized to raise competence is, approximately, the horizontal distance from AL to the point that represents a just-noticeable-difference (jnd) in press. With the subject in the passive role, environmental design should be calculated to demand behavior that is just slightly more complex or taxing than the characteristic behavior at AL. Press increments of jnd proportions seem best calculated to become translated into elevations of competence, rather than being limited to prosthetic behavior maintenance. If we imagine such a press increase to be applied to an individual operating at AL, the normal tendency will be the establishment of a new AL in the direction of the new increased stimulus by means of added tension, energy expenditure, and attempted coping. If such efforts are successful, the new adaptation will involve an increase in competence, proceeding vertically from the increased point to re-intersect the AL line of Figure 3.2. The press increment may also evoke a negative behavioral or affective response and may be experienced as chronic stress, and ultimately a decrement in competence. In actual fact, press are of many kinds and vary regularly in intensity, frequency, and duration. Under most circumstances, this range of variation is such that the total level of press stays within the limits of the maximum comfort and performance zones. However, press levels vary over time. For the high-competence person, this variation rarely goes beyond tolerable limits; for the low-competence person, normal variation will frequently bring press to excessive levels (Nahemow & Lawton, 1973).

In the case of the individual as initiator, the key is environmental choice [Kaplan (1973) has discussed this concept in some detail]. As Berlyne and Madsen (1973), Wohlwill (1972) and others have indicated, the search for tension creation (that is, curiosity, exploration, novelty) is as characteristic of people as the search for tension reduction. If given the opportunity to choose environmental changes, people will as frequently choose those that raise press level as those that lower it. They will clearly be better able than an environmental designer to know when to seek an increase and when to seek a decrease in press level. I have presented some evidence suggesting that older people applying to housing projects have a tendency to match their own competence to the type of housing they choose: Applicants to housing with many services were older, in poorer physical health, and more deprived in other ways than people applying to housing without services (Lawton, 1969). In this very active sense, people design their own environments appropriately with respect to their competence for the most part.

The mechanisms by which competence is elevated by either active or passive means are varied. They include: the utilization of unrecognized potential; the increase in self-esteem consequent to seeing oneself handle an increase in press (the feeling of competence, Perin, 1970); and the affirmation of self involved in having control over the nature and intensity of press (active mastery, Neugarten, 1968). Biological and social constraints greatly limit both environmental choice by the older person and his opportunity for controlling the environment. Intervention that widens these opportunities has the best chance to affect competence.

These avenues for therapy are theoretically possible with individuals of any level of competence. At very low levels, however, as in the case of the mentally impaired, the seriously ill, and the extremely poor, prosthesis is the more usual manner of approach. Excessively high press are far more likely for the low-competent than are excessively low press, as indicated by the displacement of the tolerable range segment to the lower left of Figure 3.2. Such people are typically treated by attempting to lower press level by such means as retirement, extending supportive services, confinement to the dwelling unit, institutionalization, and general social condescension. These treatments are sometimes appropriate, although they are just as frequently over-applied so as to force the individual into the below-AL threshold of deprivation. The narrow width of the adaptive behavior-positive affect range at low levels of competence emphasizes the fine line that separates protection from stress and environmental deprivation for the very impaired. On the other hand, an optimistic note is conveyed (if the model is correct) by the probability that a relatively small relief of stress or addition of support can bring behavior and affect back into a range that is appropriate, at least for the given level of competence of the individual.

INTERACTIVE PROCESSES

The major domains of the behavioral system have been described: behavior/affect, competence, and environmental press. Before examining some of the research findings germane to these assertions, the interactive term of the equation $P \times E$ will be discussed. This interaction subsumes two additional concepts necessary to account for the personal processing of information from the environment: personality style and environmental cognition. Personality style has been alluded to earlier as one of a number of intrapersonal processes frequently seen as belonging to the individual rather than to the environment. It is suggested here that the processes are interactive rather than intrapersonal, since they represent relatively content-free ways of converting unpatterned environmental stimuli into meaningful information consistent with the intrapsychic goals, wishes, past experience, and competence of the individual. The second interactional term, environmental cognition, refers to the specific personalized environmental content. Personality styles are enduring ways of experiencing the environment. Environmental cognition is processed environmental content, which differs from explicit physical environmental stimuli to the extent that personality style, variation in competence, and other personality factors not accounted for in this model intrude into the apprehension of the objective environment.

Personality Style

A great many personality styles have been identified in the experimental psychological literature. However, their interrelationships and their discriminant validity have not been adequately investigated. Many of them turn out to be related to one another and to non-style factors such as sex, intelligence, socioeconomic status, personality traits, and competences. Convergent validity is also less than desired; different operational measures of the same presumed style sometimes show disturbingly low relationships to one another. As was pointed out in the case of the list of higher-order environmental dimensions discussed above, much more research is needed to determine which processes are conceptually meaningful and relatively independent of other psychological processes. In some way, however, each style is meant to describe some way in which the individual utilizes environmental stimuli as a basis for pursuing life goals and responding either behaviorally or affectively to some external situation.

Environmental Cognition

One of the main streams of research on man-environment relations has dealt with the inner experience of the large-scale and moderate-scale physical environment. Traditional psychophysics and perceptual psychology examined the experiential environment in micro terms (for example, brightness, hue, form, apparent movement), utilizing as stimulus materials discrete properties of objects either explicitly removed from their contexts or with their contexts also under total experimental control. Environmental psychology, in contrast, has looked at the perceptual, cognitive, and affective experience of rooms, man-made structures, neighborhoods, cities, and natural environments. This research is based broadly in the phenomenological stream of scientific investigation whose position is that the external world attains reality only through its translation by the individual into terms that are meaningful to him and consistent with his highly personalized goals. More extended attention is given this construct by Weisman in Chapter 5 of this volume.

Empirical Data Relevant to the Environmental Docility Hypothesis

The substance of the environmental docility hypothesis had been noted by Yarrow (1963), Birren (1964), and documented by Rosow (1967). The latter author studied the social interaction patterns of elderly apartment dwellers and reported the very influential finding that the amount of contact of such older people was a direct function of the number of proximate (within the apartment building) age peers, that is, the age density of the structure. Other results of his study demonstrated the added importance of other moderator variables in determining the strength of this relationship. Higher age, female sex, unattached marital status, working class status, and to a lesser extent, poor health, made the older person more sensitive to local variations in age density. That is, such people were more dependent on having many similar-aged peers living nearby in order to maintain active social relationships. Age and health are clear examples of competence, and in our society a good case can be made for female sex as a status whose effect may frequently be tantamount to reduced competence. Marital status and working class membership, both to some extent achieved statuses, less clearly represent intrapersonal competence. However, being never-married, widowed, or having lived a lifetime identified as a working class member (Rosow determined this status by the distinction between earlier-life manual versus non-manual labor of the head of the household) have a clear social stimulus value that makes them indistinguishable from the more properly intrapersonal competences. Thus, in the terms of the model, the less competent were more vulnerable to the press of low age density than were the more competent: the younger, the males, the married, the middle class, and the healthier who lived in age-sparse settings were relatively better able than were the low-competent in these statuses to maintain a high level of social contact in spite of having to look further for such contacts.

A sociometric study of tenants in age-segregated housing for the elderly by Lawton and Simon (1968) led them to formulate the environmental docility hypothesis. In addition to demonstrating a strong proximity effect on choice of friends, which was invariant over time, this study examined the moderating effects of health, country of birth, marital status, age, sex and income on the extent to which tenants limited their choices of friends to those living on the same floor. Lowered status (or competence) on all except age and foreign birth resulted in smaller social space for friendship choices in at least one of the two sites studied.

In the ecological model, competence was indexed by the statuses above, and press by the distance to other people in the building. In the Lawton and Simon (1968) study, the outcome variable is more implicit than explicit: mutually satisfying friendships. That is, under unrestricted conditions, people search for friends who share values, interests, and earlier backgrounds (Nahemow & Lawton, 1975). Rosow's middle class sample did exactly this and were better able to search over a wider radius for such friends. Constrained by reduced competence to search only the immediate area of one's floor, the tenants in Lawton and Simon's study were probably less likely to find such mutually satisfying relationships.

It seems worthwhile to indicate schematically how these findings and others to be presented below fit into the ecological model. Figure 3.5 translates the specific variables of a number of studies into the P, E, and B (outcome) dimensions. Competence is shown on the ordinate, environmental press on the abscissa, and examples of the low-press, optimal-range area give examples of where individuals of high and low competence might stand. One can see here that the high-competence person, by being able to maintain friendships at a greater distance, has a much wider band of possible shared values and therefore satisfying friendships than does the low-competence person. The low-press situation, purely hypothetical at this point, suggests that detachment is one response to too easy access to friends.

A different approach to the investigation of the docility hypothesis was seen in one result of a study by Mangum (1971) of tenants in six specialized housing settings (Diagram B, Figure 3.5). These settings were divided into those serving high-SES (socioeconomic status) and low-SES elderly. Mangum examined adjustment (a combination of morale, housing satisfaction, and favorable attitude toward age-segregated housing) in terms of a number of personal characteristics (personal potency, self-esteem, inner-directedness, etc.) and setting-situational factors (length of residence, on-site social and organizational activity, etc.). He asked the general question as to the relative importance of personal and situational variables in determining adjustment (the affect outcome). Lawton and Simon's (1968) original statement of the environmental docility hypothesis was . . . "the more competent the organism . . . the less the proportion of variance attributable to . . . conditions around him" (p. 108), simply another way of stating the lesser sensitivity of better-equipped people to environmental press. Where the Rosow and the Lawton and Simon studies had physical measures of a specific environmental variable, Mangum dealt with the summative effect of a number of behavioral variables that related to the more general envi-

FIGURE 3.5.   Four empirical applications of the ecological model of aging.

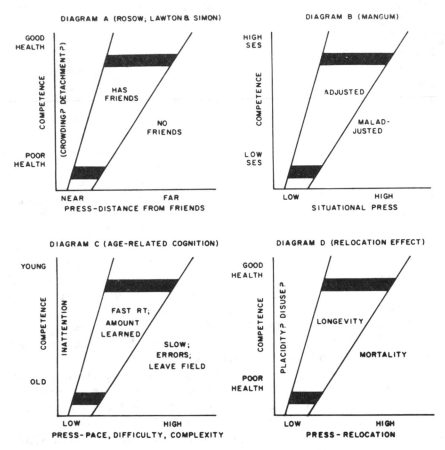

ronmental situation of specialized housing for the elderly. He found that for the high-SES tenants, personal variables accounted for a greater proportion of variance (from a stepwise multiple-regression analysis), while the situational variables accounted for more variance among low-SES tenants. In Diagram B a wide range of environmental press may end up in optimal adjustment for the high-competence tenants, while a much more limited range will have this effect for the low-competence tenants.

The strongest support for the environmental docility hypothesis comes from the large body of research reviewed by Lawton (1975) in the perceptual-motor and cognitive areas, looking at chronological age as the index of competence. Many of these studies have attempted to remove the influence of non-cognitive factors on the performance of the elderly; Diagram C of Figure 3.5 is meant to portray those studies that still show an apparent age decrement even after social, motivational, and other influences have been accounted for. Thus, adequate performance, whether measured in terms of fast response time or speed of learning, is the outcome for a wider variety of press (rate of pacing, task difficulty, stimulus complexity) among younger subjects than among older ones (see Botwinick, 1973).

The research on relocation mortality is also consistent with what might be predicted by the environmental docility hypothesis. Diagram D of Figure 3.5 illustrates the substance of these findings, although most studies involve a dichotomous definition of press, that is, relocation versus no relocation. Lawton and Nahemow (1973) summarized the research up to that point. Studies were found showing a greater excess mortality following institutional relocation among psychotics (Aldrich & Mendkoff, 1963), the less physically healthy (Goldfarb, Shahinian & Burr, 1972; Markus, 1970; Killian, 1970), those with a diagnosis of chronic brain syndrome (Goldfarb, et al., 1972), and sometimes, though not always, the older residents (Markus et al., 1970; Killian, 1970; Markus, 1970). The only groups showing no overall relocation mortality effect were those whose competence was relatively high as compared to the aforementioned studies: healthy institutional residents (Miller & Lieberman, 1965); mental patients considered good candidates for community placement (Lieberman, Tobin & Slover, 1971); and people moving voluntarily to senior housing (Lawton & Yaffe, 1970).

Research data are not at hand to clarify the low-press-high-competence sector of Diagram D. However, both Goldfarb et al. (1972) and Markus et al. (1970) found that healthier subjects showed a positive relocation effect, that is, fewer than the predicted number of deaths. If one can really say that such a change may be good for the originally most hardy, then one might infer the converse, that remaining in the same location might encourage placidity or disuse of skills, which is what Diagram D posits.

Summary

There is an abundance of data to support the environmental docility hypothesis. What is lacking are more studies utilizing specifically defined and scaled environmental attributes. Clearly not all are equivalent, and not all are relevant either to specific competences or specific behaviors/affects. Furthermore, the distinction between strength of press, as compared to the presumed goodness or badness of the press, needs to become much better defined in operational terms. Finally, the tradeoffs, compensatory mechanisms and balances among different types of press-competence outcomes need investigation. Glass and Singer (1972) have identified a phenomenon called "the latent cost of adaptation," in which behavior in response to noise stress was adaptive at one level (good motor-cognitive performance) but maladaptive at another level (post-stress low frustration tolerance). Thus, multilevel research is clearly needed.

CONCLUSION: SOME OF THE DEFICIENCIES
OF THE MODEL

The foregoing presentation has raised far more questions than it has answered. It has not hesitated to speculate in the absence of data nor to allow a generality to be used in the place of a more specific concept that does not seem operationally definable at present. In conclusion, one may list some areas in which more work is necessary in order to improve the model.

1. Competence becomes more a transactional than an intrapersonal attribute as the process becomes more complex. While it is of conceptual value to distinguish person-attributes (for example, biological health, perceptual-motor capacity, and cognition ability) from transactional attributes (for example, social status, cognitive performance, effectance, and social behavior), in practice these latter processes must themselves be treated as competences when other adaptive behaviors and affects are used as outcome or dependent variables. Measures of each type of competence are available. While these indices are far from adequate, our ability to measure competences is considerably better than in the case of environments and inner aspects of wellbeing.

2. Environmental press are still very poorly conceptualized and operationalized. The scale needs to be better specified (laboratory stimulus, specific event, generalized milieu). Clearer distinctions need to be made between idiosyncratic, phenomenal events (beta press), consensual environmental press, and physically-defined environmental attributes. The relationships among aspects of the environment need defining, and the task of organizing them into a functional taxonomy needs to be done. All of the foregoing discussion reveals persistent confusion between strength of press and the positive/negative direction of press, as defined in terms of the adaptive behavior/affect outcome.

3. Optimal range of stimulation and the concept of adaptation level are still only theoretically, rather than empirically, defined. The separate, combined, or contradictory effects of tension arousal and tension reduction need to be examined in relation to behavioral and affective outcomes.

4. Personality style has been suggested as a potentially useful addition to the model, but we do not really know whether this concept adds to prediction beyond the information gained by measuring basic competence or other personality traits. Is there a developmental aspect to personality style that aids or hinders adaptation to the biological and social changes associated with aging?

5. Knowledge about environmental cognition should clearly lead to better planning decisions for elderly individuals, a wider range of choices for them, and better community planning processes. It should also add to our general knowledge about the relationship between the personal and environmental aspects of the process of aging.

The net message to be derived from these gaps in knowledge is that the study of the ecology of aging is still emerging from a prescientific phase. Taxonomy, measurement, naturalistic research, and experimentally controlled hypothesis-testing are all necessary approaches that will aid in this process.

REFERENCES

Aldrich, C. K. and Mendkoff, E. Relocation of the aged and disabled: A mortality study. *Journal of the American Geriatrics Society*, 1963, *11*, 185–194.

Allport, G. W. *Personality: A psychological interpretation*. New York: Hall, 1937.

Baltes, P. B. and Labouvie, G. V. Adult development of intellectual performance: Description, explanation, and modification. In Eisdorfer, C. and Lawton, M. P. (Eds.), *The psychology of adult development and aging*. Washington: American Psychological Association, 1973.

Beattie, W. M. and Bullock, J. *Preface to a counseling service*. St. Louis: Health and Welfare Council of Metropolitan St. Louis, 1963. (Mimeo)

Berlyne, D. E. and Madsen, K. B. (Eds.). *Pleasure, reward, preference*. New York: Academic Press, 1973.

Birren, J. E. *The psychology of aging*. Englewood Cliffs, NJ.: Prentice-Hall, 1964.

Botwinick, J. *Aging and behavior*. New York: Springer, 1973.

Bradburn, M. *The structure of psychological wellbeing*. Chicago: Aldine, 1969.

Burgess, E. M., Cavan, R., and Havighurst, R. *Your activities and attitudes scale*. Chicago: Science Research Associates, 1949.

Cameron, P. Mood as an indicator of happiness: Age, sex, social class and situational differences. *Journal of Gerontology*, 1975, *30*, 216–224.

Carp, F. M. *A future for the aged*. Austin: University of Texas Press, 1966.

Culbertson, K., Pomeroy, L., and Cunningham, W. R. Age and the measurement of mood. Paper presented at the annual meeting of the Gerontological Society, San Juan, Puerto Rico, December 1972.

Dibner, A. S. Behavioral correlates of preference for complexity in the aged. Paper presented at the annual meeting of the Gerontological Society, Miami, November, 1973.

Edwards, A. L. *Manual for the personal preference schedule*. New York: Psychological Corporation, 1953.

Erikson, E. H. *Childhood and society*. New York: Norton, 1963.

Freud, S. Sexuality and aetiology. In S. Freud, *Collected works*, vol. 1. New York: Basic Books, 1959.

Glass, D. G. and Singer, J. E. *Urban stress*. New York: Academic Press, 1972.

Goldfarb, A. I., Shahinian, S. P., and Burr, H. T. Death rate of relocated nursing home residents. In Kent, D. P., Kastenbaum, R., and Sherwood, S. (Eds.), *Research, planning and action for the elderly*. New York: Behavioral Publications, 1972.

Granick, R. and Nahemow, L. D. Preadmission isolation as a factor in adjustment to an old age home. In Hoch, P. H. and Zubin, J. (Eds.), *Psychopathology of aging*. New York: Grune & Stratton, 1961.

Hartshorne, H. and May, M. A. *Studies in deceit*. New York: Macmillan, 1928.

Helson, H. *Adaptation level theory*. New York: Harper & Row, 1964.

Hershberger, R. G. Toward a set of semantic scales to measure the meaning of architectural environments. In Mitchell, W. J. (Ed.), *Environmental design: Research and practice*. Los Angeles: University of California, Los Angeles, 1972.

Kaplan, S. Cognitive maps, human needs, and the designed environment. In Preiser, W. (Ed.),

Environmental design research, Vol. 1. Stroudsburg, PA.: Dowden, Hutchinson & Ross, 1973.

Killian, E. C. Effect of geriatric transfers on mortality rates. *Social Work*, 1970, *15*, 19–26.

Kutner, B., Fanshel, D., Togo, A. M., and Langner, T. S. *Five hundred over sixty*. New York: Russell Sage Foundation, 1956.

Lawton, M. P. Supportive services in the context of the housing environment. *Gerontologist*, 1969, 9, 15–19.

_____. Ecology and aging. In Pastalan, L. A. and Carson, D. H. (Eds.), *The spatial behavior of older people*. Ann Arbor: Institute of Gerontology, University of Michigan, 1970.

_____. Assessing the functional competence of older people. In Kent, D. P., Kastenbaum, R. and Sherwood, S. (Eds.), *Research, planning, and action for the elderly*. New York: Behavioral Publications, 1972.

_____. Competence, environmental press, and adaptation. In P. G. Windley, T. O. Byerts, and G. Ernst (Eds.), *Theory development in environment and aging*. Washington, DC.: Gerontological Society, 1975.

_____. and Brody, E. Assessment of older people, self-maintaining and instrumental activities of daily living. *Gerontologist*, 1969, 9, 179–188.

_____. and Nahemow, L. Ecology and the aging process. In Eisdorfer, C. and Lawton, M. P. (Eds.), *The psychology of adult development and aging*. Washington: American Psychological Association, 1973.

_____. and Simon, B. B. The ecology of social relationships in housing for the elderly. *Gerontologist*, 1968, 8, 108–115.

_____. and Yaffe, S. Mortality, morbidity, and voluntary change of residence by older people. *Journal of the American Geriatrics Society*, 1970, *18*, 823–831.

Lewin, K. *Dynamic theory of personality*. New York: McGraw Hill, 1935.

Lieberman, M. Institutionalization of the aged: Effects on behavior. *Journal of Gerontology*, 1969, *24*, 330–340.

Lieberman, M., Tobin, S. S., and Slover, D. *The effects of relocation on long-term geriatric patients* (Final Report, Project No. 17–1328). Chicago: Department of Health and Committee on Human Development, University of Chicago, 1971.

Lindsley, O. R. Geriatric behavioral prosthetics. In Kastenbaum, R. (Ed.), *New thoughts on old age*. New York: Springer, 1964.

Lowenthal, M. *Lives in distress*. New York: Basic Books, 1964.

Mangum, W. P. Adjustment in residential settings for the aged: An inquiry based on the Kleemeier conceptualization. Unpublished Ph.D. dissertation, University of Southern California, 1971.

Markus, E. *Post-relocation mortality among institutionalized aged*. Cleveland: Benjamin Rose Institute, 1970. (Mimeo)

_____., Blenkner, M., Bloom, M., and Downs, T. Relocation stress and the aged. In Blumenthal, T. (Ed.), *Interdisciplinary topics in gerontology*, Vol. 7. Basel, Switzerland: Karger, 1970.

Maslow, A. H. *Motivation and personality*. New York: Harper, 1964.

Miller, D. and Lieberman, M. A. The relationship of affect state and adaptive capacity to reactions to stress. *Journal of Gerontology*, 1965, *20*, 492–497.

Moriwaki, S. Y. Self-disclosure, significant others, and psychological wellbeing in old age. *Journal of Health and Social Behavior*, 1973, *14*, 226–232.

Murphy, G. *Personality: A biosocial approach to origins and structure*. New York: Harper & Row, 1947.

Murray, H. A. *Explorations in personality*. New York: Oxford, 1938.

Nahemow, L. and Lawton, M. P. Toward an ecological theory of adaptation and aging. In Preiser, W. (Ed.), *Environmental design research*, Vol. 1. Stroudsburg, PA.: Dowden, Hutchinson & Ross, 1973.

_____. Similarity and propinquity in friendship formation. *Journal of Personality and Social Psychology*, 1975, *32*, 205–213.

Neugarten, B. L. Adult personality. Toward a psychology of the life cycle. In Neugarten, B. L. (Ed.), *Middle age and aging*. Chicago: University of Chicago Press, 1968.

_____., Havighurst, R. J., and Tobin, S. S. The measurement of life satisfaction. *Journal of Gerontology*, 1961, *16*, 134–143.

Park, E. E., Burgess, E. W., and McKenzie, R. D. (Eds.). *The city*. Chicago: University of Chicago Press, 1925.

Perin, C. *With man in mind*. Cambridge, MA.: MIT Press, 1970.

Rapoport, A. An approach to the construction of man-environment theory. In Preiser, W. (Ed.), *Environmental design research*, Vol. 1. Stroudsburg, PA.: Dowden, Hutchinson & Ross, 1973.

Rosow, I. *Social integration of the aged*. New York: Free Press, 1967.

Schooler, K. K. The relationship between social interaction and morale of the elderly as a function of environmental characteristics. *Gerontologist*, 1969, *9*, 25–29.

Sterns, H. L. The relation of age to experience, mode of evaluation and complexity in visual preference. Unpublished Ph.D. dissertation, West Virginia University, 1971.

Tuckman, J. Factors related to attendance in a center for older people. *Journal of the American Geriatrics Society*, 1967, *15*, 474–479.

Tuddenham, R. D. The constancy of personality ratings over two decades. *Genetic Psychology Monographs*, 1959, *60*, 3–29.

White, R. W. Motivation reconsidered: The concept of competence. *Psychological Review*, 1959, *66*, 297–333.

Witkin, H. A., Lewis, H. B., Hertzman, M., Machover, K., Meissner, P. B., and Wapner, S. *Personality through perception*. New York: Harper, 1954.

Wohlwill, J. F. Amount of stimulus exploration and preference as differential functions of stimulus complexity. *Perception and Psychophysics*, 1968, *4*, 307–312.

_____. *Behavioral response and adaptation to environmental stimulation*. University Park, PA.: Pennsylvania State University Department of Man-Environment Relations, 1972.

_____. The environment is not in the head! In Preiser, W. (Ed.), *Environmental design research*, Vol. 1. Stroudsburg, PA.: Dowden, Hutchinson & Ross, 1973.

_____. and Kohn, I. The environment as experienced by the migrant: An adaptation-level view. *Representative Research in Social Psychology*, 1973, *4*, 135–164.

Yarrow, M. R. Appraising environment. In Williams, R. H., Tibbitts, C., and Donahue, W. (Eds.), *Processes of aging*. New York: Atherton, 1963.

4

Environmental Dispositions: A Theoretical and Methodological Alternative

PAUL G. WINDLEY

This chapter reexamines the theoretical basis for the concept of environmental dispositions as formulated by Sonnenfeld (1969), McKechnie (1970), and Marshall (1970). The intent is to present a more integrated conceptual position that considers recent theoretical developments in the psychology of personality and environmental psychology. The usefulness of this position in understanding aging/environment relationships will then be discussed.

Environmental dispositions are defined as the unique but relatively stable ways people relate to the man-made and natural environment. Dispositions include the configuration of people's attitudes, beliefs, values, and sentiments in regard to the physical environment. Dispositions also imply a trait-like behavioral potential — a predisposition to respond and behave in a consistent fashion in the environment. In addition, environmental dispositions include individuals' reported uses and modifications of the physical environment as reflected by questions in established personality inventories (c.f. Craik, 1976, 1977).

These researchers argue that, with knowledge of environmental dispositions, phenomena such as adaptation to environmental stress, adjustment to migration, preference for different housing environments and transportation modes, and leisure style can be better understood or perhaps predicted. Such knowledge is valuable for environmental decision makers, architects and planners, as well as for behavioral scientists attempting to account for additional variance in human behavior.

McKechnie's (1974) 184 item Environmental Response Inventory is designed to assess 8 environmental dispositions: pastoralism, urbanism, environmental adaptation, stimulus seeking, environmental trust, antiquarianism, need for privacy, and mechanical orientation. The Environmental Personality Inventory developed by Sonnenfeld (1969) measures four environmental dispositions: sensitivity to environment, environmental control, mobility, and risk-taking. Little (1968) devised a fourfold typology of person–thing orientation: thing specialists, person specialists, generalists, and nonspecialists. Marshall (1970) has developed a set of scales assessing six different privacy orientations, while Windley (1972) identified four environmental dispositions among elderly individuals: need for privacy, preference for complexity, preference for environmental stability, and need for environmental manipulation.

McKechnie (1970) found correlations for several of his environmental dispositions with the California Psychological Inventory, the Myers–Briggs Type Indicator and the Study of Values. Mehrabian and Russell (1974) found that high arousal-seekers prefer more complex situations than do low arousal-seekers, and that persons who normally maintain greater distances between themselves and others are more likely to experience stress and task performance deficits in high-density conditions than those who maintain close distances. Among certain groups, internal versus external locus of control has been found to correlate with antipollution activities, preferences for greater interpersonal distance requirements, and control over the environment (c.f. Levensen, 1974; Baron, et al., 1976). Marshall (1970) found correlations between six orientations toward privacy (noninvolvement with neighbors, seclusions of home, solitude, privacy with intimates, anonymity, and reserve) and the personality dimensions extraversion-introversion, thinking-feeling on the Myers-Briggs Type Indicator, and wanted and expressed affection and inclusion on FIRO-B. These six orientations were also found to be associated with person-room density of home, neighborhood, occupation, features of the physical environment affecting potential privacy, and privacy-oriented behavior and social norms regarding privacy. Windley (1973) found, among a sample of elderly females, significant correlations between need for privacy and self-ratings of need for privacy on the one hand, and number of people with which leisure time is spent on the other. Preference for environmental complexity was found to be associated with such variables as time spent alone each day, self-ratings of activity level, size of resident's community, fear of natural hazards, and age of respondent. Preference for environmental manipulation was significantly related to activity level, age, marital status, and education level.

Although relationships such as those reported above have been found between some environmental dispositions and self-reported behavior, the position advanced here is that the concept of environmental dispositions as presently conceived is not theoretically well-founded and is unlikely to lead to substantial prediction of environmental behavior. The remaining part of this chapter will discuss this issue in more depth and will present a more tenable alternative viewpoint of how disposition-like behavior relates to the physical environment.

THE CONCEPT OF TRAITS

The traditional field of personality is concerned with identifying and studying the basic traits underlying the ways in which people relate to themselves and to others. Environmental dispositions are thought to conceptually parallel such personality traits as altruism, aggression, or authoritarianism. The majority of trait theorists are structuralists — that is, they search for stable interrelated trait networks that serve as motives for, as well as descriptive predictors of, behavior across varied situations. The structuralist stance is that traits are glued together within the individual and that cross-situational correlations should be perfect.

Assaults on trait theory have occurred in at least three areas. First, Sarason and Smith (1971), Adelson (1969), Wiggins (1968), and Mischel (1968) have seriously questioned the descriptive and predictive value of personality as such. Personality traits, individually or collectively, seldom accounted for more than ten percent of the variance in human behavior in any given instance, and they accounted for even less across different situations. Second, Sarason and Smith (1971) argued that methodological tinkering has become a preoccupation among personality theorists. For example, each new factor analysis adds new traits to the endless list, and few attempts are made to integrate these traits theoretically. Symptomatic of the methodological preoccupation is Wiggins' (1968) observation that such methodological phenomena as response set or respondent suspicion are, themselves, now considered to be personality traits. A third vulnerable point is the argument that trait structures remain relatively intact through the life cycle, with variances in observed behavior merely reflecting different response modes of the same underlying trait. These differential response modes are thought to parallel the biological curve, thus occurring roughly at the same stage in the life cycle for most individuals. However, in a recent review of personality research, Neugarten (1973) has pointed out that age differences occur on some traits and not in others, and that some of the changes are discernible in middle age, others in old age.

The search for stable and enduring individual-difference variables that would permit prediction of behavior across varied situations has yielded less than even modest success. The emerging picture is one of skepticism and frustration with the inadequacies of trait theory. Since the present concept of environmental dispositions is theoretically and methodologically patterned after trait theory, it is highly improbable that we will be able to account for any more variance in behavior with such dispositions than we have with personality traits as such.

It is felt that a new conceptualization of environmental dispositions is in order and should occur on at least four fronts:

1. a reexamination of the nature of the disposition itself;

2. the need for situation-specific hypotheses;

3. the role of moderating variables; and

4. the influence of specific attributes of situations.

THE NATURE OF DISPOSITIONS

Two alternative views of personal dispositions exist. Ryle (1949) considers dispositions to be hypothetical propositions, much like dispositional statements in the physical sciences. The statement "John is an urban person" is akin to saying "the concrete is hard"; each is likely or will probably respond in certain ways under certain conditions. On the other hand, Hampshire (1971) considers dispositions to be summarizing statements which may take the form: "As far as we can tell, John's trend of behavior suggests that he is an urban person." In this view the emphasis is not on probability of behavior given a set of circumstances, but rather it is on general trends over prolonged periods of observation.

Regardless of which viewpoint is considered, it is more useful to view dispositions as abilities rather than as behavior traits. The abilities concept requires that we focus on two issues: the capacity to respond to a stimulus, and the performance conditions of the response. If an individual negatively endorses the following test item: "A person has a right to modify the environment to suit his needs," the traditional argument is that the person has a deep and abiding disposition to respect and conserve nature. However, the individual may simply be incapable of manipulating the environment in most situations because he has so infrequently done so — environmental manipulation is generally not in his repertoire of abilities. Moreover, the individual may in some situations manipulate his environment adequately, but in others fail to do so.

Construing dispositions as abilities is not new. Wallace (1966, 1967), Kogan and Wallach (1964), and Eriksen and Eriksen (1972) have found substantial correlations between personality traits and cognitive abilities. Mischel (1968) argues that personality traits correlate higher with cognitive abilities (which show more cross-situational consistency) than they do with noncognitive referents. Although Mischel, in this critique, offered several examples of abilities as alternatives to personality traits, a more recent conceptualization has identified the following personal cognitive variables (Mischel, 1968):

1. construction competencies — ability to generate particular behavior related to I.Q., mental maturity, ego development, and social skills;

2. encoding strategies and personal constructs — units for categorizing events and for self descriptions;

3. behavioral expectancies in particular situations;

4. subjective values — placed on these expectancies; and

5. self-regulatory systems and plans — rules (standards) and self-reactions for performance.

All five of these alternatives redirect our attention from what people are like to an assessment of what they do in the environment.

Viewing environmental dispositions as response capabilities rather than as response dispositions also has different implications for both disposition measurement and change, which will be discussed later.

SITUATION-SPECIFIC HYPOTHESES

It is remarkable how each of us manages to reconcile our diverse behaviors into one self-consistent whole. An individual may insist that he have a private office at work but continually socialize with workmates during the day; he may retreat while at home on weekday evenings but frequent many social gatherings on weekends. He may thus construe himself to be a basically private person, while his peers may see him as gregarious. How does one reconcile this self-perception of continuity with the equally impressive evidence that on virtually all personality traits, substantial changes occur both over time and across situations? For example, Mischel (1968) in his review of personality trait research demonstrated that the average correlation for any given trait cross-situationally is only $+ .30$, and he argues that the unreliability found in many measurements is really not methodological noise but true individual differences across situations.

The predictive utility of environmental dispositions is greatest when tied to specific situations rather than viewed solely as structural aspects of the person. In other words, to the extent that a person would attempt to answer a traditional self-report item (usually phrased quite abstractly) without reference to actual situations, we would expect him to experience increasing degrees of uncertainty in arriving at an answer concerning himself. Neugarten (1973), in her study of the adult personality, argues a similar point both in terms of continuity across situations and stability over time. What people do in any situation is altered by seemingly minor variations in prior experience or in the social and physical attributes of the setting.

However, Bem (1974) has argued that a more accurate characterization of behavior prediction across situations is to adopt a middle-of-the-road position; that is, some people are predictable some of the time. Moreover, Bem argues that situations are as effective as personality traits in predicting behavior. Thus, the interaction of persons with situations deserves more concentrated study. Bowers (1973) has supported this point by stating that both the extreme trait and situationist positions are misleading, and that a position stressing person-situation interaction is more conceptually satisfying and empirically warranted.

MODERATING VARIABLES

Closely related to the person-situation interactionist position is the role of intervening or moderating variables. For example, in a reanalysis of data on environmental dispositions of elderly females, Windley (1972) observed that widely varying differences in correlations emerged between personal-behavioral measures and dispositions when urban and rural elderly were each analyzed separately. Thus, the effect of moderating variables is often masked when subgroups are lumped together and treated as a homogeneous sample.

The identification of moderating variables must be a prerequisite to a person-environment interaction position. It must be possible to predict on a priori grounds which moderators are likely to divide up the world into useful segments for study: What kinds of individuals might display trait-like consistency? What environmental settings might be functionally equivalent for a given group of individuals? An important point to note here is that such questions reverse the usual assumptions of trait consistency as given and inconsistency as problematic. Our future research stance should assume, however, that the concept of stability is now relevant only when refering to person-environment units rather than independently to dispositions or situations.

A TAXONOMY OF SITUATIONS

It has been argued that to increase the predictive potential of environmental dispositions they should be studied more as abilities and should be examined across a variety of environmental situations. A major difficulty in such cross-situational research is the lack of standardization of descriptive situational characteristics for comparative analysis. The need for a taxonomy or classification scheme of physical environments seems obvious.

What is a situation for a person and how should it be described? Should one consider the perceived or actual environment? Koffka's (1935) conclusion was that behavior could be more meaningfully understood if it was related to the perceived environment. Sells (1963) argues, however, that situational measures must be obtained independently of the individual's perception of them. A conclusive answer will likely require an understanding of the circumstances under which one or the other kind of data would be most useful. At a minimum, such a scheme should describe at a variety of scales objective social and physical characteristics such as area, density, and spatial configuration as well as more subjective factors such as aesthetic appeal. Although several attempts have been made to describe the environment in this manner (c.f. Craik, 1971; Frederiksen, 1972; Wallace, 1967), Moos (1973) has conceptualized six major parameters of environments, which incorporate much of the work of others and seem most promising:

1. ecological dimensions — ranging from temperature, topography, and soil conditions in the natural environment to temperature, noise level, and other design properties in the man-made environment;

2. behavior settings — stable extra-individual units that have both an environmental and behavioral component;

3. dimensions of organizational structure — size, staffing ratios, degree of organizational control, and turnover rate;

4. personal and behavioral characteristics of the milieu inhabitants — average age, ability level and socioeconomic background, which together make up the more general descriptive characteristics of social situations;

5. psychosocial characteristics and organizational climate — certain dimensions along which organizations may be compared such as maintenance or production structures, authority structures, formal role patterns, and regulatory mechanisms; and

6. functional or reinforcing properties of environments — the type of attributes that allow differing situations to reinforce or elicit differential responses from the same individual.

Implicit in the description of physical settings is the assumption that physical attributes of settings, once identified, affect and are affected by the individual's ability to respond. Thus any attempt to predict behavior across settings via dispositions must also be able to identify the situational characteristics of settings most likely to produce differential response.

Mischel (1977) has argued that in developing a taxonomy of environments, it is not sufficient to simply create a list of different situations where settings rather than people are given different labels. More important will be the job of analyzing how environmental characteristics interact with the people in them. This is consistent with the conceptual position advanced earlier in this chapter that person-environment interaction units should form the basis for environmental disposition research.

IMPLICATIONS FOR AGING/ENVIRONMENT RELATIONSHIPS

This chapter hypothesizes that chronological age per se explains very little variance in environmental abilities; rather, the major explanatory variable will be environmental, that is, a combination of the physical, social, and psychological attributes of the situation. This does not mean that age differences will not occur on some ability measures. Similar and concurrent changes in environmental situations may tend to normalize measures for specific age groups, for example, retirement at age 65, relocation, moving into housing for the elderly, or institutionalization. Likewise, similar increments and deficits in life experiences such as education, urban versus rural background, and type of occupation could lead to similarity in abilities. Thus, age-related deficits in environmental abilities are likely to be more a function of society's failure to provide and maintain supportive environmental situations than of any organismic factor. This reemphasizes the need to maximally explore the role of moderating variables of both long- and short-term experiential nature.

This hypothesis regarding the origin of environmental abilities also points up the possibility for intervention through environmental manipulation and design, provided key antecedents and moderating variables affecting environmental ability development and change can be identified. Research should concentrate on strategies that explicitly involve alterations and modifications of these key antecedents. Those environmental settings that appear most immediately promising in terms of such research would be housing, urban versus rural settings, institutional environments, senior centers, and transportation facilities.

REFERENCES

Adelson, J. Personality. In P. H. Mussen and M. R. Rosenzweig (Eds.), *Annual Review of Psychology*, 1969, 20, 217–252.

Baron, R. M., Mandel, D. R., Adams, C. A., and Griffin, L. M. Effects of social density in university residential environments. *Journal of Personality and Social Psychology*, 1976, 34, 434–446.

Bem, D. J. and Allen, A. On predicting some of the people some of the time: The search for cross-situational consistencies in behavior. *Psychological Review*, 1974, 81, 506–520.

Bowers, K. S. Situationism in psychology: An Analysis and a critique. *Psychological Review*, 1973, 80, 307–336.

Craik, K. The assessment of places. In P. McReynolds (Ed.), *Advances in psychological assessment*, Vol. 2, Palo Alto: Sciences and Behavior Books, 1971.

_____. The personality research paradigm in environmental psychology. In Wapner, S., Cohen, S. B., and Kaplan, B. (Eds.), *Experiencing the environment*. New York: Plenum, 1976.

_____. Multiple scientific paradigms in environmental psychology. *International Journal of Psychology*, 1977, 12, 147–157.

Eriksen, B. A. and Eriksen, C. W. *Perception and personality*. Moorestown, NJ.: General Learning Press, 1972.

Frederiksen, N. Toward a taxonomy of situations. *American Psychologist*, 1972, 27, 114–123.

Hampshire, S. Dispositions. In S. Hampshire, *Freedom of mind and other essays*. Princeton, NJ.: Princeton University Press, 1971.

Koffka, K. *Principles of gestalt psychology*. New York: Harcourt, Brace, 1935.

Kogan, N. and Wallach, M. *Risk taking: A study in cognition and personality*. New York: Holt, Rinehart & Winston, 1964.

Levenson, H. Activism and powerful others: Distinctions within the concept of internal-external control. *Journal of Personality Assessment,* 1974, *38,* 377–383.

Little, B. R. Psychospecialization: Functions of differential interest in persons and things. *Bulletin of the British Psychological Society,* 1968, *21,* 113.

Marshall, N. Personality correlates of orientation toward privacy. *Proceedings of the 2nd Annual Environmental Design Research Association Conference,* Pittsburgh, 1970.

McKechnie, G. Measuring environmental dispositions with the environmental response inventory. *Proceedings of the 2nd Annual Environmental Design Research Association Conference,* Pittsburgh, 1970.

_____. Manual for the *Environmental Response Inventory.* Palo Alto, CA.: Consulting Psychologists Press, 1974.

Mehrabian, A. and Russell, J. A. *An approach to environmental psychology.* Cambridge, MA.: MIT Press, 1974.

Mischel, W. *Personality and assessment.* New York: Wiley, 1968.

_____. On the future of personality measurement. *American Psychologist,* 1977, *32,* 246–254.

Moos, R. H. Conceptualizations of human environments. *American Psychologist,* 1973, *28,* 652–665.

Neugarten, B. Personality change in late life: A developmental perspective. In C. Eisdorfer and M. P. Lawton (Eds.), *The psychology of adult development in aging.* Washington, D.C.: American Psychological Association, 1973.

Ryle, G. *The concept of mind.* New York: Barnes and Noble, 1949.

Sarason, I. G. and Smith, R. E. Personality. In P. H. Mussen and M. R. Rosenzweig (Eds.), *Annual Review of Psychology,* 1971, *22,* 393–466.

Sells, S. B. An interactionist looks at the environment. *American Psychologist,* 1963, *18,* 696–702.

Sonnenfeld, J. Personality and behavior in environment. In J. Fraser (Ed.), *Proceedings of the Association of American Geographers,* 1969, *1,* 136–141.

Wallace, J. An abilities conception of personality: Some implications for personality measurement. *American Psychologist,* 1966, *21,* 132–138.

_____. What units shall we employ? Allport's questions revisited. *Journal of Consulting Psychology,* 1967, *31,* 56–65.

Wiggins, J. S. Personality structure. In P. R. Farnsworth, M. R. Rosenzweig, and J. T. Polefka (Eds.), *Annual Review of Psychology,* 1968, *19,* 293–350.

Windley, P. G. Environmental dispositions of older people. Unpublished Ph.D. dissertation. Ann Arbor: University Microfilms, 1972.

Windley, P. G. Measuring environmental dispositions of elderly females. In W. F. E. Preiser (Ed.), *Environmental design research,* Vol. 1. Stroudsburg, PA.: Dowden, Hutchinson and Ross, 1973.

5
Developing Man-Environment Models

JERRY WEISMAN

INTRODUCTION

The behavioral sciences are increasingly involved in what might be characterized as a real world revolution. Researchers are exchanging the familiar laboratory context for the complexities and uncertainties of the world outside. They are more and more often joined there by members of the environmental design/planning community who are equally concerned with the behavioral consequences of the built environment. These complementary paradigm shifts reflect the convergence of many interrelated forces: increased awareness of ecological and ethological issues; recognition of the limitations of the laboratory setting; the press of real world problems.

This emerging environment/behavior perspective has already yielded some significant insights. Within the gerontological context, for example, it has become possible to revise the previous view of the inevitable decline in intellectual functioning over the life cycle. Environmental demands and opportunities, as well as an individual's competence, are now seen as defining performance (Baltes & Labouvie, 1973).

Such important insights reflect the potential contribution of viewing human behavior and development within its environmental context. Pursuit of such an environment/behavior perspective, however, forces us to ask some difficult questions: Where do we go from here? How ought we look at, think about, and conceptualize our complex environment (Moos, 1973)? What are the key variables, among the multitude that constitute our environment, and which variables are potentially most salient? What are the patterns of interrelationships among these variables? This chapter argues that the study of environmental perception and cognition can yield significant answers to these important questions. It is suggested that human behavior within the environment is, to some considerable extent, dependent upon the mental representation or cognitive map of the environment that people build for themselves. In a sense everyone, not only environment/behavior researchers, must be able to model and conceptualize their environment. It is essential that all individuals be able to identify relevant environmental variables and develop an understanding of the relationships among them.

We will review some of what is known about how people perceive and represent their world, primarily in terms of its visual and spatial properties. Emphasis will be given to the functional importance of such cognitive maps, their relationship to both environment and behavior, and their underlying structure. While there is yet little environmental perception and cognition research that focuses specifically on aging and the aged, examples will be reviewed and implications drawn whenever possible.

HISTORICAL ROOTS OF THE COGNITIVE MAP

Environmental perception and cognition may be seen as a paradigm of rather mixed theoretical and disciplinary heritage. The temporal and spatial aspects of mental representations of the environment are familiar to architects, planners and geographers as cognitive maps (Downs & Stea, 1973; Moore & Golledge, 1976). Such models may be more familiar to psychologists as "a genetic coding system, a focus, a system of representations, a cognitive structure, a schema, or a paradigm" (Anglin, 1973, p. xxii).

Moore and Golledge, in a wide-ranging review, trace the roots of the field to pioneering efforts during the 1940s and 1950s in sociology, anthropology, geography, psychology, and urban planning. Other reviewers, in tracing earlier theoretical contributions from within psychology, tend to reach rather different conclusions. Downs and Stea see key concepts as emerging from gestalt psychology; Ittelson (1970) emphasizes the role of the transactionalists; Kaplan (1973, 1976) considers the insights of the early Twentieth Century American functionalists and of Hebb (1949); and Lee (1973) reviews the concepts of Head (1920) and Bartlett (1932).

Such attempts to trace and understand the roots and basic premises of environmental perception and cognition may clearly lead in rather different directions. Despite such variations, however, there do seem to be several key theoretical and empirical issues that reappear consistently. These three interrelated questions might be characterized in the following way:

1. What is the functional significance of environmental perception and cognition? In William James' terms (1968), what is such behavior good for?

2. How does the cognitive map relate to both antecedent environmental conditions and subsequent environmental behavior? What does this suggest about the nature of man/environment relationships?

3. How do cognitive maps relate to theoretical models of cognitive structure and cognitive abilities? How might such structure and abil-

ities change over time, and particularly in the latter stages of the life span?

Indeed it might be suggested that these three issues — function, image and structure — reflect traditional and significant behavioral concerns only now beginning to converge in the development of theory within environment/behavior and environment/aging studies.

FUNCTIONS OF THE COGNITIVE MAP

A subset of the cognitive mapping literature, specifically that emerging from an anthropological or evolutionary perspective (Kaplan, 1973, 1976; Lynch, 1960), addresses the question of function: What might be the adaptive advantage of building an image of the world within one's head? Most fundamentally, possession of a cognitive map permits purposeful mobility within a spatially extensive and demanding environment: "In the process of way-finding, the strategic link is the environmental image, the generalized mental picture of the exterior environment held by the individual" (Lynch, 1960, p. 4).

Kaplan (1973) argues that the cognitive map meets additional information-processing functions beyond those of way-finding. Such representations allow for quick and decisive handling of information and for recognition on the basis of only partial information.

The cognitive map would also appear to be important in dealing with conceptual as well as spatial information. Lynch observes that the environmental image "can serve as a general frame of reference within which the individual acts, or to which he can attach his knowledge, . . . an organizer of action . . . and may help to assuage fear, to establish an emotionally safe relationship between men and their total environment" (pp. 126–127). A number of other authors (Griffin, 1973; Hallowell, 1955) also emphasize these important links between spatial orientation and orientation in a larger social or even cosmological sense.

Thus we ought not to be surprised that people highly value and endeavor to hold onto the representations that they build of their world; the cognitive map "has wide practical and emotional importance to the individual" (Lynch, 1960, p. 4).

Disorientation and Relocation

We likewise ought not to be surprised by the strong reactions of people who come to find themselves without an adequate image of their world. Not only do many of us become lost in environments of all sorts, we often become disconcerted, irritated or even anxious. Berkeley (1973) reports the anger and indignation of users unable to find their way or to build an image of public buildings in Boston and Chicago. Bronzaft, Dobrow, and O'Hanlon (1976) report study participants feeling very insecure in selecting routes and traveling to specific destinations within the New York City subway system.

Such problems of disorientation may become particularly acute in large congregate institutions in which numbers of older persons may find themselves. Spivack (1967) describes psychiatric facilities where inordinately long and undifferentiated corridors distort one's sense of time and distance. Focusing on similar settings, Izumi (1970) makes reference to insecure situations which relate to being lost. Sivadon (1970) considers the countertherapeutic implications of such illegible, institutional settings. To the extent that most people, with increasing age, have greater contact with such health-care facilities, it becomes essential to insure that an adequate level of spatial orientation is maintained.

Clearly, relocation to a new and unfamiliar setting represents a related but likely more severe problem. The representation of one's former home is lost, and it is necessary to begin to build a cognitive map of a new setting and to function with only partial information in the interim. Fried's (1963) study of forced relocation from the West End of Boston, for example, indicates that it was those former residents who had the most extensive knowledge of the area who suffered the most extreme grief reactions.

Given that such relocation is not an uncommon occurrence among older people, this issue of adequacy of environmental information and image was explored in Bourestom and Pastalan's (1973) study of relocation of residents of a county home conducted at the University of Michigan. In addition to a consideration of those variables that might typically be seen as influencing an older person's adjustment to relocation (for example, patient, staff and environmental characteristics), this study also assessed the impact and efficacy of a preparation program. Prior to relocation, residents were taken on three separate occasions to visit the new facility to which they were to be moved. It was found that the preparation program increased the chances that the patients would survive the trauma of the move. Ongoing research by Hunt (n.d.) may be seen as a further step in this direction. He is utilizing both video and model-building techniques to stimulate a traversal of an unfamiliar environment. The simulation includes both images of specific locations and relatively abstracted diagrams of plan configurations. This issue of how we might provide people with the appropriate seeds from which they can then develop a new cognitive map would seem to be an important topic for environments and aging research.

IMAGE, ENVIRONMENT, AND BEHAVIOR

As stated at the outset, the cognitive map is seen as an important link mediating between environment and behavior.

The basic assumptions of cognitive mapping research are that there is a relationship between the spatial environment and the way it is organized and that there is a relationship between the way it is organized and spatial behavior (Lee, 1975, p. 176)

Such links to both antecedent environmental conditions and to subsequent behavioral response, however, have yet to be adequately explored. Goodey (1975) speaks of "an unfortunate hiatus between cognition as monitored and subsequent behavior" (p. 190). Similarly, Wohlwill (1973) has pointed out the dangers of becoming overly fascinated with the individual differences in environmental representations without also exploring the relationships between such variations and the characteristics of the physical environment being represented. Despite such limitations, the cognitive mapping literature can take us some distance in understanding relationships between image, environment and behavior.

Image and Environment

A substantial number of studies have explored the relationship between the objective environment and the environment as represented; much of this research has focused on the likelihood and manner of particular elements of an environment being incorporated in an individual's cognitive map. Such studies, then, have explored identity and structure, the first two of the three components for the analysis of cognitive maps proposed by Lynch. Lynch's third component, meaning, has been the focus of considerably less research (Moore, 1976).

A series of studies conducted by Lynch, his colleagues, and students, spanning more than a decade, provides some sense of how and why particular elements are incorporated as landmarks in environmental representations. The emphasis of Lynch's initial work was clearly on visual/spatial properties of the urban landscape, focusing on such variables as figure/background clarity and form singularity. Subsequent studies (DeJonge, 1962; Gulick, 1963; Harrison, 1967) brought into sharper focus those additional factors — small-scale elements of the environment, cultural values, location of activity centers, meaning and association — that determine the landmarks within an environment. Steinitz (1968), in a key study, emphasized the impact of congruence of activity and physical form in shaping an individual's knowledge of a setting. Finally, Appleyard (1969a, 1969b) assessed the impact of three environmental variables upon urban knowledge: intensity and singularity of physical form, levels of visibility, intensity and singularity of use and community significance. All three variables were found to have comparable and significant effects.

Many of these same authors explored questions of the structure of cognitive maps — the spatial interrelationships among elements — and how structure is shaped by the objective physical environment. Lynch, for example, found that Boston's Back Bay, with its regular gridiron street pattern, could be effectively structured, but not the South End; Boston's subway system was more readily structured than its streets. Appleyard's (1969b) study classified inhabitants' cognitive maps of a city along two dimensions reflecting accuracy (primitive and topological to positional) and kind of elements used (sequential or spatial). Furthermore, Appleyard emphasized the relationship between identification and structuring of an environment. In sum, the inhabitants appeared to structure the city in the same way that they selected elements: through relationships created by action, form, visibility, or significance (p. 440).

Finally, virtually all of these studies emphasize that the cognitive map is far from a perfect reproduction of a cartographic map. To the contrary, it is likely to be schematic, disjointed, simplified, incremental and, at least in parts, non-veridical (Appleyard, 1970). Much of the existing research has endeavored to understand such departures from objective reality as a consequence of such variables as length of residency, familiarity, mode of travel, and ethnic and cultural differences (Appleyard, 1969b; Devlin, 1976; Maurer & Baxter, 1972).

Clearly, with increasing age, some of these variables (for example, the shift from driver to rider) may have a negative impact upon an individual's environmental representation. There is as yet relatively little research directly exploring environment/image links among older people. In one of the few such studies, Regnier (1974) found that such environmental variables as land-use patterns, bus routes, traffic patterns and topography all influenced the definition of neighborhood as represented by a consensus mapping procedure.

Image and Behavior

If there has been some failure to adequately explore relationships between cognitive maps and antecedent environmental conditions, there has been a perhaps greater failure to assess the impact of cognitive maps upon subsequent environmental behavior. While much of the research reviewed in the preceding section calls attention to the schematic, inferential and often non-veridical nature of cognitive representations, as yet we know very little about the impact of such gaps, distortions, and errors on people's behavior. It is, likewise, almost twenty years since Lynch first advanced the proposition that legibility — the ability to identify and structure the environment — does make a difference for both affective and emotional reasons. These issues, however, have yet to be researched. They remain important, unanswered questions, certainly so within the field of environments and aging.

A number of studies at the geographical scale explore the impact of environmental cognition upon subsequent behavior; these are reviewed by Moore (1976). At the neighborhood scale, Lee's (1968) research serves as a strong example. Lee reviews the efforts of both planners and sociologists to explore the concept of neighborhood — in one case viewing it as a piece of territory, in the other only as a set of social relationships, and in neither case with much success. While the concept of neighborhood is, according to Lee, a salient concept in people's lives and is related to environmental behavior, it cannot be defined solely in either physical or social terms. An individual's neighborhood, Lee suggests, is a socio-spatial schema; it is an internal model or representation, reflecting both social and physical factors and reflected, if poorly, in the neighborhood maps drawn by housewives.

Lee's research also has some relationship to environment and aging issues, suggesting that older respondents tend to rely more on proximate neighborhood facilities and services. Regnier (1974) explores similar issues, while focusing specifically on older respondents. Beginning with individual neighborhood maps drawn by respondents, Regnier created composite or consensus cognitive maps for residents in two public housing sites in San Francisco. Results indicate a strong relationship between these consensus maps and the location and frequency of use of services.

This same consensus map approach has been pursued in more recent research efforts (Regnier, Dolak, & Hamburger, 1977), again indicating a link between patterns of service utilization and definition of neighborhood. Krauss et al. (1978) utilize both cartographic and hand-drawn maps in exploring the image of neighborhood held by older respondents.

Relatively little research has been done exploring cognitive representations and their behavioral implications at the architectural scale. A study by Weisman (1979) suggests that the inability of users of a facility to adequately conceptualize its overall layout may have a fundamental and negative impact upon way-finding behavior within that setting. As emphasized earlier, most people have strong feelings about such disorientation and it is an issue of some importance relative to older people.

STRUCTURE OF THE COGNITIVE MAP

As suggested above, considerable research has focused on individual and group variations in environmental representations. The bulk of these studies have concerned variables such as familiarity, class, and so forth. Fundamentally more important yet less explored, are a series of interrelated questions: What are the relationships between the environmental image and the cognitive structure that underlie such representations and the basic cognitive abilities that underlie the mapping process? And, with respect to the field of environments and aging, what might be the pattern of developmental changes in such structure and abilities?

Research in environmental perception and cognition by no means builds on any one model of cognitive structure. Hebb's (1949) neural net models, for example, underlie Kaplan's (1973, 1976) model of the cognitive map;

Lee (1973) extends the concept of schema as developed by Bartlett (1932) and Head (1920). A considerable amount of current research builds upon the developmental concepts of Piaget and Inhelder (1967); it focuses, not surprisingly, on earlier stages of the lifespan continuum (Acredolo, 1976; Moore, 1975). There have, however, been some efforts to extend the Piagetian framework to adults and older persons (Ohta & Walsh, 1977). It remains for researchers to explore the relationships between such laboratory-derived measures of fundamental spatial cognition and developmental changes in them, and cognition of the large-scale spatial environment.

The theoretical approach of Cattell (1963) and Horn (1967) provides another, as yet less utilized, approach to the study of cognitive structure and age-related changes. Indeed their model suggests that with age may come an increasing difficulty in creating new cognitive maps of unfamiliar settings. This can be understood in terms of what Horn and Cattell have characterized as two kinds of intelligence: crystallized intelligence and fluid abilities. Fluid abilities have the most to do with the brain's basic integrative capabilities. There are indications, though not directly validated, that aging individuals do suffer a decline in these fluid abilities, abilities that Hebb has referred to as intelligence A (Baltes & Labouvie, 1973). Horn suggests that an older person is typically able to compensate for this decrement in fluid abilities through an increased reliance upon crystallized intelligence, essentially the accumulated knowledge of one's lifetime. In Horn's terms, widsom is substituted for brilliance. Horn and Cattell claim that spatial abilities are related to the fluid abilities rather than to crystallized intelligence. It thus becomes essential to explore such age-related decrements in spatial abilities, to learn if they influence environmental cognition, and determine whether some form of educational or environmental intervention might assist in maintaining an adequate level of functioning.

SUMMARY

It would seem essential to learn more about environmental perception and cognition and their relationship to the physical environment, patterns of human behavior, and age-related changes in cognitive functioning. It likewise is of considerable importance to learn more about maximizing the abilities of older people to make ongoing use of already-developed cognitive maps. This might mean increasing efforts to maintain independent living in familiar settings. If relocation is necessary, perhaps it can be accomplished in the same or similar surroundings. Certainly the kind of institutional environment found all too often in hospitals and congregate homes is far removed from the experience of most people; such settings may be difficult places for anyone, young or old, to represent mentally and to become oriented. Pre-relocation visits and simulations may be one viable approach to assisting in the building of new cognitive maps when relocation is necessary.

An understanding of the world as people perceive and represent it should be of considerable value in explicating the relationship between the environment and human behavior. A clearer image of the elements of the environment that people include in their own representations and the characteristics and relationships of these elements, should assist in providing a focus for environment/aging research.

REFERENCES

Acredolo, L. Frames of reference used by children for orientation in unfamiliar spaces. In G. Moore and R. Golledge (Eds.), *Environmental knowing: Theories, research and methods.* Stroudsburg, PA.: Dowden, Hutchinson & Ross, 1976.

Anglin, J. M. Introduction. In J. S. Bruner (Ed.), *Beyond the information given.* New York: Norton, 1973.

Appleyard, D. Notes on urban perception and knowledge. In J. Archea and C. Eastman (Eds.), EDRA2, Proceedings of the 2nd Annual Environmental Design Research Association conference. Pittsburgh, PA.: Carnegie-Mellon University, 1970.

Appleyard, D. Why buildings are known. *Environment and Behavior,* 1969a, *1,* 131–156.

_____. City designers and the pluralistic city. In L. Rodwin (Ed.), *Planning urban growth and regional development: The experience of the Guayana program of Venezuela.* Cambridge, MA.: MIT Press, 1969b.

Baltes, P. and Labouvie, G. Adult development of intellectual performance: Description, explanation and modification. In C. Eisdorfer and M. P. Lawton (Eds.), *The psychology of adult development and aging.* Washington, D.C.: American Psychological Association, 1973.

Bartlett, F. C. *Remembering.* Cambridge: Cambridge University Press, 1932.

Berkeley, E. More than you wanted to know about the Boston City Hall. *Architecture Plus,* February, 1973, *1,* 72–77.

Bourestom, N. C. and Pastalan, L. A. *Preparation for relocation.* Relocation Report No. 3. Ann Arbor: University of Michigan, Institute of Gerontology, 1973.

Bronzaft, A., Dobrow, S. and O'Hanlon, T. Spatial orientation in a subway system. *Environment and Behavior,* 1976, 8, 575–594.

Cattell, R. B. Theory of fluid and crystallized intelligence: An initial experiment. *Journal of Educational Psychology,* 1963, *105,* 105–111.

DeJonge, D. Images of urban areas: Their structure and psychological foundations. *Journal of the American Institute of Planners,* 1962, 28, 266–276.

Devlin, A. The "small town" cognitive map: Adjusting to a new environment. In G. Moore and R. Golledge (Eds.), *Environmental knowing: Theories, research and methods.* Stroudsburg, PA.: Dowden, Hutchinson & Ross, 1976.

Downs, R. and Stea, D. *Image and environment: Cognitive mapping and spatial behavior.* Chicago: Aldine, 1973.

Fried, M. Grieving for a lost home. In L. Duhl (Ed.), *The urban condition.* New York: Basic Books, 1963.

Goodey, B. Spatial behavior and environmental imagery: Lines on the public face. In B. Honikman (Ed.), *Responding to social change.* Stroudsburg, PA.: Dowden, Hutchinson & Ross, 1975.

Griffin, R. Topographical orientation. In R. Downs and D. Stea (Eds.), *Image and environ-*

ment: Cognitive mapping and spatial behavior. Chicago: Aldine, 1973.

Gulick, J. Images of an Arab city. *Journal of the American Institute of Planners*, 1963, *29*, 179–198.

Hallowell, I. *Culture and experience.* Philadelphia: University of Pennsylvania Press, 1955.

Harrison, J. *Components of imageability: A case study.* Unpublished M.A. thesis. University of Denver, 1967.

Head, H. *Studies in neurology.* Oxford: Oxford University Press, 1920.

Hebb, D. O. *The organization of behavior.* New York: Wiley, 1949.

Horn, J. Intelligence — why it grows, why it declines? *Trans-action*, 1967, *4*, 23–31.

Hunt, M. *The effectiveness of a simulated site visit to familiarize the elderly with a new environment.* Unpublished. Ann Arbor, MI.: Institute of Gerontology, University of Michigan, n.d.

Ittelson, W. The perception of the large scale environment. Paper presented to the New York Academy of Science, 1970.

Izumi, K. Psychosocial phenomena and building design. In H. Proshansky, W. H. Ittelson, and L. Rivlin (Eds.), *Environmental psychology: Man and his physical setting.* New York: Holt, Rinehart & Winston, 1970.

James, W. *Psychology: The briefer course.* New York: Harper, 1968 (originally published 1898).

Kaplan, S. Cognitive maps in perception and thought. In R. Downs and D. Stea (Eds.), *Image and environment: Cognitive mapping and spatial behavior.* Chicago: Aldine, 1973.

_____. Adaptation, structure and knowledge. In G. Moore and R. Golledge (Eds.), *Environmental knowing: Theories, research and methods.* Stroudsburg, PA.: Dowden, Hutchinson & Ross, 1976.

Krauss, I., Awad, A., Ohta, R., and Regnier, V. Neighborhood imagery and service use among the urban elderly. Paper presented at the annual meeting of the American Psychological Association, Toronto, Canada, August 1978.

Lee, S. Cognitive mapping research. In B. Honikman (Ed.), *Responding to social change.* Stroudsburg, PA.: Dowden, Hutchinson & Ross, 1975.

Lee, T. Psychology and living space. In R. Downs and D. Stea (Eds.), *Image and environment: Cognitive mapping and spatial behavior.* Chicago: Aldine, 1973.

Lee, T. Urban neighborhood as a socio–spatial schema. *Human Relations*, 1968, *21*, 241–267.

Lynch, K. *Image of the city.* Cambridge, MA.: MIT Press, 1960.

Maurer, R. and Baxter, J. Images of neighborhood among Black, Anglo and Mexican-American children. *Environment and Behavior*, 1972, *4*, 351–388.

Moore, G. The development of environmental knowing: An overview. In D. Canter & T. Lee (Eds.), *Psychology and the built environment.* London: Architectural Press, 1975.

_____. Knowing about environmental knowing: The current state of theory and research on environmental cognition. Working paper. Milwaukee: Publications in Architecture and Urban Planning, University of Wisconsin, Milwaukee, 1976.

_____. and Golledge, R. *Environmental knowing: Theories, research and methods.* Stroudsburg, PA.: Dowden, Hutchinson & Ross, 1976.

Moos, R. Conceptualizations of human environments. *American Psychologist*, 1973, *28*, 652–665.

Ohta, R. and Walsh, D. Age-related differences in spatial perspective-taking ability. Paper presented at the annual meeting of the Gerontological Society, San Francisco, 1977.

Piaget, J. and Inhelder, B. *The child's conception of space.* New York: Norton, 1967.

Regnier, V. Matching older persons' cognition with their use of neighborhood areas. In D. Carson (Ed.), *Man-environment interactions: Evaluations and applications.* Milwaukee: Environmental Design Research Association, 1974.

_____., Dolak, M., and Hamburger, J. The use of cognitive mapping measures to direct environmental design intervention. Paper presented at the annual meeting of the Gerontological Society, San Francisco, 1977.

Sivadon, P. Space as experienced: Therapeutic implications. In H. Proshansky, W. H. Ittelson, and L. Rivlin (Eds.), *Environmental psychology: Man and his physical setting*. New York: Holt, Rinehart & Winston, 1970.

Spivak, M. Sensory distortions in tunnels and corridors. *Hospital and community psychiatry*, 1967, *18*, 24–30.

Steinitz, C. Meaning and congruence of urban form and activity. *Journal of the American Institute of Planners*, 1968, *34*, 233–248.

Weisman, J. Way-finding in the built environment: A Study in architectural legibility. Unpublished Ph.D. dissertation. University of Michigan, 1979.

Wohlwill, J. The environment is not in the head. In W. Preiser (Ed.), *Environmental design research*, Volume 2. Stroudsburg, PA.: Dowden, Hutchinson & Ross, 1973.

6

Response of the Elderly
to Environment: A Stress-
Theoretical Perspective

KERMIT K. SCHOOLER

INTRODUCTION

We frequently appear to be impatient with the labors of others who have attempted to generate theory. Too often we act as if something new must be developed without previously exhausting the opportunities for test and elaboration of the existing theories. This chapter attempts, in a small way, to amend the situation by exploring the utility of an already existing theory about stress for explaining responses of the elderly to their environment. The chapter will be organized as follows: First, the theory will be described; second, the fit between the theory and some existing data will be examined; and finally, the chapter will address itself briefly to the kind of research that could be undertaken to further demonstrate the utility of the theory.

THEORY

Multivariate relationships among characteristics of the environment, responses of the elderly, and other variables that have an intervening or otherwise mediating role have been suggested by several investigators. As attempts are made to develop theory to account for these relationships, a number of prior questions need to be addressed. For example, is this to be a theory of the aging process? Or is it to be a theory of the impact of environment or of environmental change? What about stress theory, in which an event in the environment may presumably be considered the stressor and the dependent variables may be classified as adaptive or maladaptive responses? Or, could not the search for theory begin as an attempt to explain in psychological terms how those events, environmental attributes, or stressors are mediated, antecedent to response or adaptation? Finally, what will determine whether a causal model is preferred to a systems model, or what will determine the causal priorities of the set of variables with which we are dealing? All of these questions have been addressed explicitly or implicitly, with the result that in the present effort to explain observed variations in adaptive responses of the elderly — specifically health and morale — the theory invoked will attempt to account for the impact of physical environment and changes in physical environment as only two out of a multiplicity of factors possibly accounting for these variations. The scope of this theoretical development is further delimited by imposing the concept of stress, mediated by cognitive processes, between environment on the one hand and the adaptive responses on the other.

As the theory is described, it will become apparent that this author is indebted to Lazarus (1966, 1974) and to Cassel (1977). Lazarus introduces his theory of psychological stress by noting "some of the key issues to be resolved by psychological-stress theory, and (summarizing) briefly the concepts of the theoretical system" to which he addresses himself. The central issues alluded to are:

(1) What are the conditions and processes that determine when stress reactions will be produced and when they will not? . . . (2) What happens when a stimulus is reacted to as stressful? . . . (3) What are the patterns of reaction that define the presence of stress? . . . Psychological stress analysis . . . is distinguished from other types of stress analysis by the intervening variable of *threat*. Threat implies a state in which the individual anticipates a confrontation with a harmful condition of some sort. Stimuli resulting in threat or non-threat reactions are cues that signify to the individual some future condition, harmful, benign, or beneficial. These and other cues are evaluated by the cognitive process of *appraisal*. The process of appraisal depends on two classes of antecedents. The first class consists of *factors in the stimulus configuration*, such as the comparative power of the harm-producing condition and the individual's counter harm resources, the imminence of the harmful confrontation, and degree of ambiguity in the significance of the stimulus cue. The second class of antecedents that determine the appraisal consists of *factors within the psychological structure of the individual*, including motive strength and pattern, general beliefs about transactions with the environment, intellectual resources, education, and knowledge. . . . Once the stimulus has been appraised as threatening, processes whose function it is to reduce or eliminate the anticipated harm are set in motion. They also depend on cognitive activity but because they are influenced by special factors we term the cognitive activity related to coping *secondary appraisal*. Three main classes of factors are involved in secondary appraisal. The first is *degree of threat*. The second consists of *factors in the stimulus configuration* such as the locatability and character of the agent of harm, the viability of alternative available routes or actions to present the harm and situational constraints which limit or encourage the action that may be taken. A third class of factors influencing the secondary appraisal process is *within the psychological structure* — for example, the pattern of motivation which determines the price of certain coping alternatives, ego resources, defensive dispositions, and general beliefs about the environment and one's resources for dealing with it. Secondary appraisal based upon the above factors determines the form of coping pro-

cess, that is, the coping strategy adopted by the individual in attempting to master the danger. The end results observed in behavior (for example, affective experiences, motor manifestations, alterations in adaptive functioning, and physiological reactions) are understood in terms of these intervening coping processes. (pp. 24–26)

Thus, in accordance with this capsule version of Lazarus' theory, elements of the environment, changes in elements of the environment, and individual mobility (sometimes resulting in change in the environment) constitute, for the purposes of this chapter, the factors in the stimulus configuration. To the extent that these elements of the environment and environmental change are appraised as threatening, they may be thought of as stressors. And the end results observed in behavior might well be those alterations in adaptive functioning that are labeled poor health. According to Lazarus, the appraisal of threat depends not only on the stimulus configuration itself, but on psychological characteristics of the individual.

The concern here is with the impact of environment on the elderly. It is interesting to note that motive strengths, beliefs about transactions with the environment, intellectual resources, education, and knowledge are included in Lazarus' conception. All of these may be presumed to vary with chronological age. Indeed, they have been the subject of direct as well as indirect concern in gerontological research. Thus, to understand the impact of environmental change according to this formulation, an understanding of cognitive process and the correlates or determinants of cognitive process is required. Lazarus is a psychologist. It is understandable, therefore, that most of the emphasis in the elaboration of his theory is psychological and biological. While he includes the possibility of the importance of social factors at this particular point in the paradigm, a clearer indication of the place of those factors derives from the work of Cassel (1977), who recognized the complexity of the process linking environment and health, and who gave a more prominent place to the social dimensions in that process.

Noting that under some circumstances "the spread of infectious disease is facilitated by crowding," Cassel draws greater attention to the fact that this relationship is not always demonstrable. Relying on Rene Dubos (1965), Cassel asserts:

In a large number of cases clinical manifestations of disease can occur through factors that disturb the balance between the existing ubiquitous organisms and the host that is harboring them. It may well be that under conditions of crowding this balance may be disturbed, but this disturbance is not simply a function of the physical crowding (that is the closeness of contact of susceptibles to carriers of the microorganisms) but of other processes. (p. 131)

On this basis, Cassel goes on to propose that the presence of other members of the same species, that is, social relationships, may constitute the environmental factors that affect homeostatic mechanisms. Cassel's theory, then, is compatible with the larger theory of stress outlined by Lazarus, in that not only psychological, but also sociological phenomena may determine the cognitive process that allows environmental characteristics and environmental change to be perceived as threatening and stressful. One principle suggested by Cassel derived from the research on animals, however, is that "not all members of a population are equally susceptible to the effects of these social processes" (p. 139). In Cassel's terms, another derived principle is concerned with the available protective factors, those devices that buffer or cushion the individual from the physiological or psychological consequences of these social processes. He points out that these buffers may be of either a biological or a social nature. Of particular significance is his statement that "under biological would be included the adaptive capacities of all living organisms, the capacity, given time, to adjust physiologically to a wide variety of environmental circumstances" (p. 135). In regard to the social processes, he refers to the nature and strength of the group supports provided to the individual. A final general principle deriving from animal research is that "variations in group relationships, rather than having a specific etiological role, would enhance the susceptibility of disease in general. The specific manifestations of disease would be a function of genetic disposition and the nature of the physical, chemical, and microbiologic insults they encounter" (p. 136).

At this point a synthesis of the parts of the Cassel formulation with the larger system proposed by Lazarus is offered. According to Lazarus, as shown schematically at Stage I, Figure 6.1, some aspects of the stimulus configuration (in this case either some characteristic of the environment or change in the environment) may be assessed as threatening. Appraisal of threat is determined by the interaction of the stimulus configuration with attributes of the individual, which themselves are psychological or social in origin (Stage II, Fig. 6.1). Cassel's concern for social and biological buffers becomes relevant in regard to the relation between stimulus and stress: His formulation leads to the prediction of relationships (for example, the more social supports, the less illness) but neglects to explain the process (that is, how social supports are mediated). It is contended, therefore, that the Stage II process in Cassel's formulation is identical to the Stage II process in Lazarus' formulation, namely the predisposition to appraise a situation as threatening.

According to Lazarus, if the situation is appraised as threatening, another appraisal process (secondary appraisal) ensues. It is at this point (Stage III, Fig. 6.1) and through this process, that the person's armamentarium of coping skills and mechanisms is ransacked to produce an appropriate response to the threat (Stage IV, Fig. 6.1). The schematic diagram shows again that both the social and psychological factors interact with the stimulus configuration to result in a selection of coping responses. In short,

FIGURE 6.1. Schematic diagram of stress process.

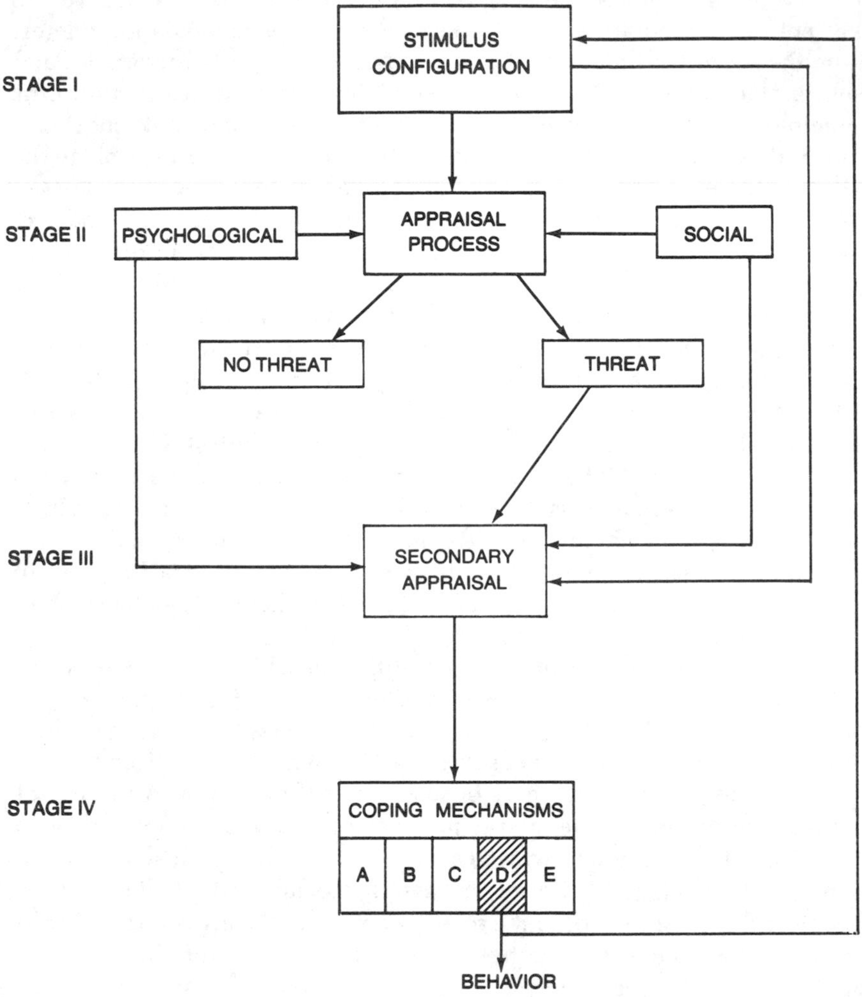

cognitive mediation of the environment, influenced by the interaction with social and psychological factors, will result in negative or positive changes in morale and health, or perhaps a static condition ("behavior" in Fig. 6.1).

RELEVANT DATA

In the preceding section a general theory of stress was described, suggesting that characteristics of the residential environment (and, in particular, some aspects of environmental change) may be thought of as the stimulus configuration which, in combination with cognitive styles of the older person, may be appraised as threatening and, consequently, stress-producing. According to this formulation, responses of the elderly in the form of decline in health and morale may be observed as a consequence of such stress. The task of this section is to describe some research findings in a manner that may demonstrate the tenability of the theory as stated.

The study on which the data to be reported here are based has been described in detail elsewhere (Schooler 1969, 1970, 1975, 1976, 1977). Nevertheless, a brief summary may be in order. These studies reported data on a sample of approximately 4,000 noninstitutionalized elderly in the United States (continental limits). The purpose of that study was to explore relations among such classes of variables as characteristics of the residential environments, social relationships, morale, and health. A working hypothesis was that environment would affect health which would affect morale, and that this process would in some way be mediated by the maintenance of social relationships. The interview schedule, which took approximately two hours to administer, also contained questions pertaining to the more or less common demographic characteristics — knowledge and use of social services — and a handful of other items of particular interest but not easily assumed under the rubrics mentioned. A variety of forms of data analysis were employed, but of a special interest at this point is the use of factor analysis. Each of the domains (environment, social relations, morale, and health) was factor analyzed separately, and factor scores were subsequently computed for each individual on each of the usable factors extracted. Many of the analyses after that point employed those factor scores as principal variables. Approximately three years later a follow-up study was undertaken, administering essentially the same questionnaire to a subsample of 521 of the original sample. Again, factor analysis was undertaken and a number of analyses employing controls on demographic and other attributes were performed.

Initially it seemed important to be able to show that environmental characteristics are associated with the outcome variables, morale and health. Small but statistically significant relationships could be demonstrated to exist between some of the environmental factor scores and the morale scores. In a similar way, environmental characteristics were shown to be statistically related to measures of health. Although several factors were extracted in each domain, the environmental factor having to do with condition of dwelling units, the several morale factors, and the health factor called general health, are of special interest. The report of findings will be confined to those factors. Table 6.1 shows these factors and some of the items with the highest loadings. Moreover, while some aspects of the theory under discussion might readily be tested by cross-sectional data, it would appear that a more convincing demonstration would be derived from panel or longitudinal data permitting the measurement of change.

TABLE 6.1. Examples of Items in Environmental, Morale, and Health Factors

DOMAIN	FACTOR TITLE	EXAMPLES OF ITEMS	LOADINGS
Environment	Condition of Dwelling	Condition of Building	.773
		Care of Home Interior	.692
		Building Need Repairs	.683
		Desc of Furniture	.676
		Style of Furniture	.673
		Condition of Grounds	.615
Morale	Morale 1	Do you get upset easily?	.741
		Do you take things hard?	.672
		Worry so much you can't sleep?	.593
		Little things bother you more this year?	.580
		Get mad more than you used to?	.557
		Afraid of a lot of things?	.504
	Morale 2	The lot of the average man is getting worse.	.721
		A person doesn't really know who he can count on	.708
		Little use in writing to public officials because they aren't interested in problems of the average man.	.640
		Hardly fair to bring children in the world.	.615
	Morale 3	Age Image	-.582
		As you get older you are less useful.	-.576
		You have as much pep as you did last year.	-.532
		Resp Understanding	.483
		Things keep getting worse as you get older.	-.428
	Morale 4	How much do you feel lonely?	.543
		You see more of your friends and relatives.	.502
		You have a lot to be sad about.	.482
		You are as happy now as you were when you were younger.	.470
		How satisfied are you with your life today?	.428
		If you could live where you wanted, where would you live?	.426
		Most days you have plenty to do.	.412
Health	General Health	Inactive due to health	-.715
		NMB Days Inactive	.704
		Health Today	-.589
		Lasting Health Problems	-.586
		Hosp, Nurse Home Last Year	-.543
		Lgth Time Health Problem	.536
		Freq Health Restricts	-.525
		Main Reason for Visits	-.522

It is becoming commonplace to demonstrate that residential mobility frequently results in some form of decline, presumably because of an insult to the system. At the same time, the theory proposed here suggests that it is the changes in the characteristics of the environment that produce in some manner the changes in health and morale. It seems appropriate to find some method of disentangling the two confounded variables; that is, residential mobility per se and change in environmental characteristics. More-over, the need to separate the effects is accentuated by the relationship shown in Table 6.2. An examination of this table shows that, in the aggre-gate, the quality of residential environment is much more likely to change for the worse among those older people who do not move than among those who do move. Thus, if changes in morale or health were shown to be associ-ated with moving, without control for the change in the environment, or if, conversely, the simple bivariate relation between environmental change (based on reports and perceptions of the respondent) and change in the de-pendent variable were to be shown without accounting for mobility, one might expect that, in the first instance, the negative effect of moving would be offset to some extent by the positive effect of improved environment; or conversely that, in the second instance, a positive effect of improved envi-ronment would be dampened by the insult of the move. In both cases the result would be spuriously low zero-order relationships.

The analytical strategy would then be, first, to perform the tabulations and statistics to demonstrate and measure the relation between:

(1) mobility and morale/health; and

(2) environmental change and morale/health.

Second, we would perform the analyses of (1) and (2), controlling in each instance for the other independent variable, thus:

(3) mobility and morale/health, controlled for environmental change; and

(4) environmental change and morale/health, controlled for mobility.

A change in magnitude of the relationships found in analysis (1) when anal-

TABLE 6.2. **Relation Between Residential Mobility and Environmental Change**

	Mobility between 1968 and 1971	
	Moved	Did not Move
Change in Quality of Dwelling	%	%
Declined	21.3	57.7
Improved or remained the same	78.7	42.3
	100.0	100.0
	N = 126	395

ysis (3) is performed would then not only show that the two independent variables are confounded, but it would also demonstrate the effect of mobility with the effect of environmental change removed. The conclusions based on a comparison of analyses (2) and (4) are obvious and analogous. This strategy has been employed and, as the following discussion demonstrates, the anticipated results were obtained: Mobility and environmental change are confounded but their unconfounded effects on health and morale are demonstrable. Tables 6.3 through 6.7 show the bivariate relations between residential mobility and changes in the four morale factors and in health, without controlling for environmental change. In most instances, some relationships of relatively modest magnitude are seen. Similarly, the relations between change in environment and change in morale and health, without controlling for residential mobility, are of equally modest magnitude (tables not shown). As the preceding discussion argues, what is called for initially is an analysis of the relation between the dependent variables and either mobility or environmental change, while controlling for the other. This has been accomplished.

The relevance of such analysis for the theory proposed is as follows: If mobility is shown to relate to morale and health, independent of the perceived characteristics of the environment, one might infer the possibility of physiological or psychological stress following the appraisal of threat due to dislocation. On the other hand, if change in the environment, independent of factual residential mobility, can be shown to be related to change in morale or health, we could infer stress resulting from the perceived change in the surrounding stimulus configuration. Table 6.8 summarizes the effect of the interaction between mobility and environmental change on changes in the dependent variables. The left-hand column shows that three of the zero-order relations between mobility and the dependent variables were trivial, and two of them were of some magnitude. The next two columns

TABLE 6.3. Residential Mobility by Change in Morale
Factor I (Transient Response)

	Mobility	
	Moved	Did not Move
Change in Morale I	%	%
Declined	14.3	22.0
No change	66.7	45.4
Improved	19.0	32.7
	100.0	100.1
N =	126	395
gamma = .138		

TABLE 6.4.   Residential Mobility by Change in Morale Factor II (Anomie)

	Mobility	
	Moved	Did not Move
Change in Morale II	%	%
Declined	32.5	30.7
No change	27.8	35.7
Improved	39.7	33.7
	100.0	100.1
N =	126	395
gamma =	.062	

TABLE 6.5.   Residential Mobility by Change in Morale
Factor III (Age-Related Morale)

	Mobility	
	Moved	Did not Move
Change in Morale I	%	%
Declined	20.6	33.2
No change	50.0	30.7
Improved	29.3	36.2
	100	100
N =	126	395
gamma =	.006	

TABLE 6.6.   Residential Mobility by Change in Morale
Factor IV (Sustained Unhappiness)

	Mobility	
	Moved	Did not Move
Change in Morale IV	%	%
Declined	22.2	34.9
No change	41.3	41.0
Improved	36.5	24.1
	100	100
N =	126	395
gamma =	.251	

TABLE 6.7.   Residential Mobility by Change in General Health

		Mobility	
		Moved	Did not Move
Change in Health		%	%
Declined		23.0	31.6
No change		42.1	28.7
Improved		34.9	39.7
		100	100
	N =	126	395
	gamma =	.009	

show, however, that when change in environment is taken into account, the magnitude of the relationship changes, in most instances increasing in absolute magnitude, and in some instances changing sign.

It is important at this point to show the relations between change in environment and change in the dependent variable separately for movers and nonmovers. The anticipated result is shown in Table 6.9, which is comparable to the one preceding. Two of the zero-order coefficients were not statistically significantly different from zero, while three of them were. This result is shown in the left-hand column of Table 6.9, where the coefficients vary in magnitude from .072 to .374. The next two columns of the table show the relations between the change in environment and change in the dependent variables separately for those who moved and those who did not move. It should be pointed out that a positive coefficient in this table indicates that improvement in the environmental variable was associated with improvement in the dependent variable. (For reasons that will be shortly elaborated, coefficients having to do with change in the third morale factor

TABLE 6.8.   Relations Between Mobility and Changes in Morale and Health

	zero-order (gamma)	Controlled for Environmental Change	
		Decline in Environment (gamma)	No Decline in Environment (gamma)
Change in:			
Morale I	.138	.270	.174
Morale II	−.062	−.342	.191
Morale III	−.006	.419	−.196
Morale IV	−.251	−.301	−.085
Health	.009	.507	−.144

TABLE 6.9. Relations Between Environmental Change and Changes in Morale and Health Controlled for Mobility

Change in:	zero-order (gamma)	Mobility	
		Moved (gamma)	Did not Move (gamma)
Morale I	.113	.187	.225
Morale II	.374	−.428	.540
Morale III	.072	.675	−.096
Morale IV	.277	.016	.218
Health	.194	.615	.062

should be disregarded for movers). It is especially interesting to note the tremendous increase in magnitude of the coefficient in the case of the general health factor among movers. That is to say, there was a very strong positive relation between change in the quality of environment and change in health among those who changed their residences but a trivial relationship between change in environment and change in health among those who did not move. The inference to be drawn from both of the preceding tables is that change in environment and residential mobility can be separated, and their effects can be determined separately. It would appear that each had effects independent of the effects of the other. But more important is the support for real interaction, paralleling the statistical interaction demonstrated. That is, in a manner consonant with Dubos' notions as described by Cassel (1977), the conditions necessary for deterioration may already be in the host organism, but activated or made sufficient by changes in the environment.

Up to this point we have employed two separate concepts, each of which may mean change in environment. The first of these was residential mobility, which may be thought of as real change. The second, which has been labeled "change in environment," was used to indicate perceived change, even when there had been no mobility. Of course, included in this class are those changes that take place in the environment around a person while the person remains in place. In analyzing that type of change, the notion of direction of change has been included. That is, the environment has been described as having worsened or improved. In the context of Cassel's writings, however, it becomes important to conceive of environmental change as being nondirectional. That is, if one has patterns of interaction with the environment and has learned how to negotiate an environment, any change can be thought of as a potential impact or influence on the person, irrespective of whether the change is for the better or for the worse. An attempt to test that proposition is illustrated in Table 6.10. This table shows the relation between the dependent variables and change in the environment without regard for the direction of change (that is, a dichotomous variable consisting of categories of change and no change). Table 6.10 shows that among movers there were no statistically significant relations between change in the environment and change in the dependent variables, with the exception of the relation for change in the third morale factor, which will be shown to be spurious among movers. On the other hand, four of the five relationships were statistically significant among nonmovers. The interpretation of this table is not overwhelmingly obvious, but it does suggest that change, without regard for the direction of change, is a meaningful concept, and perhaps the reason that the relationships among movers appear to be nonsignificant is that the effects of mobility themselves are far more critical than the effects of environmental change per se.

Table 6.11 shows comparable data: the relations between mobility and changes in the dependent variables where environmental change (nondirectional) has been held constant. Where there has been environmental change, three of the four morale-related coefficients were reduced, and the relationship to the health factor was of the same magnitude but with reversed sign. Where there was no environmental change, all the coefficients increased in magnitude and no signs were reversed.

The preceding analysis of data purports to show that elements in the stimulus configuration and, specifically, changes in that configuration were shown to be related to morale and health of the elderly. These relations are compatible, to say the least, with a stress theory relying heavily on Lazarus and on Cassel for the formulation. But Lazarus introduced the concept of threat and the awareness of threat as necessary antecedents of stress. It is regrettable that the data under discussion here were not collected with the initial intention of testing Lazarus' stress theory. Conse-

TABLE 6.10. Relations Between Non-Directional Change in Environment and Changes in Morale and Health Controlled for Mobility

	zero-order (gamma)	Mobility	
		Moved	Did not Move
Change in:		(gamma)	(gamma)
Morale I	−.385	.003	−.479
Morale II	−.079	−.214	−.039
Morale III	−.395	−.577	−.327
Morale IV	−.269	−.048	.348
Health	.157	−.077	.231

TABLE 6.11.   Relations Between Mobility and Changes in Morale and Health Controlled for Environmental Change

Change in:	zero-order (gamma)	Environmental Change	
		Change (gamma)	No Change (gamma)
Morale I	.350	-.011	.472
Morale II	-.128	-.015	-.191
Morale III	-.022	.161	-.154
Morale IV	-.465	-.215	-.558
Health	-.113	.103	-.205

quently, some elements of the theory can be only tangentially tested. Nevertheless, some of the analysis is relevant. Suppose that appraisal of threat is associated with the anticipation of a move. In that case, if an older person anticipates making a residential change, the cumulative effect of awareness of threat should reinforce the effect of the move itself. The attempt to demonstrate the tenability of that proposition has not been entirely successful. Considering just those who moved between 1968 and 1971, it was found that, in regard to some of the morale variables, those who anticipated moving showed greater decline than those who did not anticipate moving while in the case of other morale variables, the reverse was true. In all instances the differences were relatively small. However, it was noted that a large and significant difference did occur when the health variable was similarly analyzed. That is, if only movers are considered, those who anticipated moving show a greater decline with respect to health than those who did not anticipate moving. This relationship was accentuated when the analysis was confined to the older segment of this sample, where approximately 67 percent of those who anticipated moving showed a decline in health, compared to approximately 40 percent who did not anticipate moving. Thus, modest support for the contention that appraisal of threat is a necessary precondition of stress is obtained.

The cognitive element is critical for the Lazarus formulation and may be inferred to be necessary in the Cassel formulation. Lazarus refers to the process of appraisal, and, specifically in connection with the coping processes, he refers to secondary appraisal. Cassel, meanwhile, refers to the situation in which individuals do not receive evidence from the environment that their actions are leading to anticipated consequences. It would seem that any evidence relating environmental change to cognitive process would support the stress theory that is suggested here.

Both Lazarus and Cassel recognize the possibility of buffers. In Lazarus' terms, buffers would be especially important in the process of secondary appraisal. In both the Lazarus and Cassel formulations, the presence of social relationships may serve the purpose of mediating stress-provoking circumstances in the environment. Here again the study provides considerable evidence to support the contention about the importance of social relationships in mediating stress-provoking circumstances. The most convincing statement is found in Pastorello (1973). The analysis of environmental change is only peripheral to the main thrust of this thesis, but after a sound theoretical development, Pastorello used the data of the Schooler studies to demonstrate convincingly that "having a confidant who is not a member of one's immediate family of procreation proves to be the most efficacious social-relations variable in contributing positively to age-related self-conception among the elderly" (p. 128). While testing a set of path models derived from a symbolic–interactionist formulation, he shows the importance of the confidant relationship in mediating threats to the older person's self-esteem. At one point he concludes,

> Therefore, poor environmental conditions tend to be consistently associated with low levels of life satisfaction — happiness — although to various degrees. Interestingly and in support of previously stated hypotheses, the presence of a confidant successfully reduces the impact of environment on life satisfaction — happiness to zero. . . . The confidant, therefore, serves to mitigate the impact of environmental stress upon life satisfaction–happiness. (1973, p. 139)

A similar function is performed by the confidant relationship in regard to the health factor.

The analysis shows that, for example, when the relation between change in health and change in environment is subsequently analyzed separately for movers versus nonmovers and for change in membership in clubs and organizations (few organizations in 1971 versus same or more organizations in 1971), the expected change in magnitude of relation ensues. That is, among movers as well as nonmovers, the relation between changes in environment and health is positive where the social support has declined, but not significant where that support has remained static or has improved. Similarly, when the social support variable — change in amount of contact with the confidant — is substituted for membership in organizations, the effect of social support is to buffer the impact of environment on health. These findings are summarized in Table 6.12.

CONCLUSION

In summary, a theory proposed by Lazarus (1966, 1974) has been presented to attempt to explain the impact of environmental change on older people. That theory has been somewhat modified here by the inclusion of inferences drawn from Cassel (1977) regarding the buffering effect of social

TABLE 6.12. Relations Between Change in Environment and Change in Health Controlled for Residential Mobility and Selected Social Variables

| | Movers | | Non-Movers | |
| | Decrease | Static or Increase | Decrease | Static or Increase |
	(gamma)	(gamma)	(gamma)	(gamma)
Membership in Organizations	1.00	n.s.	.16	n.s.
Contact with Confidant	1.00	n.s.	.11	n.s.

relations on the impact of environmental change. The Lazarus theory defines stress as a consequence of the appraisal of threat inherent in a stimulus configuration. Appraisal of threat is in part determined by the interaction of psychological and social phenomena, as well as by the attributes of the stimulus itself. Then, through the process of secondary appraisal, a coping process is attained, selected from the array of such processes available to the individual. Secondary appraisal is further determined by psychological and social phenomena.

The argument is not that this particular theory has been totally confirmed, but rather that, as modified, the theory seems plausible and deserves further testing before being ignored. Its terms, therefore, have been held up against empirical data deriving from a national study of the elderly. The stimulus configuration in this analysis consists of attributes of the physical environment, changes in those attributes, and residential relocation. Stress is inferred from the observed change in morale and health status. The buffering effect of the maintenance of social relationships, that is, having a confidant, is also demonstrated. The data presented suggest that the theory is tenable, but numerous areas of investigation and analysis still remain. A thorough examination of awareness of threat as a basis for inferring appraisal is of paramount importance. Lazarus addresses this problem in his formal statement (1974, pp. 75–83). However, the relevant literature has not been concerned with sustained threat (for example, the prospect of relocating, extending over long periods of time) nor with aged samples (who, it may be presumed, have had opportunities to be conditioned over a lifetime to threatening, stress-provoking situations). Also needed — but within reach — is the investigation of the role of psychological factors on buffering the appraisal of threat. Finally, a serious methodological problem exists: In contrast to the laboratory methodology of measuring physiological response, attention to a methodology of clinical, attitudinal, and behavioral assessment of change over time is needed in order to account fully for the responses to the cumulative and long durational nature of the stressful stimulus configurations.

REFERENCES

Cassel, J. The relation of urban environment to health: Toward a conceptual frame and a research strategy. In L. E. Hinkle and W. C. Loring (Eds.), *The effect of the man-made environment on health and behavior*. Atlanta: Center for Disease Control, U.S. Public Health Service, 1977.

Dubos, R. *Man adapting*. New Haven, CT.: Yale University Press, 1965.

Lazarus, R. *Psychological stress and the coping process*. New York: McGraw Hill, 1966.

Lazarus, R., Averill, J. R., and Opton, E. M. The psychology of coping: Issues of research and assessment. In G. V. Coelho, C. A. Hamburg, and J. E. Adams (Eds.), *Coping and adaptation*. New York: Basic Books, 1974.

Pastorello, T. Intimacy in nonfamilial relations: An exploration of the social conditions of successful adjustment among the aged. Unpublished Ph.D. dissertation. Syracuse University, 1973.

Schooler, K. K. The relationship between social interaction and morale of the elderly as a function of environmental characteristics. *Gerontologist*, 1969, 9, 25–29.

Schooler, K. K. On the relation between characteristics of residential environment, social behavior, and the emotional and physical health of the elderly in the United States. *Gerontologist*, 1970, 10, 194–197.

Schooler, K. K. A comparison of rural and nonrural elderly on selected variables. In R. Atchley (Ed.), *Rural environments and aging*. Washington, D.C.: Gerontological Society, 1975.

Schooler, K. K. Environmental change and the elderly. In I. Altman and J. Wohlwill (Eds.), *Human behavior and environment: Advances in theory and research*. New York: Plenum Publishing Corporation, 1976.

Schooler, K. K. and Bellos, N. S. Residential environment and health of the elderly: Use of research results for policy and planning. In L. E. Hinkle and W. C. Loring (Eds.), *The effect of the man-made environment on health and behavior*. Atlanta: Center for Disease Control, U.S. Public Health Service, 1977.

7

A Congruence Model of Person-Environment Interaction

EVA KAHANA

INTRODUCTION

Understanding the effects of environmental settings on older people and searching for optimal environments have become major concerns within the field of social gerontology in recent years. This concern has paralleled that of other behavioral scientists who have become increasingly aware of the fact that substantial proportions of the variance in human behavior are accounted for by situational and environmental variables (Moos, 1969). However, systematic guidelines for providing the optimal environmental input to meet needs of the aging individual have been largely absent. Moreover, the range of conceptual approaches for understanding the ways in which environments affect older people has also been limited.

This chapter will discuss a conceptual model that has been developed in the last few years in an effort to find regularities within the complexities of person-environment interaction and develop a model that is salient to older people and that takes into account the environmental docility of many aged, primarily those requiring special settings. A congruence model of environmental characteristics and individual needs is proposed as a means of understanding the impact of environmental settings on the wellbeing and adjustment of older people.

In conceptualizing the impact of environments on the older person, gerontologists have typically concentrated on specifying and measuring the direct impact of the environmental setting on the majority of those inhabiting the setting. Studies using this approach have ranged from an emphasis on the physical characteristics of the environment (of special interest to architects) to emphasis on organizational climate or structure and to studies focusing on the suprapersonal environment, that is, personal and behavioral characteristics of individuals inhabiting the environment (Lawton, 1970). The latter approach has underscored the notion that the nature of the environment is strongly influenced by the typical characteristics of its members. Recently, consideration of relevant environmental characteristics has also included attempts at measuring more complex gestalt-type environmental attributes, for example the social psychological milieu. Studies that sought to define optimal environmental features have pointed to the special importance of issues of environmental homogeneity (Lawton, 1973), privacy and private domain (Pastalan & Carson, 1970), proximity (Lawton & Simon, 1968), totality (Goffman, 1961), and need gratification (Kahana & Harel, 1971).

Having documented the significance of environmental variables in influencing attitudes, activities, and wellbeing of the elderly, gerontologists have recently become concerned with specifying the ways in which environmental variables exert their influence. This has aided in further specifying the suprapersonal environment and in focusing on social characteristics of older people which may mediate environmental effects.

Gubrium (1970) has emphasized the importance of physical and financial resources in mediating between environmental characteristics and individual outcomes. In her studies of housing, Carp (1968) has found that voluntary activity patterns versus work-related patterns differentiated residents who adjusted well from those who did not. In institutional settings, Turner, Tobin, and Lieberman's (1972) study focused on the importance of personality traits as intervening variables between the impact of institutionalization and outcome.

All of these studies reflect the recognition that one must go beyond asking the question: Which environments contribute to the wellbeing of older people? Recognizing that apparently helpful environmental characteristics may be harmful to some elderly people while apparently undesirable features may benefit others, we must ask not only, is it good? but also, good for whom? Furthermore, we must follow up our interest in the impact of environments and consider the process by which they make their impact.

It is largely in response to these questions that the model of person-environment congruence is found to be an especially promising one. Rather than focusing on single environmental or individual dimensions as major causal variables while holding other aspects of the environment constant, this model permits simultaneous consideration of a variety of salient environmental and individual attributes and measures them along parallel and commensurate dimensions. By combining person and environment measures arithmetically, this approach produces a direct index of person-environment fit along given dimensions. In addition to determining whether personal outcomes may be predicted by the discrepancy or congruence between individual needs and the environment, this approach also makes possible the consideration of two additional issues. It is possible to determine what areas or dimensions of person-environment fit are most salient for adjustment, and what is the best quantitative representation of the relationship between person-environment fit and adjustment.

Although the model is relevant to elderly individuals in diverse environmental settings, it has been developed and tested in institutional facilities where the impact of the environment on the elder individual may be most dramatically observed. Residents of institutions for the aged represent only a small portion (5%) of the total population of elderly in the United States. Nevertheless, this is an important group exemplifying the problems of the vulnerable years in their most extreme form. It is also a group that utilizes a high proportion of the financial, manpower, and other resources of the community. As the proportion of the very old increases, the problem of institutional care and its cost may assume even greater importance. In the following discussion, then, principles especially relevant to institutional settings will be emphasized. It should be kept in mind, however, that the institutional setting is merely an illustrative setting for the principles discussed.

THE CONGRUENCE MODEL OF PERSON-ENVIRONMENT FIT

The congruence model of person-environment interaction proposed here has its roots in Lewin's (1935) notion that behavior is a function of the relationship between the person and his environment and in Murray's (1938) need-press model of human behavior. Descriptions of environmental press are posed as inferred connections among otherwise discrete events. According to the congruence model, individuals with certain types of needs are most likely to seek and be found in environments that are congruent with their needs. Dissonance between press and need is seen as leading to modification of the press or to the individual's leaving the field in a free-choice situation. When such choice is unavailable and the individual must function in a dissonant milieu, stress and discomfort follow (Stern, 1970).

The disadvantages of the older years in terms of reduced income, frequently impaired health, and loss of social roles, reduce the options and choices available to the older person in maintaining or finding an environment in keeping with his preferences. It is often because of these very losses that the aged enter special care settings. Based on the above considerations, it is hypothesized that a close fit between environmental characteristics and individual preferences and needs should contribute to a sense of wellbeing and adequate functioning of the elderly individual. It is suggested that the individual's profile of personal needs and preferences must always be considered in conjunction with the profile of the environment in evaluating residential settings.

In the rapidly expanding field of social ecology a congruence model of person-environment interaction has been advocated by French, Rodgers, and Cobb (1974). They define adjustment as goodness of fit between characteristics of the person and properties of his environment. Furthermore, they underscore the notion that in order to quantify person-environment fit, they must be operationalized as commensurate dimensions, that is, one must be able to measure them on the same scale. Using the terminology of environmental and individual supplies and demands, French and colleagues consider a deficiency of environmental supplies relative to individual needs as having a negative effect, whereas excess supplies are expected to have no effect. The present model does not make this assumption. Furthermore, in the present conceptualization of congruence, goodness of fit is seen as antecedent to wellbeing rather than as synonymous with it. Whenever there is a lack of congruence between the individual's needs and life situation — due to either change in environment (especially new housing or institutionalization) or a change in needs or capacities — various adaptive strategies are called upon to increase the fit between person and environment. Adaptive strategies may serve to reduce mismatch either by changing needs or by changing the environment. Depending on the success of these adaptive strategies, wellbeing or lack of wellbeing may result.

The relationship between person-environment fit and positive outcome may be empirically tested in cross-sectional studies, whereas the congruence adaptation model can only be tested in longitudinal investigations. Congruence between environmental characteristics and individual needs may be expected to be most important where environmental or individual options are limited. Three factors may be expected to result in limitation of such options: (1.) restrictiveness in environmental characteristics, (2.) limited degrees of individual freedom, and (3.) internal preception of limited degrees of freedom. Restrictive environmental characteristics may be exemplified by a total institution; limitations of individual freedom may be seen in terms of personal vulnerability [as postulated in Lawton's (1970) environmental docility hypothesis]; and self-perceptions of limited freedom may be reflected in external locus of control.

Some approaches to defining congruence (for example, Stern, 1970) are problematic in that measurement of the environment and individual are not conducted independently of one another. That is, the individual respondent serves as the informant both about his needs and the environment. It is, therefore, quite likely that reports of the environment may be influenced by individual need. This methodological problem may be overcome by obtaining independent assessments of the environment. Based on recent work by French and co-workers (1974), it would appear that the discrepancy between subjective assessments of the environment and its objective attributes may in and of itself represent an important aspect of congruence.

Diverse aspects of the environment may contribute to the environmental press along a given dimension, including the physical and the social environment, and what Lawton (1970) termed the suprapersonal environment. It must also be recognized, however, that the impact of the larger environment is mitigated by the personal life space of the individual. Thus, in residential settings for the aged, it is possible that even residents whose needs are not met by the larger environment of the home may find a nook (physical or social) that may shelter them from a generally incongruent environment. Conversely, it is possible that, even if programs and general characteristics of a setting are ideally suited to a resident, presence of a significant figure, for example, a roommate who is not congenial to the resident, may have a deleterious influence.

In utilizing the congruence model, one of the first tasks is to delineate salient environmental and individual dimensions that may be measured on a parallel basis. Let us turn now to a discussion of dimensions that may be viewed as salient in measuring person-environment congruence in settings for the aged. It should be emphasized that a different set of dimensions may be found salient for other types of settings or populations (Moos, 1973).

Dimensions of Congruence

Based on theoretical considerations salient to special settings for the aged, two broad areas of congruence between environment and individual characteristics appear to be especially important: dimensions based on environmental differences and dimensions based on individual differences.

Dimensions based on environmental differences. The first set of variables are the dimensions along which settings for the aged may be characterized. The segregate, congregate and institutional control dimensions used by Kleemeier (1961), and the elaborations presented by Pincus (1968; Pincus & Wood, 1970) provide a comprehensive method of classifying the impact of the setting on the lifestyle of the residents.

To the extent that most residential and behavior settings for the aged may be characterized along the above dimensions, it may be of special interest to study the effects of the extent of congruence between the setting and resident characteristics along these dimensions. These parallel characteristics appear useful both in describing institutions as a whole and in relating to specific activities.

1. The segregate dimension was originally used by Kleemeier (1961) to refer to "the condition under which older persons may live exclusively among their age peers having little contact with other age groups" (p. 281). In broader terms, however, the concept may refer to the heterogeneity or homogeneity of the setting in terms of sex, health status, and level of functioning of the participants. It may, thus, contrast living or participating with a group of persons much like oneself to living with persons who are different from oneself.

2. The congregate dimension refers to "the closeness of individuals to each other and to the degree of privacy possible to attain in the settings" (Kleemeier, 1961, p. 282).

3. The institutional-control dimension refers to the extent of staff control of residents, the use and importance of rules, and the degree of resident autonomy tolerated.

In absolute terms, environments that are highly controlling and homogeneous and restrict privacy (that is, they are segregate, congregate, and institutionally controlled) may in addition often disregard individual needs and have little positive value. The majority of settings for the aged do not represent such an extreme. At the same time, there are few institutions with a complete absence of totalistic features and that present many options to their residents and permit them to shape their own personal environments according to their needs. To the extent that options are many, congruence of the macroenvironment with individual needs may once again lose saliency. According to Bennett (1964), residential settings for the aged typically fall around the middle range of totality. Hence, such settings would be ideally suited for testing the congruence hypothesis.

Some elderly individuals have especially strong needs for privacy, while others may enjoy being with others and participating in group activities much of the time. Thus the fear of being alone experienced by some aged has long been familiar to clinicians. Similarly, some elderly persons have great needs for autonomy or independence, and a controlling institutional environment with many rules and regulations would be inconsistent with their self-image, previous lifestyles, and present needs. Others, however, have a great need for structured situations, clear-cut rules as to what is expected of them, and may have entered the institution expecting that the burden of making decisions will be taken from them. It may, therefore, be expected that congruence of individual needs and characteristics of the setting along these dimensions should lead to a sense of wellbeing, satisfaction, and adequate functioning in the institution.

Dimensions of Congruence Based on Characteristics
of the Aged Individual

Age-related changes have been established in previous studies along several dimensions of cognitive functioning and of personality organization (Burgess, 1960; Korchin & Basowitz, 1956; Neugarten, 1964). These changes are frequently in the form of a decrement in the ability to cope with the environment. Thus, inability to tolerate ambiguity, inability to delay gratification, flattened affect and avoidance of stimuli have been observed among the elderly in the above studies.

One may expect that incongruity between environmental expectations and the needs and characteristics of the aging individual may be especially difficult to cope with in these areas. The very existence of psychological changes may present the aging person with an incongruity between his needs and his environment, placing stress on his weakened coping abilities. Utilization of a residential or institutional living situation may often be precipitated or hastened by those changes. An important role of the environment, then, is to accommodate as much as possible the changing needs of the aging individual. To the extent that the environment provides a setting that can accommodate the new resident's needs, stress is reduced and the pace of decline may be checked.

Table 7.1 summarizes seven dimensions of necessary congruence between environmental settings and individual preferences. These are comprised of the three environmentally-based dimensions of segregate, congregate, and institutional-control features and four individually-based dimensions. Each is further subdivided into its component aspects. Based on previous theory and empirical work in social gerontology, these seven dimensions appear to be especially salient for matching individual needs or preferences and environmental characteristics in institutional settings for the aged.

Subdimensions of Congruence

In operationalizing the seven dimensions of congruence, however, it became clear that they do not represent unitary aspects of needs or environments. The seven dimensions were therefore expanded and further subdivided into eighteen subdimensions considered basic to characterizing institutional environments. Further subdivisions were, in some cases, based on environmental aspects, while in others refinements were based on closer examinations of individual need. These refinements were necessary because in existing conceptualizations (Kleemeier, 1961; Stern, 1970), operationalization of a single dimension often included conceptually discrete elements; for example, conformity and dependency were subsumed under the common category of institutional control.

Segregate dimension — subdimensions. In the present study, the segregate dimension was treated as consisting of three subdimensions, all related to various aspects of sameness versus varying environmental qualities and corresponding individual preferences. The dimension encompasses both temporal and spatial features.

The first subdimension, homogeneity–heterogeneity, is defined similarly to Kleemeier's notion of segregation, although characteristics of residents other than their age are considered to be salient. One can refer to the heterogeneity or the homogeneity of the setting in terms of the sex, health status, ethnicity, and level of functioning of the participants. The heterogeneity–homogeneity subdimension thus contrasts living or participating with a group of persons much like oneself to living with persons who are different.

The concept of segregation or homogeneity may also be extended beyond characteristics of other persons to encompass both a temporal dimension and the content of activities. The monotony or variability in activities is thus considered to constitute a second subdimension of congruence. The changeability versus sameness of the environment is conceptualized in terms of the presence or absence of daily routines and the frequency of

TABLE 7.1. Environmental and Individual Dimensions and Subdimensions of Person-Environment Congruence

1. Segregate Dimension

Environment

Individual

A. Homogeneity of com-
position of environ-
ment. Segregation
based on similar-
ity of resident
characteristics
(sex, age, physical
functioning and men-
tal status).

A. Preference for homogeneity, i.e., for associat-
ing with like individuals.
Being with people similar
to oneself.

B. Change vs. sameness.
Presence of daily and
other routines, fre-
quency of changes in
staff and other en-
vironmental char-
acteristics.

B. Preference for change vs.
sameness in daily rou-
tines, activities.

C. Continuity or simil-
arity with previous
environment of resi-
dent.

C. Need for continuity with
the past.

2. Congregate Dimension

Environment

Individual

A. Extent to which privacy
is available in setting.

A. Need for privacy.

B. Collective vs. indi-
vidual treatment. The
extent to which resi-
dents are treated
alike. Availability
of choices in food,
clothing, etc. Op-
portunity to express
unique individual
characteristics.

B. Need for individual expression and idiosyncracy.
Choosing individualized
treatment whether that
is socially defined as
"good" treatment or not.

C. The extent to which
residents do things
alone or with others.

C. Preference for doing
things alone vs. with
others.

TABLE 7.1. *(continued)*

3. Institutional Control

Environment

A. Control over behavior and resources. The extent to which staff exercises control over resources.

B. Amount of deviance tolerated. Sanctions for deviance.

C. Degree to which dependency is encouraged and dependency needs are met.

Individual

A. Preference for (individual) autonomy vs. being controlled.

B. Need to conform.

C. Dependence on others. Seek-support, nurturance vs. feeling self-sufficient.

4. Structure

Environment

A. Ambiguity vs. specification of expectations. Role ambiguity or role clarity, e.g., rules learned from other residents.

B. Order vs. disorder.

Individual

A. Tolerance of ambiguity vs. need for structure.

B. Need for other and organization.

5. Stimulation - Engagement

Environment

A. Environmental input (stimulus properties of physical and social environment).

B. The extent to which resident is actually stimulated and encouraged to be active.

Individual

A. Tolerances and preference for environmental stimulation.

B. Preference for activities vs. disengagement.

(continued)

TABLE 7.1. Environmental and Individual Dimensions and Subdimensions of Person-Environment Congruence *(continued)*

6. Affect

Environment	Individual
A. Tolerance for or encouragement of affective expression. Provision of ritualized show of emotion (e.g., funerals).	A. Need for emotional expression--display of feelings, whether positive or negative.
B. Amount of affective stimulation. Excitement vs. peacefulness in environment.	B. Intensity of affect, e.g., need for vs. avoidance of conflict and excitement (shallow affect).

7. Impulse Control

Environment	Individual
A. Acceptance of impulse life vs. sanctions against it. The extent to which the environment gratifies needs immediately vs. postponed need gratification. Gratification/deprivation ratio.	A. Ability to delay need gratification. Preference for immediate vs. delayed reward. Degree of impulse need.
B. Tolerance of motor expression--restlessness, walking around in activities or at night.	B. Motor control; psychomotor inhibition.
C. Premium placed by environment on levelheadedness and deliberation.	C. Impulsive closure vs. deliberate closure.

changes in staff and other environmental characteristics. Visual monotony has been described as a salient dimension along which to characterize urban environments. Within the institutional setting, monotony or variability in the furnishing of residents' rooms represent a relevant factor. At the psychosocial level, monotony of social interactions and behavior patterns may be related to individual preferences for change versus sameness as predictors of outcome.

The third subdimension of segregation considered relevant was that of continuity with the past. The maintenance of earlier life patterns has been seen as especially important for the aged. Rosow (1976) suggested that the greater the disruption of previous lifestyles, activities and relationships, the greater the risk of personal demoralization, since a major readaptation is required from them at an age when their adaptive capacities are diminished. There are individual differences in the need for continuity with the past. Many older persons after retirement or widowhood may express a desire to make a clear break with the past. Thus, the degree of discrepancy between the institutional environment and the older person's previous environment is considered to represent another important factor of the segregate dimension.

These three segregate dimensions are assumed to form a cluster, in that individuals who prefer environmental homogeneity are also likely to prefer sameness to change and to express needs for continuity with their past.

Congregate dimension — subdimensions. The first subdimension of congregate characteristics is broadly conceptualized as the extent to which privacy is available in the setting, that is, opportunities for or needs to be alone (Pastalan & Carson, 1970).

The notion of batched treatment of groups of individuals derives in part from Goffman's (1961) characterization of the total institution. The individual treatment subdimension includes considerations of the extent to which residents are treated alike, the availability of choices in food, clothing, or activities, and the presence or absence of sanctions for the expression of unique individual characteristics.

The third congregate subdimension, referring to the extent to which residents do things alone or with others, combines elements of both privacy and individual expression. The opportunity to engage in private activities is taken as an indication of institutional tolerance of individual idiosyncracy and private behavior.

Institutional control dimension — subdimensions. The institutional control dimension, as posited by Kleemeier (1961), refers to the extent of staff control of residents, the use and importance of rules, and the degrees of resident autonomy tolerated. Thus, the amount of control over institutional resources and individual behavior that the staff exercises at the expense of individual autonomy constitutes one subdimension of institutional control. The degree of conformity required by rules and sanctions for deviance constitutes another separate subdimension of institutional control.

Lack of autonomy has also been formulated in previous gerontological work (Goldfarb, 1969) in terms of dependency fostered by the environment. Environments that fulfill or foster dependency needs may be seen as paralleling individual needs for nurturance.

Structure dimension — subdimensions. The ability to tolerate ambiguity has often been posited as a personality dimension of particular salience to one's relations with one's environment. Evidence suggests that there are few clearcut social expectations and norms for older persons following retirement (Burgess, 1960; Neugarten, 1964), thus making the individual's tolerance of ambiguity a salient consideration for older people.

A related subdimension is the need for order or tolerance of disorder. The order–disorder dimension has also appeared as important in differentiating psychiatric treatment milieux (Moos, 1973).

Stimulation dimension – subdimensions. In the psychological literature, the importance of environmental stimulation has long been underscored (Wohlwill, 1966). Two subdimensions are particularly salient in homes for the aged. The stimulating properties of the physical and social environment constitute one subdimension. The corresponding individual characteristic relates to tolerance of environmental input or need for a stimulating milieu. This subdimension does not presuppose need for actual involvement in activities but rather refers to preferences for complexity, noise, or light and may include the spectator role in the social sphere.

Another subdimension refers to the extent to which the resident is actually stimulated and encouraged to be active. Activities may be viewed as a particular form of environmental stimulation.

Affect dimension – subdimensions. Cumming and Henry (1961) and Neugarten (1964) have demonstrated a tendency toward emotional as well as social withdrawal among some older people. This observation suggests that older individuals may differ in their needs for expressing affect and for being exposed to affective stimulation. Two subdimensions have been differentiated relating to affective expression and affective stimulation. In terms of environmental counterparts, the tolerance or encouragement of affective expression may be manifested in sanctions on behavior and in the provision of opportunities for ritualized shows of emotion such as those portrayed at funerals. The second subdimension, general level of affective stimulation available in the environment, may range from tranquility to excitement and may be a function of both staff and resident behavior.

Impulse control dimension – subdimensions. Age-related decline in ability to control impulses has been demonstrated in several studies (Kahana & Kahana, 1966; Pollack & Kastenbaum, 1964). Sometimes this decline is expressed in terms of loss of motor control or, at other times, it is manifested in the need for immediate need gratification. Impulsion–deliberation or reflectivity is a third dimension of impulse control, one that appears in Murray's (1938) taxonomy of needs and press.

In examining the proposed dimensions and subdimensions, the preliminary nature of this conceptualization should be emphasized. These dimensions are not seen as mutually exclusive. For example, environmental heterogeneity and change also imply stimulation; high degree of environmental control would also be likely to imply a lack of ambiguity in the environment. The overlap among personal and environmental dimensions is not simply a function of fuzzy thinking or errors in measurement, but reflects the complexity and convergence of facets of the social/psychological milieu. It should also be noted that dimensions included are not to be considered exhaustive, and they may have differential salience for different milieus and different individuals. The aims in the empirical study conducted to test the above conceptualization were to determine the differential salience of different dimensions and subdimensions of congruence for elderly residents of institutional settings. The complexity of issues does not stop here.

Different Levels of Measuring Congruence

The congruence hypothesis may be empirically tested at several different levels. One may consider and measure individual components of congruence in terms of personal preference, of external characteristics of the individual, or of inferred intrapsychic need dispositions. Thus, on the simplest level overt reported preferences may be considered for different types of settings and relate those to environmental characteristics. In addition, characteristics or capabilities of individuals may be related to environmental demands as Lawton (1970) has suggested. Finally, using a more clinical approach, intrapsychic needs may be considered as relevant individual characteristics in measuring congruence.

Similarly, Murray's (1938) model of environmental press includes at least two levels of analysis. Objective, ecological dimensions of the environment are alpha press, while subjective perceptions of the environment are beta press. In our own studies objective assessments, resident perceptions, and consensual indices of staff perception as separate measures of environmental characteristics were considered.

The environment of the residents may also be conceptualized and studied on two levels. On the one hand, the term refers to the larger institutional environment along specified dimensions; on the other hand, it may be used to describe the personal life space (physical and social environment) of each individual resident.

ALTERNATIVE CONCEPTUALIZATION OF THE CONGRUENCE MODEL

Many provocative questions must be considered in this regard. Does the environment have to fit the person's needs in every area? Can mismatch in one area be made up for by match in another area? What are the effects of extreme mismatch? While the answers to these questions are not yet known, it is instructive to consider the alternative conceptualizations that they would yield. Several models are possible for considering the relationship of congruence to outcome. Essential variations in possible models relate to several central issues. Along any one dimension one may consider continuous versus discontinuous models, directional versus nondirectional models, symmetrical versus asymmetrical models, and linear versus curvilinear models. Different methods may also be proposed for summarizing $P-E$ fit or congruence along several dimensions. The implications of different models for testing the congruence hypothesis along a single dimension will be outlined first, followed by the issue of simultaneous consideration of congruence along a number of different dimensions. It also may be noted that linear or curvilinear models may, alternatively, best fit different congruence situations.

In order to deal with issues of alternative congruence models more clearly in the present discussion, a single dependent variable will be utilized. In reality, however, multiple outcomes are often considered. A given degree of mismatch or congruence may have differential effects when considering diverse dependent variables.

The Cumulative Difference Model

The first set of models assumes mismatch to be cumulative and continuous but varying in directionality. The greater the differences between personal needs or preferences and environmental characteristics, the more negative the anticipated outcomes. Close fit between environment and person is assumed to lead to maximum satisfaction, with a zero mismatch hypothesized to be associated with the most positive outcome. Congruence may be computed using these models by considering the simple difference between personal and environmental measures on the parallel scales.

The nondirectional cumulative difference model. The conceptualization of the nondirectional congruence hypothesis assumes that noncongruence is uniformly detrimental to adjustment. Regardless of whether the individual prefers more or less of a particular environmental attribute than is actually provided, and regardless of the nature of that preferred situation, the fact of noncongruence causes discomfort, dissatisfaction, and maladaptive behavior. The relationship is linear. The greater the difference between environmental press and individual need in terms of oversupply or undersupply, the more negative the anticipated outcome. For example, if the environment provides more or less stimulation than that desired by the individual, dissatisfaction will result. The greater the difference, the greater the dissatisfaction. The effects of congruence on outcome using this model may be tested by obtaining the absolute difference between personal and environmental characteristics and relating them to outcome.

The one-directional cumulative difference model. A second related conceptualization of the congruence model considers only the effects of negative differences between person and environment, that is, an undersupply. This is the incongruence proposed by French, Rodgers, and Cobb (1974). The greater the negative mismatch, the more negative the anticipated outcome. While French and co-workers acknowledge that an overabundance of environmental supplies is possible, this is not seen as resulting in negative consequences. Such a conceptualization may accurately fit only certain areas of congruence. Thus, in a setting for the aged where there is little privacy and residents must share rooms and baths, the individual with high privacy needs may be especially likely to suffer negative consequences. It may be plausible to argue, however, that even if maximum opportunities for privacy were to be provided with private rooms and baths, an oversupply of privacy is unlikely, and negative outcomes should not be expected to arise.

The two-directional cumulative difference model. Another conceptualization assumes that the consequences of noncongruence differ depending upon whether the individual prefers more or less of a given characteristic than the environment provides. For instance, one may assume that the consequences of preferring more stimulation than the environment provides are different from the consequences of preferring less stimulation than is provided. Thus, too little stimulation may result in apathy and lack of responsiveness to the environment; too much stimulation may result in anxiety. The effects of the mismatch must be considered separately for conditions of positive or negative mismatch. Incongruence may result not only in qualitatively different types of outcome.

The Critical-Difference Model

A second set of models may consider the possibility of a critical mismatch. This approach would assume that effects of incongruence are problematic or detrimental only beyond a certain critical point or range. If the critical point or range can be specified, the effects of mismatch may be predicted. The critical point or range may be either constant over individuals, or it may differ from one individual to the next (that is, it may be a floating point).

The notion of critical differences presupposes either a noncontinuous model when the effect of mismatch must be differentiated from the effect of match or congruence, or a continuous model with a point demarcating the critical difference. It should be noted that we are still assuming that the effects of noncongruence are consistently negative. The critical-difference approach may also be subdivided in terms of a nondirectional, one-directional, or two-directional orientation.

The nondirectional critical-difference model. In the case of a nondirectional model, once a critical point or range is reached, for example, too much or too little stimulation, a negative outcome would result. If a discontinuous model is being considered, basic or extreme differences in outcome would occur precipitously at this point.

The one-directional critical-difference model. The assumption of French and co-workers (1974) that only undersupplies are detrimental is, in this model, simply combined with the notion that the critical difference must be specified in order for undersupply to have an impact.

The two-directional critical-difference approach. In this model, a critical difference either in over- or under-supply would be sought. Employing a noncontinuous model and the example of stimulation, outcome scores would be compared for individuals who are critically understimulated, for those who are within the congruence range, and for those who are critically overstimulated. Using a continuous approach the magnitude of negative mismatch beyond the critical-difference point would be related to outcome on the one hand, and the magnitude of positive mismatch beyond the critical-difference point would be related to outcome on the other.

The Optimal Discrepancy Model

In both the cumulative-difference and the critical-difference models, incongruence is assumed to have a negative effect, while complete congruence is seen as resulting in positive outcomes. This congruence hypothesis is analogous to a tension-reduction model. One may also consider the possibility of a model in which complete congruence between an individual's needs and the environment may have a negative outcome, just as an extreme mismatch may be negative. Thus, some optimal amount of discrepancy or congruence would result in positive outcomes. A basic feature of this model is its assumption that complete congruence results in negative outcomes. The optimal congruence model set forth here also relates to Helson's (1964) adaptation-level model; this model is further discussed in Wohlwill (1966). Helson's model suggests that environmental variation within a specified range of deviation from the individual's adaptation level (congruence) is positive, whereas beyond that range, deviation has negative consequences.

Adaptation-level theory does not presuppose, however, that complete congruence would have negative effects — rather its effects are seen as indifferent, that is, neutral. The latter notion may fit the stimulation subdimension particularly well. Thus, it is conceivable that a complete match or a very slight discrepancy between expressed needs for stimulation and environmental characteristics would have indifferent effects. Having somewhat more (or somewhat less) stimulation would represent a pleasant change but extremely more or less stimulation would be unpleasant or result in equally negative outcomes.

One-directional model. Some support for this model may be found if one considers the example of dependency. If older persons expressing dependency needs are provided with an institutional environment that completely meets their dependency needs (a maximum prosthetic environment), the patients may be expected to continue at a low level of functioning, rehabilitation may be unlikely, and a decline in competence may follow. If, however, the environment does not meet all needs completely and a certain amount of noncongruence is created, the patient may adapt by striving to improve his competency and positive outcome may be likely. Conversely, an environment may meet very few of the dependency needs of the resident, resulting in considerable mismatch. Such excessive mismatch will once again result in a negative outcome, with the resident being asked to perform at an impossible level. This example is a one-directional optimal congruence model. That is, providing more care than the dependency needs expressed by the resident is either unlikely or would result in negative outcomes. This model would not assume that an oversupply of a prosthetic environment is likely.

Two-directional model. One would thus expect that no difference between the amount of nurturance wanted by a resident and that given by his environment will result in negative outcomes, but extreme under- or over-supply will have negative consequences of different types. In considering the relationship between person-environment differences and outcome, the optimal congruence notion would lead to expectations that a zero difference would result in negative outcome, a moderate difference would result in positive outcome, and an extreme difference would also result in negative outcome.

CONSIDERING CONGRUENCE ALONG SEVERAL DIMENSIONS

Having outlined the models possible in considering congruence along any one dimension, let us turn to the issue of considering the effects of congruence along several dimensions and subdimensions. It is unlikely that an environment would fit with individual needs in every area or that it would be incongruent with needs in all areas. How, then, do we relate the whole person and the whole environment? Four such strategies for considering these issues are suggested.

Focus on the Number of Areas of Mismatch

First, one may consider an additive model, which is readily quantifiable and parsimonious. The greater the numbers of areas of mismatch, the more negative outcomes may be anticipated. This approach presupposes that the relationship between person and environment is dichotomized along each dimension as congruent or noncongruent. The number of congruent dimensions would be used to predict outcome. A variation of this approach would count the number of areas of critical mismatch.

Focus on Cumulative Mismatch

Here the degree of mismatch observed in each area would be added to mismatch observed in other areas to derive a cumulative noncongruence score considering both amount and intensity of mismatch in an additive fashion and yielding a cumulative difference score.

Focus on Salient Areas of Mismatch

A third approach may focus on mismatch along only salient dimensions. The assumption being made in this instance is that not all areas of need are equally important. Thus, even large amounts of mismatch may be tolerated in areas that are less salient for the individual. However, match or mismatch is exceedingly important in salient areas. The focus may be on the empirical definition of which areas are salient to a group of aged, or consider salience on an individual basis, asking each older person to specify areas of the environment valued as most important to him.

Focus on Profile of Mismatch

A fourth approach utilizing elements of those previously outlined would focus on profiles of mismatch. This approach would consider the configuration of all aspects of person and environment as comprising the total picture of match–mismatch.

THE EMPIRICAL STUDY

The conceptualization outlined above has been put to empirical test by the author and her associates in a series of analyses (Felton, 1975; Kahana & Harel, 1971; Kahana, Liang, & Felton, 1977; Kiyak, Kahana, & Fairchild, 1977).

The analyses by Kahana and Harel (1971) and Felton (1975) provided a preliminary examination of the data collected by Kahana (1972). Utilizing a regression approach, a more recent study (Kahana, Liang, & Felton, 1977) analyzed the same data set by considering all dimensions simultaneously. Since this study extends these earlier studies while at the same time providing greater insights into the congruence concept, its findings will be presented in some detail. In addition, a brief description of another investigation (Kiyak, 1977) will also be included. Kiyak's study is unique in the sense that it presents an alternative approach in measuring congruence and further extends 3 of Kahana's 18 subdimensions.

Study One

The focus of the study conducted by Kahana, Liang and Felton (1977) was the examination of the relative predictive power of various congruence measures in the context of different congruence models. Data regarding individual preference for various environmental characteristics were obtained from a sample of 124 institutionalized elderly. Independent assessments of the commensurate dimensions of environment were also gathered from staff of the three environments in which the elderly respondents resided. Subsequently, congruence measures were derived to test the utility of three specific congruence models. They included: (1) the non-directional model; (2) the one-directional model; and (3) the two-directional model.

The environments. Elderly respondents were selected from three institutions. They included one traditional nonprofit home for the aged, sponsored by a Protestant church (Grace Hill), one Jewish home for the aged (Ethnic Home), and a nonsectarian, proprietary nursing home catering to well-to-do residents who paid for their own care (Country Club).

In rating the three homes along dimensions of institutional totality (Bennett, 1966), the Jewish professional home received the highest score on totality, the commercial home rated a close second, and the church-sponsored home showed few totalistic features.

The homes thus selected represented different types of ownership and sponsorship patterns, different environmental features, and resident populations with diverse cultural and ethnic backgrounds. The major reason for the exclusion of homes in which adequate physical comfort and care were not available was that such environments would, by definition, be noncongruent with basic needs of all residents. Therefore, testing of the congruence hypotheses would be, for all practical purposes, impossible.

Sample. Only well residents, that is, those without incapacitating physical or mental impairment, were included in the sample. Exclusion of ill residents insured that subjects were able to respond to a rather extensive interview. In addition, severe illness might have diminished the potential importance of congruence along project dimensions and thereby invalidated the test of the hypotheses. The selection of relatively intact residents was generally a simple matter since all three homes housed residents on different floors according to their levels of physical and mental functioning.

Thirty interviews were completed at the commercial nursing home, 44 at the nonprofit Jewish home, and 50 at the Protestant church-related home (total of 124 interviews).

Measures of congruence between individual preference and environmental characteristics along commensurate dimensions were the major independent variables. Morale was the dependent variable.

Congruence scores were derived by using parallel measures of individual preferences and environmental characteristics. First, 70 items pertaining to individual preferences were administered to the respondents. These items were generally modeled after Stern and Pace's (1963) measures of individual preferences. Along the seven proposed dimensions of congruence, composite measures of individual preferences were constructed by combining items exhibiting an item-total correlation above .10. Due to its inadequate reliability (alpha = .37), the measure of one dimension, structure, was excluded from the analysis. Second, environmental characteristics were assessed by 141 staff members from the 3 homes. This method is similar to that developed by Pincus and Wood (1970). Assessments were made regarding the policies and norms of the home as well as the model activities of the staff and residents.

Residuals resulting from the regression of environment scores on individual preferences were used as measures of person-environment congruence. This approach was initially developed in research concerning status inconsistency (Brod & Lutz, 1974). It has the advantage of differentiating the main effects of person and environment from that of congruence (Blalock, 1969). In particular, a least-squares solution that predicted the value of environment from that of individual preference along each dimension was obtained. The extent to which this prediction is accurate can be used as a measure of commonality or congruence between person and environment. In most cases, the congruence (or correlation) will not be perfect; this lack of fit is described by the value of the error term. Thus, the error term or residual constitutes a measure of mismatch or incongruence; that is, the smaller the residual, the greater is the congruence. Since the residual is a measure of incongruence or mismatch, subsequent analyses are presented by using incongruence scores rather than congruence scores as predictors.

Two types of incongruence scores were generated to test different models. First, the absolute value of the residual was used to test the nondirectional model. This analysis assumed that incongruence, regardless of direction, was negatively related to morale. Second, to evaluate the two-directional model a modified dummy-variable technique was used to distinguish positive incongruence (oversupply) from negative incongruence (undersupply). As implied by the two-directional model, different types of incongruence differ in their effects. Since the one-directional model is a special case of the two-directional model, the usefulness of the one-directional model is implicitly examined while testing the two-directional model.

Results. The empirical question posed by this analysis was: Do incongruence scores explain any variance in addition to that explained by individual preferences and environmental characteristics? To answer this question, a stepwise regression analysis was conducted by including not only incongruence measures but also measures of person and environment. Since there was a relatively large number of predictors (18 to 24) in relation to the sample size (N = 124), only the first five or six variables entered into the regression equation were retained as predictors. This was necessary to avoid serious capitalization on chance (Cohen & Cohen, 1975, pp. 103–104). According to the findings, the two-directional model exhibited a slightly greater predictive power than did the nondirectional model.

In general, the results from both the nondirectional model and the two-directional model were fairly similar. Incongruence measures along congregate and institutional control dimensions were found to be significantly correlated with morale, as was individual preference along the affect dimension. As indicated by analysis of the nondirectional model, incongruence within the congregate dimension was positively related to morale

(β = .46, p < .01). On the other hand, according to the analysis of the two-directional model, an undersupply of opportunities for congregate activities had a greater positive impact (β = .57, p < .01) on morale than did an oversupply (β = .36, p < .01).

In the case of institutional control, it was found that nondirectional incongruence had a negative correlation (β = .44, p < .01) with morale, and further, in the two-directional model, only an undersupply of institutional control had a negative influence (β = .85, p < .01) on morale.

Individual preference along the affect dimension was also a significant predictor of morale. This was substantiated by the nondirectional model (β = .42, p < .001) as well as the two-directional model (β = .41, p < .001).

Results from these two models, nevertheless, differed in two respects. First, mismatch in terms of segregation was found to be a significant predictor (β = .34, p < .05) of morale only in the two-directional model. Second, environmental stimulation was correlated (β = .72, p < .001) with morale only in the nondirectional model. These differences may be a function of the different operational procedures used to measure incongruence in the two models examined. Different transformations of the incongruence measures may conceivably affect the intercorrelations among the predictors included in the analysis.

In summary, mismatch along congregate and institutional-control dimensions was found to play an important role in explaining morale. This was true even when the measures of individual preferences and environmental characteristics were controlled. These results indicate that the concept of congruence is indeed useful in understanding adjustment.

Study Two

A recent study by Kiyak (1977) extended the work of Kahana and colleagues. Three individual preference dimensions (privacy, activity/stimulation, order) were intensively studied within a multitrait–multimethod framework. Both person and environment were assessed in diverse ways; congruence was conceptualized and analyzed differently from the approach utilized by Kahana and Harel (1971), Felton (1975), and Kahana, Liang and Felton (1977).

The three dimensions chosen for this study were those which could be assessed more readily in both the physical and the social environment, as well as in the individual. Items derived from Kahana's Individual Preferences Questionnaire (1972), Marshall's Privacy Preference Questionnaire (1970), and from other personality and preference measures comprised the revised measure. It was administered to a sample of 450 college students and both community-resident and institutionalized elderly. A factor analysis of their responses resulted in five factors. Although order and activity/stimulation remained relatively intact, privacy emerged as three factors: physical privacy, isolation, and social solitude. The development of this thirty-item scale, labeled Environmental Preferences Questionnaire (EPQ), is described in Kiyak (1978).

Using Murray's (1938) need-press framework, environmental press or opportunities for satisfying needs were measured by environmental items parallel to the EPQ items. Recognizing that the perceptions of individuals who reside in a particular environment may diverge widely from those of trained observers, it was necessary to assess the environment from both perspectives. Furthermore, the larger institutional (distal) environment should be expected to impinge on the individual in a different manner than the individual's immediate (proximal) environment. For this reason, environment was assessed by four different instruments: observers' rating scales for the proximal and distal environment, and users' rating scales of proximal and distal environment. Each of these environmental measures could then be separately matched with the EPQ to determine the effects of congruence along each of the five dimensions.

The environmental preference and perception questionnaires were administered to 107 elderly residing in 8 homes for the aged. Respondents had resided in the homes for the aged between 3 and 32 months, and they represented a wide range of socioeconomic, religious and ethnic orientations.

The distal environment of each home and the proximal environment of each respondent were assessed by research staff observers. Scores on the preference and perceived-environment measures were trichotomized, such that each respondent received a score of high, medium, or low on each of the measures within each dimension. For each person-environment combination, a three × three matrix was created, and each respondent was placed into one of the resulting nine cells. Through a series of one-by-nine analyses of variance of the person-environment congruence scores, the utility of the concept of congruence was tested.

A detailed description of the findings is presented in Kiyak (1977), Kahana and Fairchild (1977), and Kiyak (1978). The findings suggest that congruence is a useful predictor of satisfaction, morale, and desire to stay, particularly within the dimensions of physical privacy, isolation, and stimulation/activity. Congruence accounted for more variability in the dependent variables than did person or environment measures alone on four of the five study dimensions. Solitude was the only dimension for which person or environment explained a greater proportion of variability in well-being than congruence scores. The results support the desirability of assessing environment in a multidimensional manner. On some dimensions, congruence between preferences and the proximal environment was important, while on others the distal environment was more critical for congruence. In general, both perceptions and objective observations of the environment were useful components of congruence, although the former emerged as a significant factor in more dimensions than did the latter.

The importance of considering a two-directional model was also supported by the findings. Thus, an oversupply of order, physical privacy and isolation in the distal environment relative to one's needs resulted in greater wellbeing than did congruence or an undersupply. In contrast, a level of environmental stimulation that was congruent with one's preferences resulted in greater satisfaction and morale than did an undersupply of stimulation.

The studies described above provide the next steps in the development of a model of *P–E* congruence. Their findings support the utility of the concept of congruence, but suggest the need to examine diverse elements of congruence in a more detailed manner.

THE APPLIED RELEVANCE OF CONGRUENCE MODELS

The congruence model outlined in this chapter is a rough one. There are many loose ends and unanswered questions. The complexities still appear greater than do the observed regularities. Nevertheless, this approach represents one step in the much needed direction of systematizing our efforts for understanding the impact of environments on older people.

The congruence model seems useful because it permits alternative conceptualizations and flexibility and permits the consideration of complex environmental individual patterns. The model is quantifiable and may be tested in an empirical fashion.

In addition to these considerations it is also a model of common sense. Clinicians, architects, and planners have long been striving to match environments to the needs of the individuals whom they serve. There have been some recent accounts of such attempts to clinically match older people with a range of functional abilities (Snyder, 1969). The formal model and resulting research presented in this chapter may provide the systematic guidelines sought by practitioners, environmental designers, and planners in accomplishing such a match.

The model may be used in various settings in order to predict those residents who are most likely to make an easy adjustment upon entering. As such, the notion of congruence may be helpful to practitioners in the placement of residents in any one of a number of settings. In addition, this model may be also used to guide practitioners' efforts in channeling residents to available activities, programs, and facilities within residential-care settings.

REFERENCES

Bennett, R. The meaning of institutional life. In M. Leeds and H. Shore (Eds.), *Geriatric institutional management*. New York: G. P. Putnam's & Sons, 1964.

_____. Socialization and social adjustment in five residential settings for the aged. Paper presented at 7th International Congress of Gerontology, Vienna, June 1966.

Blalock, H. M. *Theory construction.* Englewood Cliffs, NJ.: Prentice Hall, 1969.

Brod, R. L. and Lutz, G. M. Some contributions of residual analysis to methodological problems in status inconsistency research. Paper presented at the annual meeting of the American Sociological Association, Montreal, Canada, 1974.

Burgess, E. W. *Aging in Western societies.* Chicago: University of Chicago Press, 1960.

Carp, F. M. Person-environment congruence in engagement. *Gerontologist*, 1968, 8, 184–188.

Cohen, J. and Cohen, P. *Applied multiple regression correlation analysis for the behavior sciences.* Hillsdale, NJ.: Lawrence Erlbaum, 1975.

Cumming, E. and Henry, W. E. *Growing old.* New York: Basic Books, 1961.

Felton, B. Person-environment fit in three homes for the aged. Unpublished PhD. dissertation. University of Michigan, 1975.

French, J. P. R., Rodgers, W., and Cobb, S. Adjustment as person-environment fit. In G. V. Coelho, D. A. Hamburg, and J. E. Adams (Eds.), *Coping and adaptation.* New York: Basic Books, 1974.

Goffman, E. *Asylums: Essays on the social situation of mental patients and other inmates.* Garden City, NY.: Doubleday-Anchor Books, 1961.

Goldfarb, A. The psychodynamics of dependency and the search for aid. In R. Kalish (Ed.), *The dependencies of older people.* University of Michigan Institute of Gerontology, Ann Arbor, 1969.

Gubrium, J. F. Environmental effects on morale in old age and the resources of health and solvency. *Gerontologist*, 1970, 10, 294–297.

Helson, H. *Adaptation level theory: An experimental and systematic approach to behavior.* New York: Harper and Row, 1964.

Kahana, E. The role of homes for the aged among needs of the elderly. Progress report submitted to the National Institute of Mental Health, 1972.

Kahana, B. and Kahana, E. Age changes in impulsivity among chronic schizophrenics. Vienna: *Proceedings of the Seventh International Congress of Gerontology*, 1966.

———. and Harel, A. Social psychological milieu in residential care facilities for the aged. Paper presented to the annual meeting of the Gerontological Society, Houston, October 1971.

Kahana, E., and Fairchild, T. Measurement of adaptation to changes in health and environmental change among the aged. In W. G. Peterson and D. Mangen (Eds.), *Handbook of Research Instruments in Social Gerontology.* Minneapolis: University of Minnesota Press, in press.

Kahana, E., Liang, J., and Felton, B. Alternative models of P–E Fit and wellbeing of the aged. Paper presented at the annual meeting of the Gerontological Society, San Francisco, November 1977.

Kiyak, A. Person-environment congruence as a predictor of satisfaction and wellbeing among institutionalized elderly. Unpublished Ph.D. dissertation. Wayne State University, 1977.

Kiyak, A. A multidimensional perspective of privacy preference. In W. E. Rogers and W. Ittelson (Eds.), *New Dimensions in Environmental Design Research.* Washington, D.C.: Environmental Design Research Association, 1978.

Kiyak, A., Kahana, B., and Fairchild, T. Privacy as a salient aspect of P–E fit: Implications for institutional planning. Paper presented at the Annual Meeting of the Gerontological Society, San Francisco, November, 1977.

Kleemeier, R. W. The use and meaning of time in special settings. In R. W. Kleemeier (Ed.), *Aging and leisure.* New York: Oxford, 1961.

Korchin, S. S. and Basowitz, H. The judgment of ambiguous stimuli as an index of cognitive functioning in aging. *Journal of Personality*, 1956, 25, 81–95.

Lawton, M. P. Ecology and aging. In L. A. Pastalan and D. H. Carson (Eds.), *The spatial behavior of older people.* Ann Arbor: The University of Michigan Institute of Gerontology, 1970.

———. Assessing the competence of older people. In D. P. Kent, R. Kastenbaum, and S. Sherwood (Eds.), *Research, planning and action for the elderly*. New York: Behavioral Publications, 1972.

_____. The relationship of age mixing to security in housing for the elderly. Paper presented to the HUD Conference on Security in Multi-family Housing. Washington, D.C., September 10, 1973.

_____. and Simon, B. The ecology of social relationships in housing for the elderly. *Gerontologist*, 1968, *8*, 108–116.

Lewin, K. *Dynamic theory of personality*. New York: McGraw-Hill, 1935.

Marshall, N. Environmental components of orientation toward privacy. In *EDRA 2, Proceedings of the 2nd annual Environmental Design Research Association Conference*. Pittsburgh: Carnegie-Mellon University, 1970.

Moos, R. Sources of variance in response to questionnaires and in behavior. *Journal of Abnormal Psychology*, 1969, *74*, 405–412.

_____. Conceptualization of human environment. *American Psychologist*, 1973, *28*, 652–665.

Murray, H. A. *Explorations in personality*. New York: Oxford University Press, 1938.

Neugarten, B. L. A developmental view of adult personality. In J. E. Birren (Ed.), *Relations of development and aging*. Springfield, IL.: Charles C Thomas, 1964.

Pastalan, L. and Carson, D. (Eds.). *Spatial behavior of older people*. Ann Arbor: Institute of Gerontology, University of Michigan, 1970.

Pincus, A. The definition and measurement of the institutional environment in homes for the aged. *Gerontologist*, 1968, *8*, 207–210.

_____. and Wood, V. Methodological issues in measuring the environment in institutions for the aged. *Aging and Human Development*, 1970, *1*, 117–126.

Pollack, K. and Kastenbaum, R. Delay of gratification in later life. In R. Kastenbaum (Ed.), *New thoughts on old age*, New York: Springer, 1964.

Rosow, I. Status and role change through the life span. In R. H. Binstock and E. Shanas (Eds.), *Handbook of aging and the social sciences*. New York: Van Nostrand Reinhold, 1976.

Snyder, S. The geriatric continuum. Paper presented at the Eighth International Congress of Gerontology, Washington, D.C., 1969.

Stern, G. G. *People in context*. New York: Wiley, 1970.

_____. and Pace, C. *Activities index and college characteristics index. Measuring person-environment congruence in education and industry*. Syracuse: Psychological Research Center, 1963.

Turner, B. F., Tobin, S. S., and Lieberman, J. A. Personality traits as predictors of institutional adaptation among the aged. *Journal of Gerontology*, 1972, *27*, 61–68.

Wohlwill, J. The physical environment: A problem for a psychology of stimulation. *Journal of Social Issues*, 1966, *22*, 29–38.

8

Research in Environment and Aging: An Alternative to Theory

LEON A. PASTALAN

INTRODUCTION

In 1970 Pastalan and Carson posited a strategy regarding data collection in the newly emerging area of environment and aging. The strategy behind the collection of data was organized around four logically interrelated areas:

1. physical characteristics and physiological considerations of organismic functioning;

2. personal characteristics including demographic, personality, and cultural factors;

3. psychosocial considerations of interpersonal properties;

4. environmental factors.

In the absence of a well-established theoretical system, it was thought that organizing data in this way would provide at least some assurance that a systematic data baseline would be used by investigators.

While most of the major research findings regarding environments for the elderly can fit within the broad categories mentioned above, the weaknesses inherent in pursuing research activity that are not focused or directed by a unified frame of reference are obvious. The frame of reference most of us think of immediately is a theory of some kind. It is possible, however, that there are other alternatives. The intention here is to demonstrate how the loss continuum concept has influenced this author's research activity, and how it is possible to carry on directed systematic research without invoking a traditional theoretical framework.

THE LOSS CONTINUUM CONCEPT

The loss continuum holds that as a person continues to age beyond the sixth and seventh decade of life, a number of crucial age-related losses occur and accumulate until ultimately the person will lose all semblance of an autonomous being and will depend entirely on others to sustain life. The loss continuum maintains that personal competence is age-related and, if other things, for example, a given level of environmental press, are held constant the older a person is, the less competent he is likely to be. This is basically a human developmental perspective. Birren and colleagues (1963) conclude from their study of the psychomotor functioning, sensory changes, and higher integrative skills of healthy older people that there are some biological and psychological changes associated with aging that are independent of state of health, for example, financial deprivation or loss of social supports through relinquishing affective ties with the external world.

Each of us has what might be described as a life space or home range. This concept is defined as a complex of familiar objects and people distributed in space with meaningful functions and relationships sensed by the perceiver. The physical dimensions and the complexity of a given person's home range are linked to his position on the human development continuum. The developmental continuum refers to the stage of a person's lifetime physical development. At infancy, for instance, one's home range scarcely extends beyond the body. If the infant is warm, well-fed, and reasonably comfortable, his world literally does not extend beyond the skin. He is almost totally unaware of what is occurring around him; he is primarily concerned with his immediate environment. However, as a child develops physically and intellectually, his home range begins to expand. For instance, the child begins to make sense out of his surroundings in his crib, his nursery, and so on. He begins to sort out the various arrangements of objects and spaces that he can see and relate to. As the child begins to develop his ability to walk, his home range expands even further, going beyond the crib, his nursery, out into the other rooms of the house, and soon the child is exploring not only spaces within the dwelling unit but outside as well; he begins to sort out and respond to those areas immediately outside the dwelling unit. As he increases in age and development, he continues to expand his home range until he reaches maturity, at which point he has almost an unlimited home range in the sense that he experiences relationships with a large number of spaces, objects, and people. Once the person reaches full adult capacity, his home range is fairly stable for a long period of time until sometime in the 70s. At this age a person begins to experience a reduction in sensory acuity, health, energy levels, and activities of daily living. A whole series of losses occurs as a person begins to age.

These losses can be subsumed under human development and characterized as the loss continuum. For example, upon retirement a major life role terminates; income is markedly reduced; health becomes a greater concern; energy levels diminish; death of spouse and/or significant other(s) may occur; acuity of sensory modalities becomes reduced; physical mobility decreases; and a general but steady reduction in the scope of that person's world occurs. The reduction is progressive until the person's world may be no larger than one's bed. Response to these losses can take a number of different directions. However, for the sake of this discussion, let us assume that at least one of the following two courses can take place: Extra personal support systems may be added; or limitations in the range of behavior may be conceded and accepted. The decision to take the former or latter course of action can rest with the individual, with the social system, or with a combination of these two. If, as one continues to age, the environmental support systems remain constant, an increasing incompetence on the part of aging persons is bound to occur. Thus, it becomes necessary to generate a knowledge base that addresses itself to the question of environmental fit and individual competence. The goal of a guiding framework for research activity would be to evolve appropriate physical, social, medical, and personal support networks that would intervene as each of the crucial age-related changes occurs. By this means, the effects of those changes as they occur either singly or in combination would be mitigated. These support networks would be available to, but not necessarily mandatory for, each and every elderly person. The choice or option would still be individual. If the networks were to become available, then the choice or option to take or not to take advantage of them would be real.

The loss continuum has served as a guide to a number of important research efforts. In the interest of brevity, this chapter will discuss two of these efforts, both of which have personally involved this author. The two projects in question deal with forced relocation and the empathic model.

FORCED RELOCATION

The relocation study had two objectives. One was to investigate the impact of involuntary relocation on the patient outcomes of mortality and morbidity; the other was to mitigate the consequences of relocation through a preparation-for-relocation program. Since the intervention aspect of the study will be emphasized here, it should be mentioned briefly that relocation had a disastrous impact on the study population. The mortality rate doubled in the 12 months following relocation from a previous 5-year average (Bourestom & Pastalan, 1975). While it is impossible to forestall the kinds of developmental losses discussed in terms of the loss continuum and the attendant personal incompetence, it is not impossible to reduce the demand level of a given environmental situation. This is essentially the reasoning followed in the intervention procedure of the preparation for relocation program.

Two different programs of pre-move preparation for patients undergoing involuntary relocation were designed and evaluated (Bourestom & Pastalan, 1975). The programs involved 51 residents in a county medical-care facility in Michigan, all of whom were being relocated to another facility. The mean age of the patient population was 73.7 years. Sixty-four percent were female. The average length of continuous hospitalization was 3 years, 9 months. Almost all patients suffered from long-term dysfunctions, with the majority suffering diagnosed cardiovascular, neurological, and musculoskeletal impairments.

Due to a series of administrative decisions based on state health department requirements and county fiscal restraints, these patients were to face a drastic environmental change from the old county medical-care facility to a new proprietary nursing home. Following the suggestion of the research staff, state and county officials agreed that a program should be devised to prepare patients for the move. Since little was known concerning the design of such programs, it was decided to explore the efficacy of two different methods of pre-move preparation. The goals of both programs were the same, that is, to assure each patient that there would be a continuation of adequate care and concern for him in the new setting; to reduce the anxiety of the unknown; to acclimate him to the new milieu; and, finally, to ease the psychological and environmental transition through a programmed support network. The strategies by which these goals were to be accomplished differed in the two programs mainly in terms of the type and amount of exposure to the new setting. The duration of both programs was 10 weeks, the last 2 weeks encompassing the move itself. The county facility staff, in consultation with the research staff, carried out both programs.

To meet the goals of both preparation programs required not only preparation of the patients, but also involvement of the medical-care facility staff, the nursing-home staff, and the relatives of the patients.

Patient Preparation for the Move

Twenty-six pairs of patients were matched on the basis of age, sex, and vulnerability, rated by a physician. In Phase I all patients who were medically able were taken in small groups for a site visit to the new facility and given a general tour. Following the visit, the patients met in small groups, led by a county medical-care facility staff member, to discuss the visit. In Phase II the programs for each group differed. Group A visited the new setting once each week for 3 weeks in subgroups of 5. The visits were task-oriented, and were directed toward familiarizing the patients with a specific aspect of the new facility. The visits included the dining room area and lunch, the recreational and workshop areas, and a meeting with the staff regarding general procedures. In addition, opportunities were provided to get acquainted with patients already residing at the new facility. Each visit, approximately 1 hour in duration, was followed by a small-group discussion intended to reduce apprehension and anxiety and to refresh the patient's memories of the visit.

Group B did not visit the new setting again until moving day. Instead, they participated in three, weekly small-group discussions based on slides of the new setting and new staff, photographic prints of the slides, and a visit by the administrator of the new home who discussed policies and procedures.

Other types of assistance were given to both groups during Phase II. Each patient had the opportunity to express preference for room, roommates, and bed position in order to build a sense of control over his fate. A calendar was posted on each patient's wall with his moving date circled. Informal counseling was given to patients on an individual basis as deemed necessary.

The third phase — the move itself — was identical for both programs. County medical-care facility staff escorted all patients to the new facility on moving day. They helped patients according to their expressed or perceived needs. This assistance ranged from escorting patients to the front door to feeding the patient his first meal. Patients were moved in groups of five or six per day.

The small-group discussions of both Groups A and B were similar in content and structure. Content analysis was accomplished from cassette tape recordings of the sessions, supplemented by reports from staff group leaders regarding the nonverbal behavior and other observations that might not be obvious from the tapes. Patients seemed, at first, to find it difficult to express their feelings and anxieties regarding the move. Instead, discussion often centered around the furnishings in the new facility, particularly those that might influence their mobility and independence, for example, ability to fit wheelchairs in the dining room, or the ability to alter the height of beds. Policies and procedures for meals, laundry, visitors, and so forth, formed another major topic category for the discussion groups. As these concrete questions were answered, and as staff members probed further, more patients began to express strong feelings regarding the move. Often this occurred near the end of a group meeting. Other patients, however, consistently denied the reality of the move. For these more confused patients, a longer period of preparation might have been more effective.

Reactions to the preparation programs were quite varied. Many patients felt that it helped to know what to expect. Some took comfort from the respect for their feelings and needs implied by the program, even though the move itself was involuntary. Others seemed to direct their anger about the move toward the preparation program. Still others expressed impatience with the program, feeling it only served to extend their period of discomfort after they had reluctantly adjusted to the necessity of the move. Only a small group was apathetic and neutral. It was felt that this emotional response — even a negative response — was healthy for people caught up in a difficult situation.

The Results of Preparation

The multivisit, task-oriented program (Group A) had a more dramatic effect in reducing mortality rates than did the single-visit program (Group B). Within 1 year of the move, 52 percent (13) of Group B had died, whereas of the group making 4 visits, only 27 percent (7) died.

As previously noted, Groups A and B were matched on age, sex, and vulnerability. In addition, subsequent analysis showed no significant difference in activity of daily living ability, physical limitation, mental status, or level of behavior. Differences in mortality rates are thus not attributable to these factors.

The preparation program had its greatest impact on those patients who were rated by the physician as being most vulnerable to death. These were patients judged as "likely to die" or having a 50/50 chance of dying within 1 year of the move. Of these patients, 76 percent (10) in Group B died, while only 45 percent (5) in Group A did not survive.

This fact speaks strongly in favor of people with lower competence being differentially sensitive to environmental press and of the value of reducing environmental press to a level at which it causes only a moderate departure from a previous adaptation level, thus making the experience a positive one (survival) (see Lawton, Chapter 3 in this volume).

THE EMPATHIC MODEL

The second research activity dealt with the empathic model (Pastalan, Mautz, & Merrill, 1973) which is related to the loss continuum in a number of important ways. The model simulates age-related sensory losses and is primarily a research tool that enables one to experience the physical surroundings as many older people might.

A basic strategy regarding the empathic model was to develop devices that simulated only normal loss and to steer clear of pathologies, at least until some baseline information was established for normal losses. Thus, visual, auditory, olfactory, and tactile appliances simulated only losses that occur within the context of the normal aging process. An attempt was made to simulate the condition of a person in his late 70s in the belief that this would represent an average in terms of progressive losses, keeping in mind the wide range of variation within the elderly population.

The simulated visual loss was the problem of light scatter or glare. A technical description of this condition will not be given here; suffice it to say that, for all practical purposes, the lens of the human eye typically begins to lose its elasticity and gradually starts to become opaque from about the mid-50s, and the condition continues to progress with age.

Hearing loss for the elderly typically occurs above the 2,000 cycles range, and decibel loss averages around 30 for those 65 years of age or older (Morrissett, 1950; Farr, 1967). Through the cooperation of Ronald Rogers, a speech and hearing specialist with the University of Michigan, a material was tested which, when used in the form of ear plugs, simulated the above loss very precisely. Each of the researcher-subjects had individualized ear plugs made from this material, and each was tested for their hearing before the study.

The literature is rather sketchy in the area of age-related olfactory loss; since there was no reliable guideline or practical instrumentation available to establish the magnitude of loss, it was felt that simple cotton wadding introduced into the anterior of the nasal passage would reduce olfactory stimulation sufficiently to give the researchers some idea of the kinds of environmental messages lost by the inability to acutely smell. This device was the most primitive and perhaps the least successful. Certainly the challenge of refining this simulation is a priority task for the future.

There is also very little information in the literature regarding age-related tactile loss. The research team developed its own instrumentation, standardized the losses with an aged population in the community, and experimented with a number of liquid and spray fixatives until the appropriate coating procedures were established. The procedure involved coating the finger tips with this fixative until the proper thickness was secured to elicit the necessary desensitization.

The procedures regarding the execution of the research consisted of each person's experiencing 3 standardized settings for at least 1 hour each day. That is, 1 setting would be experienced for 1 hour on 1 day, the next day the second setting would be experienced, and so on. Experiencing means something other than simple observation and reportage; it is, rather, akin to discovery and evaluation as simultaneous processes. The entire cycle would take, on the average, 3 days, and then the cycle would begin again. The experiment was carried out on a trial-and-error basis for a number of weeks in order to work out a standardized routine, and it was then pursued on a full-scale basis for approximately six months. The 3 settings consisted of a dwelling unit, a multi-purpose senior center, and a shopping center. Each of the researchers kept a daily record of his experiences for the duration of the study. During the course of the study, periodic meetings with the research team were convened, and discussions were conducted comparing experiences and reactions. Ultimately, general categories of experiences were derived from these periodic reviews, which served as bases for the first tentative summary of experiences.

The study demonstrated that age-related sensory decrements can seriously constrain a person from freely using buildings and other environments as they are presently designed. While it is apparently impossible to forestall age-related sensory losses, this experience suggests that through appropriately programmed environmental stimuli, the environment can be made to function as a more effective support network and can mitigate the consequences of sensory losses.

THEORY AND MISSION

The two research activities have been presented to illustrate the fact that both are linked to the loss continuum, and that this concept developed not as a response to a gap in knowledge, but as a response to a human need. As a gerontologist with an interest in man-environment relations, I subscribe to a general mission: How do we, or can we, evolve appropriate physical, social, medical, and personal-care support networks to mitigate the effects of age-related changes as they occur?

The empathic model, for instance, is viewed primarily as a tool of evaluation; that is, while it simulates age-related sensory changes at a given point in the aging process, at the same time it gives one an idea of what in the environment constitutes a problem. If a directional sign in a public building is illegible, steps can be taken to make it more legible. The level of environmental support in this case is increased so that the person with the increased decrement can still function in that setting at a competent level. The motivation regarding the research activity with the empathic model is less concerned with gaps in knowledge and more concerned with gaps in human need. It is essentially mission-oriented research.

A mission can be, in a certain sense, more effective in generating research activity than it can in generating theory. Mission may mean a commitment to research activity concerned with a particular problem area or need, for example, better design of housing for the elderly. A mission may be articulated in a number of different ways, as in the shared efforts of a group of like-minded researchers. It may also take the form of influencing the policies articulated by public agencies. This is not to suggest that all research activity be undertaken within a mission context. Certainly the basic disciplines in the area of human behavior would continue to accumulate empirically-based knowledge motivated by a theoretical frame of reference of one kind or another. However, so-called applied areas of research have been, generally speaking, poorly served by theory. A theory is said to define the major orientation of a particular discipline by delineating the kinds of data which are to be generated; it organizes facts into empirical generalizations and systems of generalizations; it makes predictions and points to gaps in knowledge. However, one could argue that theory in the social sciences does not really predict facts or point to gaps in knowledge. Theory does help to interpret facts, but all too frequently, alternative interpretations are just as plausible. Theory has traditionally served as an after-the-fact frame of reference to summarize that which has gone on before; it has been a kind of map to indicate where we have been, not necessarily where we are going.

Perhaps, if we frame our research activity in terms of human needs, the outcomes may become more directly useful to other applied areas such as the design and social service professions. We continuously couch our research design in terms of knowledge gaps rather than need gaps. We are frequently reminded that our findings are not directly applicable in real world situations. Altman (1973) reports that the reason designers and behavioral scientists tend not to understand each other is that designers deal in product data (data that are specific and directive, such as "lounges should not be put at the end of corridors"), whereas the behavioral scientist typically deals with process data (data that are relational in nature and are not specific and directive, such as "institutions can have a negative impact on patients' self identity"). Merrill (1974) has found empirical evidence of this dichotomy in a survey that asks designers to rate the value of behavioral research facts in a continuum ranging from product-type data to process-type data. Merrill's study indicated a clear preference for product data.

Four logically interrelated areas that are relevant to data-collection strategies in environment and aging were mentioned at the beginning of this chapter. It was also stated that, in the absence of a well-established theoretical system, organizing the data in this way would provide at least some assurance that a systematic data baseline was being established. In analogous fashion, it might be said that if a set of well-defined needs and a consensual commitment to bring about satisfaction of those needs were provided, the research activity would logically flow from those requisites.

Some researchers have suggested that serious behavioral research conducted along with systematic data accumulation without some kind of theory to guide that activity is heretical. This may be true. However, the questions to ask ourselves before we are committed to a premature or irrelevant course of action is Who are we? What are we doing? and What do we want to do?

REFERENCES

Altman, I. Some perspectives on the study of man-environment phenomena. In W. F. E. Preiser (Ed.), *Environmental design research*, Vol. 2. Stroudsburg, PA.: Dowden, Hutchinson, and Ross, 1973.

Birren, J. E., Butler, R. N., Greenhouse, S. W., Sokoloff, L., and Yarrow, M. *Human aging*. Public Health Service Publication No. 986. Washington, D.C.: National Institute of Mental Health, 1963.

Bourestom, N. C. and Pastalan, L. A. Forced relocation: Setting, staff, and patient effects. Final report to the National Institute of Mental Health. Ann Arbor: University of Michigan Institute of Gerontology, 1975.

Farr, L. E. Medical consequences of environmental home noises. *Journal of the American Medical Association*, 1967, *202*, 171–174.

Lawton, M. P. Ecology and aging. In L. A. Pastalan and D. H. Carson (Eds.), *Spatial behavior of older people*. Ann Arbor: University of Michigan Institute of Gerontology, 1970.

Merrill, J. L. Factors influencing the use of behavioral research in design. Unpublished Ph.D. dissertation. Ann Arbor: University of Michigan, 1974.

Morrissett, L. E. Plight of the nerve-deaf patient: The uselessness of all present therapy, the practical usefulness of aural rehabilitation. *Archives of Otolaryngology*, 1950, *51*, 1–24.

Pastalan, L. A. and Carson, D. H. (Eds.). *Spatial behavior of older people*. Ann Arbor: University of Michigan Institute of Gerontology, 1970.

Pastalan, L. A., Mautz, R. K., and Merrill, J. The simulation of age-related losses. In W. F. E. Preiser (Ed.), *Environmental design research*, Vol. 1. Stroudsburg, PA.: Dowden, Hutchinson, and Ross, 1973.

9

Aging-Environment Theory: A Summary

AMOS RAPOPORT

INTRODUCTION

It is a very difficult task to summarize and integrate six diverse theoretical chapters (Chapters 3, 4, 5, 6, 7, and 8 in this volume). In this chapter I will first discuss the six chapters in a general way in terms of theory and man-environment relations. Underlying this discussion is a stress on wider issues and models, since theory is about integration and linkages. Second, I shall relate the chapters to the categories identified in an earlier work on theory in environment and behavior (Rapoport, 1973). Striking gaps emerge from this analysis. These gaps relate to sociocultural and hence to symbolic aspects of the man-environment interaction and therefore to meanings of activities, mechanisms, and environments. This gap is also reflected in corresponding disciplinary and methodological gaps that might be identified using shorthand terms as anthropological and geographical perspectives. Stressing these alternative approaches, I will then relate the chapters under discussion to the missing point of view and illustrate the way in which this perspective changes, broadens, and deepens their significance. Finally, I will suggest the way in which the chapters relate to one another within this framework.

Generally speaking, these chapters avoid the largest, most important question, that is, how, through the mediums of theory, models, or paradigms, research in gerontology becomes related to man-environment studies (MES) generally.

Of course, my area of expertise is MES, not gerontology, and my background is in architecture and planning, not social science. Gerontology, in this connection, interests me as a specific field of MES research and one that may have major insights for MES because of the more extreme conditions and, consequently, the heightened responses with which it deals. It is worth remarking on similar approaches in the field of psychology, in which much work began with extreme conditions and moved to more typical ones; and in the field of anthropology, which focused on primitive cultures (the equivalent of extreme conditions) before moving on to complex socie-ties. Thus, gerontological research may suggest models, approaches, or hypotheses that can be tested in other situations; conversely, other MES work might suggest hypotheses and models that might be useable in geron-tology.

I have, in addition, further prejudices and commitments: one of these is to model- and paradigm-building and generalization (as described in Rap-oport, 1973), and the second is to the use of many models to triangulate reality and to generate meta-models. Finally, there are some models that I regard as most important because they are among the broadest (see Rapo-port, 1974). I also have a prejudice against the New Columbus Syndrome (Sorokin, 1956); therefore, relating ideas and problems to a wide range of existing empirical and theoretical work seems to me to be essential. Because all of these prejudices will play a role in this brief attempt at integration and synthesis, it is important that they be made explicit.

GENERAL DISCUSSION OF THE SIX CHAPTERS

At the highest level of generality, three of the chapters approach man-environment directly (Pastalan, Chapter 8, Windley, Chapter 4, Weis-man, Chapter 5), while three begin with environment-behavior (Lawton, Chapter 3, Schooler, Chapter 6, Kahana, Chapter 7) and from that per-spective aim at a general understanding of MES.

Figure 9.1 shows the models that I had suggested as being found in MES research (Rapoport, 1973). For the present purpose, I assigned each of the six papers a rating denoting the extent to which each paper dealt with each MES model, according to the legend at the bottom of Figure 9.1. Major agreement was found in dealing with three of the models:

competence and adaptation — 14 points
perception and complexity — 10 points
cognitive/image — 9 points

There is then a group of models with only moderate agreement:

behavior setting — 7 points
preference, choice — 6 points
information flow — 5 points
ecological — 5 points
performance-based — 5 points

Various other models are weakly represented, but the weakest seem to be the sociocultural and symbolic models which, although they seem to be most important, are effectively neglected.

FIGURE 9.1.   Major theoretical models in man-environment studies.

MES model	Kahana	Windley	Weisman	Schooler	Lawton	Pastalan	Total
Perception and complexity	○	X	○	□	○	●	10
Cognitive image	□	□	●	○	○	X	9
Behavior setting	□	○	○	X	○	X	7
Communication symbolism non-verbal communication	X	X	X	X	X	X	0
Competence and adaptation	●	X	○	●	●	●	14
Information flow	X	X	X	○	□	○	5
Ecological models	□	○	X	X	○	X	5
Ethological models	X	X	X	X	X	○	2
Evolutionary models	X	X	○	X	X	X	2
Socio-cultural models	X	X	□	X	□	X	2
Preference in environmental quality-choice	○	X	X	X	○	○	6
Performance-based	□	X	X	□	X	●	5

● = strong & direct (3)
○ = weak & direct (2)
□ = implicit (1)
X = absent (0)

Identifying the Gaps

It is, therefore, possible to identify gaps in terms of the twelve models presented. The single lowest score is environment as communication, symbolism, meaning, etc. (zero points) and sociocultural models (two points) which can be grouped together; also, evolutionary models and ethological models (two points each) can also be grouped. These categories can be arranged in this way because they link into major areas, as elaborated below.

First, both the symbolic and sociocultural models are concerned with people as members of groups and what these groups might be, that is, the criteria and characteristics of groups and the way people thus see themselves (and are seen by others) as being distinct. What are the world views, values, lifestyles, and activities of such cultures and subcultures, and what are their specific ways of doing things? In relation to this question, the difficulty of using concepts like culture, world view, and values arises because of the general nature of these concepts. I would, therefore, suggest that one start with activities and lifestyle. Regarding these two issues, the importance of latent and symbolic aspects still needs to be stressed. It follows that meanings of the environment and its parts and the importance of symbolic and communicative aspects of the environment are generally important and may be of special importance for the elderly.

Second, ethological and evolutionary models are linked in order to derive baselines, limits, and regularities. In this way, we may be able to deal with constancies and regularities, as well as variability and change, and to distinguish between species-specific and culture-specific aspects. From the ethological model we might also derive the importance of habitat selection and control over the environment. This area seems to have been neglected, so that one finds increasing confusion between housing institutions and the larger human settlements. The research stress on institutions is the more strange since institutions house only five percent of the elderly; in addition, gerontology was among the first to stress the very different effects of institutional and non-institutional settings.

These two areas — the symbolic and sociocultural, and the ethological-evolutionary — are related through the notions of variability, cross-culturally and through time on the one hand, and through baselines, constancies and limits on the other.

In addition to these major gaps, identified by analyzing the chapters in relation to the models used in MES, other gaps can also be identified that bear on the relationship, or potential relationship, of gerontology to the larger field of MES. Some of these would seem to follow from the major gap already identified, while others can be identified through direct inspection.

There is a gap in specificity of context, the group of people concerned, the setting. One example already mentioned is the blurring of the distinction between institutions and other settings. Another is a lack of identification of the groups of people involved, their lifestyles, culture, and so on. Another very important missing concept is the specifics of the environment; these will be discussed separately due to their importance in deriving design criteria.

There is a major gap in terms of the importance and the specifics of the physical (built) environment. This aspect is either neglected or it is described as residual. Yet it would seem that the nature of the built environment may affect other environmental aspects (for example, the social environment) and may also affect people generally, especially if criticality is raised as we would expect from the literature on environmental docility, lowered competence, and so forth. There is, thus, not only a blurring of institutions and housing, but there is a lack of specificity between: low-rise and high-rise; what form each has; location, in terms of city, town, suburb, countryside; the space organization of the environment; the way in which it relates to the larger setting; the linkages, transport, and proximity to services; the way in which people select and obtain environments; the way in which they change and adapt to them; the meaning, status, and other symbolic aspects of the environment. Also neglected is the relationship of the dwelling to the cluster, the neighborhood, the settlement, the region (that is, the house/settlement system) in terms of environment, behavior, meaning, symbols, activities, and also social groups.

A major gap also exists, both here and in MES generally, in terms of temporal aspects. It is interesting to note that while time has been frequently mentioned, it has been only in terms of its duration. I would argue that time is much more basic and fundamental in two major ways. First, in the larger sense, time can be understood in terms of orientation such as past versus future, linearity versus cyclicity of time. This orientation is culturally variable; for example, among the Maya, the Maenge, and the Pueblo Indians concepts vary; even between the United States and Great Britain large differences are found. Such cultural variation has major implications for design and for understanding man-environment interaction and choices, especially with regard to the elderly. I have suggested elsewhere the possibility of time lag in images (Rapoport, 1974).

The second way in which time must be considered fundamental is in tempos and rhythms and their synchronization among different groups. While this issue is, once again, a general issue, there may be specific differences between the elderly and nonelderly and also among different groups of elderly. Such differences may lead to stress due to the wrong rhythm or tempo, changes in temporal routines and the non-synchronization of tempos and rhythms of various groups. These changes may lead to differential use of the environment, lack of contact between such groups, or exposure to the wrong groups. A consideration of these more general temporal aspects raises questions about too rapid a rate or too frequent change which may, once again, be salient for the elderly merely as a more extreme case. This arena of thought has implications for research, planning, and design generally (roots, place, mobility), but there are also interesting possible implications in the view that nomadism may be the normal, evolutionary human state and hence a link to the evolutionary/ethological model. In this connection, it may well be that some of our discussion is wrongly conceived. Mobility per se may not be the source of problems, but rather may arise in regard to changes that are undesirable to particular groups; settling nomads may be equivalent to moving people in our culture. Thus a clear need to discover general MES laws before tackling specific problems for specific groups and subgroups in specific contexts exists.

It follows from the major gap in cultural, symbolic, and similar aspects that a lack of an anthropological perspective (using the term broadly) exists among these chapters. Variables such as culture, differences among groups, values, lifestyles, and the like are not considered. Most approaches represented can be classified as psychological (with some minor sociological support). I will try to show later how the perspective that I am suggesting affects some of the chapters so that a broader view of congruence, of cognition, and of environmental docility as a matter of heightened criticality, will soon lead to new links and hence possibly to a metamodel. While I believe that such a model is emerging, it is not yet clear enough nor formed enough to be expressed or articulated in this context. For example, in discussions about what social groupings replace the family, one needs to ask how these groupings vary in different groups. This question may have implications for design and may be affected by design: How does design affect communication among people, linking and separating different groups and individuals?, and How do different groups of people, even with similar temporal rhythms and tempos, interact?

CULTURE AND THE PHYSICAL ENVIRONMENT

Returning to the physical environment we can say that the built environment can be seen as the organization of space, meaning, time, and communication. It seems to me that many of these aspects have been neglected in the chapters. Taking the broader view of cognition, for example, as giving meaning to and imposing order on the world, we can say that cognition plays a role both in encoding and decoding of information.

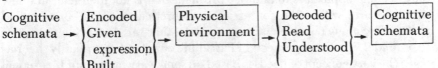

I suggest that culture can possibly be seen in the following terms:

culture → world view → values → lifestyle → activities

Of these concepts, activities seem the easiest with which to start. It can be further suggested that any activity can be understood as composed of four elements: the activity proper; the specific way in which it is done; the associated activities; and the symbolic aspects of the activity. Differences in these elements and the relative importance given them lead to differing environments. It can also be suggested that the latter two aspects of activity may be the most variable and the most important. In the chapters under discussion, these latent aspects of activities tend to be neglected, yet their variability and the specific way in which activities occur lead to differences in form.

The major mechanisms for dealing with activities and eventually with lifestyle, values, world view, and ultimately culture are symbolic and sociocultural; this principle applies as much to density, crowding, privacy, and stress as to other environmental aspects. Similarly, these aspects seem important with regard to congruence, competence, evaluation, preference, performance, and so forth. Therefore, if one wants to be able to state objectives and goals regarding location, landscapes, neighborhood, and dwelling, one must consider a theory that includes all the aspects thus far discussed. Such a theory would then affect the evaluation essential to building a cumulative body of knowledge so that a "mission-oriented" (Pastalan, Chapter 8) need approach and solution can be applied to another need set.

CRITIQUE OF THE SIX CHAPTERS

Given this meta-analytic framework, I would now like to briefly discuss each chapter within this perspective and try to show that each, while retaining its characteristic approach, becomes more general, more MES-oriented, and takes on new features when viewed in this light.

Chapter 8 — Pastalan

In view of my reiterated belief in theory and the need for integration and synthesis, I am forced to disagree with the views expressed in Chapter 8 of this volume. I have already commented that a need-oriented approach can only become applicable to another problem that is not identical (and few problems are) within the context of a theoretical position. Briefly, and eliminating many possible discussion points, there are two principal points to be made. First, many aspects of Pastalan's chapter are implicitly theoretical. The very concept of needs is based on some very important theoretical issues; one can demonstrate a similar situation with respect to many of the statements and arguments in the chapter. Second, a mission-oriented approach and theory are not only not incompatible, but they are mutually interdependent. Theory helps tackle and define problems, and, in turn, reintegrates solutions into other missions, which, given the differences among problems, would be impossible if the findings and results are not, in some way, generalized.

In terms of ideology it is interesting to point out that what Pastalan is advocating is the traditional architectural approach (which was idiographic), the result of which was a lack of generalization and advance. The whole man-environment movement can be seen as an attempt at a more nomothetic approach. In effect, then, while many architects are going in that direction, Pastalan is going in the other. Maybe we will meet en route.

Chapter 4—Windley

I think it can be suggested that more generally and at the group level, the idea of consistent approaches seems valid (hence also at the individual level, that is, members of a particular group will tend to be more alike than members of other groups). Even when attitudes change over time they will change in different ways, at different rates in different groups, and it is quite clear that group attitudes to landscapes, resources, nature, the city, how one builds, and group standards vary greatly. This variability provides a useful explanatory model for the presence of different cultural landscapes, that is, the built environment. Constancy over different contexts is related to the idea of culture as a system of regular choices and is demonstrated by the differential actions of migrants, for example. The notion, therefore, that there are certain regularities in people's responses, preferences and choices about food, manners, behavior, resources, and building is very important. The trait approach, seen more broadly and in cultural terms, or in terms of world view, lifestyle, and so on, seems very useful and has been used in geography, social ecology, and in studies of the built environment. Clearly the use of resources by Hopi, Navajo, Aborigines, or Americans are widely different and reflect widely differing attitudes and orientations to the environment, so that it does become possible to speak of national character and culture and personality.

Situations and settings themselves are partly due to what can be seen as dispositions. Different groups will define different settings and will use them differently, avoiding or seeking out specific situations. This would apply further to systems of settings (for example, the house-settlement system). We thus find that groups have different preferences and respond to environments through habitat selection. This selective process results in different populations which then tend to develop different traits and personalities. In other words, after initial selection by disposition, choice, and so on, different environments are developed which in turn affect cognitive styles, cognitive mapping, behavior, and so on, in a feedback system. Windley's example of privacy would fit into this model. Privacy definitions and the devices used to achieve privacy are group-specific and related to particular dispositions and traits. These traits may differ culturally, by age, or whatever, and they will tend to be specific and fairly stable across situations. Thus it is necessary to define groups, look at them cross-culturally in terms of lifestyles, culture, and personality.

If we consider the house-settlement system, we find different importance attached to the dwelling versus the neighborhood by different groups; differences in the type of neighborhood, house choice; differences in the way the dwelling is treated and handled; landscaping; and other symbols of social identity. If we see the environment as a group of nonverbal communication, there must be group agreement on the way in which to comprehend it. It is, in fact, possible to study these choices—and they are all trait-like. The symbolic and meaning aspects, the positive and negative valences attached to features and relationships, are reasonably stable at the group level.

With regard to decision making, hidden assumptions need to be made explicit, and they may even affect programming and information seeking. These assumptions could be articulated through a theory of group values. It is, of course, true that the behavior of any individual or group may not be congruent with the ideal construct, so that people do, in fact, reconcile diverse behaviors and values. Given this broader and more cultural view of traits, I would argue that Windley's argument is too extreme (whatever the problems of trait theory — and I hold no brief for that body of work), and that the notion of traits per se may still be useful.

Chapter 5 — Weisman

A similar argument as that made concerning Chapter 4 (Windley) may be made about Weisman's chapter on cognition. It is possible to take a broader view of that subject by examining it cross-culturally. While one of the purposes of cognition is, in fact, to simplify the world (a more general one is making the world meaningful), it is done differently by different cultures using different taxonomies, splits, templates, schemas, or whatever. Weisman's view is too narrow and too physical in its interpretation of schema and image. If one adopts an historical, cross-cultural approach, one finds many different ways of construing environments and giving them meaning and, as already pointed out, schemata play a role both in the design and understanding of the environment. These schemata and images contain a major symbolic component; while schemata differ among different groups, they tend to be regular and consistent for specific groups, so that such groups have selective attention and culturally and subculturally related schemata. While there is generally a lawful relationship between the objective and subjective world, this relationship will be different for various groups — that is, such groups have distinct cognitive styles, which links Weisman's chapter with Windley's. It is important to separate out the species-specific and culture-specific aspects of cognition. A link is provided to relate the two groups of models that I have identified as being inadequately represented in these chapters — the ethological/evolutionary and the socio-cultural/symbolic. It may then be possible to see cognition as a universal activity, but one done differently by different people (including researchers).

The notion of domains also goes beyond the specifics described by Weisman. A general concept of cognitive domains exists and plays a fundamental role. It is thus, for example, incorrect to say, as does Weisman, that describing the "what" and "where" of behavior settings does not require consideration of cognitive variables. It does. In fact, the behavior setting is

a cognitive domain both as a taxonomic unit and in terms of the often un-
written rules about what behavior takes place where, with whom, excluding whom, when, and so on. That is, the definition of the setting is a cognitive act and, seen in this fundamental way, the cognitive model has much
more power because it links concepts such as privacy, family, house-settlement system, home-range behavior, and hence the kinds of mental maps
that people have.

Seen more broadly, a cognitive act affects the elements selected and the
way in which they are organized. This process in turn affects (as one example) the perception of cues for behavior, the understanding of these cues,
and the obeyance of these cues. Again, this chain has many implications for
the design of the environment and represents a form of congruence between
the conceptual and the physical domains (a matching of images and reality).
The cognitive act also affects the physical elements selected to be incorporated in mental maps (which in themselves may be variably organized). With
regard to new settings the question might well be how one can obtain congruence rapidly, that is, how well do behavior settings facilitate new mental maps or how can they fit existing ones? In the case of the elderly there is
also the question of the costs of relearning mental maps (which relates
Weisman's chapter to Lawton's and Schooler's). This point is related to my
question about time lags in images; and it raises the question as to whether
in traditional societies the effects of aging are less or delayed, because existing schemata fit new environments better (in fact new environments equal
old environments in the most traditional societies). Thus, relocation (as described by Pastalan and/or Schooler) may be stressful not only because it is
change (sedentarization of nomads may be equivalent), but because it demands the relearning of schemata and mental maps. Since images contain
symbolic and affective aspects (these are possibly the most important components), we find that new environments may be unsuitable because they
do not match the values attached to specific elements and relationships, are
at odds with definition of standards, relative habitability, or environmental quality generally. Thus, the importance of symbolic and meaning aspects which are neglected by all the authors under discussion but which
seem to be an essential component of any cognitive MES model, may affect
the significance of physical elements. Also, if one looks at linguistic ana-
logues, symbols may be generally implicit in cognition. This approach
could be applied to the discussion of complexity, the relation of chunking
and coding related to meaning and value, and the symbolic meaning of environments that the researcher or designer may wrongly evaluate as extremely negative and undesirable. There is a persistent gap between schemata and behavior or, as discussed in geography and anthropology, the actual
versus the ideal. Thus, although people relate to the objective environment,
environmental representations seem to affect behavior; this fact seems important for gerontology and MES generally.

Chapter 6 — Schooler

The model presented by Schooler, relating to threat, buffers, and stress, can be seen as part of a much larger model derived from geography and anthropology (as well as some emerging models in MES). Chapter 6 dovetails with Weisman's since the essential point of the geographical literature on threat is that it is perceived threat that is significant (there is a large body of literature on perceived threat, hazard and opportunity in geography). The result is that different groups perceive different threats, evaluate them differently, and act differently, so that there is a cognitive link. Thus some "factors in the stimulus configuration" may be stressed, and others neglected (that is, as in the previous discussion, different elements are selected by the process of cognition). Thus, there are likely to be cross-cultural differences that may well be related to cognitive styles and hence to dispositions and traits. In other words, different groups have differing susceptibilities to environments and differing abilities to adapt to or to use environments creatively. Groups will so differ depending on their ability to absorb stress (which is variable); the amount of previous stress already present (assuming a limit); the stressfulness of particular items; and the presence of buffers. This applies to any group in terms of their perception of stress — not merely to the elderly — and therein lies its more general MES relevance.

Threat seen as stress is definitional, that is, cognitive, and so are buffers. Hence to the psychological and "possibly social" aspects of buffers mentioned in Schooler's paper must be added cultural ones, which, as in the case of crowding and privacy, may be the most important. Appraisal can also be seen in terms of congruence in my sense, that is, congruence with an ideal state; this, once again, provides a link among the chapters. For example, low crowding may be as bad as high crowding, since crowding is the negative perception of a particular number of people per unit area, that is, an undesired interaction level. Any stress is definitional, and cognitive mediation plays a major role in such definitions. One can say that environmental docility, that is, heightened susceptibility to environmental stress, can be based on cultural variables and can have cultural components. Thus, if Chinese or Pueblo Indians are crowded the effects should be less severe then if Americans or Navajo are equally crowded. If non-place-bound people are relocated, the effects should be less severe than if place-bound people are moved. One can even see moving as a way of escaping stress; again, for nomads, being fixed in place may be the stress equivalent that moving is for others. Similarly, in the United States, mobility and environmental change (Schooler's two forms of change) may be subjectively equivalent. Both are a function of a mismatch between schemata or images and reality, and hence stressful or threatening, even though they may be objectively different.

Mobility and environmental change are very molar concepts and cannot really be tested without considering the symbolic elements against which they are being tested. Change is a general problem, and the elderly represent only a more extreme case. This also implies that alpha and beta press cannot really be separated without considering symbolic and meaning aspects (see Lawton below). In addition, different groups may use different coping strategies once threat has been perceived. They may change values (to reduce cognitive dissonance); they may move; they may change the meso-environment (buildings, etc.); they may change behavior; or they may change their semifixed or non-fixed-feature environment (furniture, clothing).

The whole argument about buffers in terms of confidants — kin or non-kin — would again seem to be a function of culture and the relative importance of the family and the way in which it is defined; that is, different measures are used in different cultures regarding both self-esteem as a function of dependence on family or kinship as defining a stimulus configuration. (For example, crowding in Chinese contexts is affected by whether or not others are defined as kin.) Also, while the buffering agent may indeed be social relations (or special social relations), the environmental form itself may affect social relations (environment as organization of communication), that is, the environment may make some forms of social relations impossible (through design, zoning, management, and so on). There are also differences in the ideal as regards the organization of time or the organization of meaning (all of which are affected by the organization of space). Finally, the built environment may be a surrogate for some of these other buffers and may, in itself, act as a buffer and even reduce the degree of perceived threat, hence reducing the potential stress.

Chapter 3 — Lawton

In Lawton's terms (Chapter 3), behavior is a function of competence, environmental press, and the environment. The person in this equation is partly evolutionary and partly cultural. Competence, as I have extended its meaning, may be cultural. The built environment is a largely cultural product; hence the person-environment term is culturally affected. This means that different groups vary with regard to press, competence levels for particular contexts, the way in which they cope with stress, and their degree of environmental docility (see some of the discussion regarding Schooler's chapter above).

Environmental stress is subjectively defined so that symbolic and meaning aspects become important. For example, habitability is a relative concept, as are slums, unsatisfactory housing, and so on. Familiarity may make environments of widely varying quality "good" and, therefore, one must consider meaning. Symbolic meaning also relates to congruence (see discussion on Kahana), since stress can be understood in terms of non-congruence with expectations and norms. Hence, the same environment may have totally different press value for different cultures, and different elements in the environment may constitute identical press. The result is that it becomes difficult to distinguish between alpha and beta stress because, in effect, it is difficult to define the objective environment; the environment that affects people is the perceived and cognizable environment and, in my view, it must be approached phenomenologically. For example (using Lawton's example), seconds are not universal, and the anthropological literature is full of examples where the fine division of time into units is not important (see discussion of time above). Centimeters are similarly unimportant in situations in which the house, or whatever, needs to be understood not in terms of dimensions but concepts like sacred or profane. Distance, generally, as is clear from recent studies in environmental cognition, is *subjective* distance (at least in terms of its effects on behavior). Thus many physical characteristics of the environment are also phenomenological. For example, the press of distance is not simply solved by buses, as Lawton suggests, since we know that, at least in the case of children in Britain, bussing may be worse than walking in terms of mother-separation anxiety and, hence, effects on learning. Even if one can measure the objective environment, the standards and limits are definitional, and even more variable are the meanings and significance attached to environmental features; this variability is, however, lawful for groups (so that the variability within groups should be less than across groups).

Similarly, needs are variable at all levels. Even if the hierarchy of needs suggested by Lawton is useful (and I have serious reservations about whether this might be useful other than under the most extreme conditions) it would be variable; that is, the relative hierarchy would vary. All of this, of course, relates to the notion of cognitive style discussed above: coding, taxonomies, meanings attached, what elements are selected or ignored, and how they are organized. This cognitive style may well be related to personality style so that one gets a consistent and habitual set of choices (see discussion of Windley above). There is, thus, a relationship between culture and personality (this is at least a likely and partially accepted hypothesis), which also affects complexity in the environment due to different coding practices, different chunks and symbols used, different adaptation levels, differences in noticeable differences, and so on. In other words, the way that one copes with excessive information (one source of press and stress) is variable as are the desired levels. The discussion of complexity thus relates to both Windley's and Weisman's chapters. The elderly may represent a different cognitive style in terms of their wish to experience the world so that interior exploration (interiority) may be more general.

Although all of these ideas relate to coping, they do so in response to the congruence between the conceptual and the physical environments. Questions arise as to Who encodes what in the environment? and What are the assumptions of one set of people (designers or researchers) versus another set (users)? For the purposes of this discussion, researchers and designers may be seen as a specific cultural group. In terms of the model previously suggested (cognition → physical environment → cognition), preference and press become important determinants of the congruence of two sets of images. In the case of decision-making, the question posed immediately above (whose assumptions are encoded?) is most important and relates to the topic already raised of relative habitability, variability of standards, and the like. In fact, this variability even applies to competence at the least complex (biological) end of the spectrum since there is clearly variability in lighting and heating standards, great variability in primitive housing in extreme cold and hot climate zones, differences in the sensory modalities which play a major role in reacting to the environment, and so on. It follows that the variability at other, less biological, levels is greater still.

Thus, all terms of the equation with which Lawton is dealing are culturally variable, and the gap with which I began clearly plays a significant role. Incorporating cultural approaches would add generally to the relevance of gerontology to MES.

Chapter 7 — Kahana

In the course of these comments thus far I have had occasion to mention the concept of congruence several times. This is, of course, in line with my general argument but it is possibly even more marked here. Congruence is an extremely broad concept and may, in fact, act as almost a metamodel if seen in this way. As I shall try to suggest below, it is, in fact, found in many other contexts.

Congruence involves matching needs, desires, and so forth with environments, involving various human characteristics (both species-specific and culture-specific, as described by Windley) and fitting environments to them. The major mechanism is, of course, habitat selection, that is, choice expressed by moving. One might argue that if a person is stuck, then he has blocked habitat selection, hence stress. Thus, congruence can concern choice itself; having choice may be more important than the specific congruence or, alternatively, too much choice may be incongruent with needs. By looking at habitat selection in terms of migration groups, one can obtain insight into this phenomenon. Since migrants often try to match ideal or symbolic landscape with reality, Kahana's model seems to neglect the case of congruence with the symbolic and meaning aspects of the environment. This raises questions about the way in which congruence is defined in different contexts, that is, the variability and similarity of different processes, mechanisms, or elements. This line of thinking suggests that one cannot optimize environments. At best, one can get a better fit for the individual, but we need to ask such questions as good for whom, under what conditions, and what is good?

When we consider the elderly, a time element in the congruence process may exist so that congruence is being sought with an image of the past. At the same time, some of the dimensions involved are subjectively defined so that complexity (as already discussed) and order/disorder are variable concepts and not self-evident. In Chapter 7 as in other chapters, there is a gap regarding the physical environment in addition to the gap regarding symbolic and meaning aspects, and it is very abstractly conceived, without design examples or implications.

The gap in the symbolic domain is clear from the way in which the variables of the model are defined. Congruence with latent functions, as discussed before with symbolic landscapes, with symbols defining place and social identity, and so on needs to be considered. Similarly, congruence must also be sought with the house-settlement system, not just the dwelling or any single setting. The importance of congruence, and the elements with which it is sought, are of varying criticality for different groups. Environments designed as open-ended may make congruence much easier. By understanding the elements for which congruence is most critical, it may be possible to fix certain elements of the physical design.

As I have already stated, congruence seems a much broader concept than Kahana implies or than is found in the other chapters, and it is implicit in many of my comments thus far. At a higher level of generality, congruence seems central to MES, especially in terms of cultures and subcultures, images, and congruence of physical and conceptual environments. Congruence as a mechanism may thus apply to many models. There may be congruence in perception, in cognition, in the sociocultural realm, in information rates and flows, and in performance. Through habitat selection, congruence operates as seeking environments congruent with needs, in migration, in ecological, and in ethological models; it also plays a major role in shaping built environments to match images.

In anthropological study, one may examine cultures in terms of the congruence between world view and religion. In psychological study, levels of complexity and ambiguity and ability/preference are relevant. Sociologists study attitude theory dealing with belief congruence. Social psychologists have developed the concept of cognitive dissonance. Ecologists have found congruence with a value orientation in a larger sense, for example, environment as resources, as place, and as symbol of interest. MES has investigated the following: the notion of misfit as lack of congruence; congruence between physical form and social activity; congruence between subjectively-defined area and designed area (for example, neighborhood); congruence (synchronization) of temporal rhythms and tempos; and congruence of physical environments and ideal environments (images).

The list could be extended, but the centrality of the idea of congruence seems clear. It would be important to discover the way in which the notion of congruence fits or relates to these larger models as well as the way in which it relates to the other chapters (for example, Pastalan on perception,

Lawton on press, Weisman on cognition and Schooler on stress). Congruence would seem to be a most useful concept because it may well be a meta-model that includes and involves others, so that various aspects of congruence are dealt with by various smaller models.

As I have suggested above, the press/congruence model may lead to either habitat selection (migration), modification of need (dissonance reduction), or other strategies, although it is not at all clear that anyone seeks to eliminate all stress. In fact, the creation of a new type of stress may be a way of reducing another stress to a desirable and manageable level.

More generally, various strategies and choices are involved in obtaining congruence — whether physical, symbolic, or whatever. One mode is to re-design or change the environment. This active stance can occur at various scales — at the macroscale where one changes location (migration), at the mesoscale of either fixed-feature or semi-fixed-feature (building or furnishings, and so on), or at the microscale (non-fixed-feature, for example, clothing or behavior). In each of these cases, the change may be at the physical or the symbolic level so that the conflict may not be merely due to non-congruence of the objective and subjective environments, but rather it may be due to the presence of differing subjective environments, or it may be between subjective and objective environments.

I have already raised the issue of criticality. One could argue that congruence becomes more important as options become more limited. This is, of course, Lawton's environmental docility hypothesis and by my extension, applies to the cultural realm. One can extend this principle using Homans' (1950) exchange theory, in which the idea of adaptation as a positive outcome may not work when the costs of adaptation are too high, that is, the benefits (profit–cost) are either zero or negative.

Much of the discussion in this chapter should be modified, given my definition of cognition and use of the phenomenological approach in general. In this light, the model here proposed seems somewhat too mechanistic. The congruence model needs to be applied to the symbolic and meaning aspects of activity as well as to the manifest aspects. Similarly, the criteria for homogeneity and heterogeneity (defined in terms of the meanings of actions and environmental cues) need to be further defined.

The concept of congruence needs, at this point, to be applied to taxonomies, nonverbal communication systems, lifestyles, values, images, and so on. This suggests that the matching process proposed is too simplistic, since each term (for example, ambiguity, stimulation, privacy) is extremely variable. Thus, before one can consider privacy congruence, the term must be defined, its levels established, and the mechanisms and defenses governing its operation discovered. The result is that it is possible to obtain an over-supply of privacy (and, in fact, it is the elderly in some forms of housing who often complain about this situation).

Many other specifics about the characteristics of the elderly — tolerance of ambiguity, the codes used, and so forth — need to be approached cross-culturally through a consideration of sociocultural and symbolic aspects before one can proceed to discuss congruence. Each element to be made congruent may vary; levels of stimulation and complexity, meaning, the associational aspects of the environment, and manner of coding into chunks or symbols may also vary. Thus, in each case, and for the various models discussed by Kahana, one needs to define the significant elements, the way that they are arranged, and the criteria or schemata against which congruence is attempted and evaluated.

One final point is that, although conceptually attractive, the congruence model has several inherent problems. It is difficult to tailor congruences since an attempt to obtain fit in one element may cause new problems elsewhere. Also, congruence tends to be a static rather than a dynamic concept. Finally, congruence relates to the whole question of the effect of the environment on behavior — the separate effects of a variety of such complex processes as symbolic meaning, criticality, perception of noticeable differences, thresholds, choices available, cultural context, adaptation levels, and pacer frequencies.

In spite of the aforementioned problems, the congruence model seems to be most promising when seen in its broadest terms. Although one can link the chapters discussed in a number of different ways, I will propose one particular linkage that begins with the congruence model since it does appear to be most promising.

SUMMARY OF THE SIX CHAPTERS

All people try to achieve congruence (Kahana) with the environment and its characteristics. They do this by matching reality against ideals, images, and so forth. They use different strategies: migration, design, change of environment, change of values, or whatever. Both the ideal sought and the strategies used are variable; group-specific or idiosyncratic environmental dispositions may be found (Windley). The congruence process and much else is mediated via broadly seen cognition (Weisman), so that people react to perceived threat, buffering it in different ways (Schooler). If people cannot cope with subjectively defined problems, the result is stress. Some people, in fact, cannot cope as either individuals, as members of particular groups, or as residents of specific settings (for example, institutions) (Lawton), which leads to notions of competence or environmental docility (or criticality). Unsuccessful coping may be a result of attitudes, values, incongruent coping strategies, certain cognitive styles, previous stress already encountered, state of health, cultural health factors, or whatever. In terms of sensory capacities or physically reduced competence, one can work in a specific area with prosthetic or supportive environments in order to obtain congruence (Pastalan).

REFERENCES

Barker, R. G. Explorations in ecological psychology. *American Psychologist*, 1965, *20*, 1–14.

Homans, G. C. *The human group*. New York: Harcourt, Brace, 1950.

Rapoport, A. An approach to the construction of man-environment theory. In W. F. E. Preiser (Ed.), *Environmental design research*, Vol. 2. Stroudsburg, PA.: Dowden, Hutchinson and Ross, 1973.

_____. Urban design for the elderly: Some preliminary considerations. In T. O. Byerts (Ed.), *Environmental research and aging*. Washington, D.C.: Gerontological Society, 1974.

Sorokin, P. *Fads and foibles in modern sociology and related sciences*. Chicago: Henry Regnery, 1956.

10
Conceptual and Methodological Conflicts in Applied Interdisciplinary Research on Environment and Aging

JOHN ARCHEA

INTRODUCTION

What governs the conduct and application of interdisciplinary research on environment and aging? Many have assumed that the wide range of disciplines that have begun to address the relationships between environment and behavior provide a cornucopia of concepts and methods to enrich our prospects for productive interdisciplinary research and application. In contrast to this view, I see a situation in which discrete packages of knowledge and distinct rules for proper scientific conduct have been inherited from such diverse parent disciplines that no internally consistent position on what to look for or how to look for it can attract enough advocates to enforce its own standard for scientific content or conduct. Without widely accepted rules for inclusion or exclusion, the interdisciplinary enterprise can quickly degenerate into a play on generic catchwords virtually devoid of shared meaning. Witness the repeated use of the terms environment and behavior to focus our mutual concerns. Not only are these two of the most ambiguous terms in the English language, but their use invests written and verbal exchanges among researchers or professionals with an appearance of understanding that invariably betrays conflicting precepts that underlie and distinguish divergent positions.

The fundamental problem confronting researchers who are concerned with environment and behavior is not the apparent misfits between buildings and their users, but rather the more basic disparities between the different conceptual frameworks that scientists and technologists of various persuasions have used to characterize such misfits. What is more, this hydra-headed conceptual heritage appears to be enmeshed in a series of methodological controversies that are potentially even more divisive. Without coming to grips with these fundamental conceptual and methodological distinctions, the convergence of researchers from a number of disciplines on the multi-faceted relationships between environment and behavior could turn out to be nothing more than an interesting coincidence with minimal payoff for the aged or for anyone else.

This issue of alternative modes of research guidance is critical to the effective conduct of all applied and interdisciplinary research. Such an issue does not arise in normal science where the rules for the conduct of inquiry are explicit and beyond challenge and where the current or expected results of proper inquiry are systematically organized as theories or approximations thereof (Kuhn, 1962). By considering the legitimacy of distinctly different modes of systematic inquiry, we imply that research on environment and aging represents an abnormal science where the rules for proper scientific conduct are, themselves, open to challenge. This is far more serious than saying that our theories are out of date and must be supplemented or replaced. Rather, we are coming close to saying that the scientific tradition, having long been regarded as the exemplary mode of formal inquiry, may be an inappropriate model for applied or interdisciplinary science. In order to establish a context for elaborating this last point, I should like to present an outline of the environment-behavior field's diverse conceptual and methodological heritage.

CONCEPTUAL FRAMEWORKS

In one sense, the issue that I see as dividing and confounding us is not what we say about the relationships between environment and behavior, but rather those things that our respective professional and scientific disciplines have led us to believe "go without saying." These are our ontological commitments, our views of reality, our conceptual frameworks. These pretheoretical belief systems serve as the conceptual rallying points from which prototypic research problems are identified, categories of admissible inferences are established, and formats for organizing findings are determined. Imbedded in each of these frameworks is a series of unstated assumptions and implicit definitions that set them apart from one another. These notions cannot attain the status of a theory until the assumptions and definitions implied by a given conceptual framework are explicitly formulated for a particular content area. To date, few theories or approximations thereof to systematically elaborate specific relationships between the organization of the physical environment and patterns of individual or collective behavior have emerged. Although several theories that were originally developed in other content areas have been reinterpreted as accounts of the relationships between environment and behavior (Stokols, 1978), the great bulk of the research in this area seems to be more appropriately characterized as the spontaneous pursuit of implicit conceptual commitments rooted in our various parent disciplines, as opposed to self-conscious explorations of explicit theoretical tenets.

In an attempt to stimulate a consideration of our conceptual differences, I have identified ten frameworks that appear to be current in the field of environment and behavior. These have been selected according to their ability to handle aspects of behavior and features of the physical environment within an internally consistent frame of reference and according to the degree to which each has attracted a constituency of committed researchers. This list is similar to the set of models elaborated in a parallel effort by Rapoport (1973). (See also Chapter 9 in this volume.) For each framework I have attempted to identify: (1) the basic prototype, model, or exemplar that typifies the presumptions shared among its advocates; (2) the general case of the environment, behavior, and their relationships as these are implied in the framework; and (3) some of the theories or approximations of theory that explicate linkages between environments and behaviors in accord with that framework's inherent presumptions. As far as possible, I have abstracted each position in a manner that is more generic than the focus of the particular disciplines or specific theories with which it is associated. I doubt that anyone will find this treatment entirely to his liking, particularly where his own concerns appear to be inappropriately subdivided or confounded with those of others. Nonetheless, I find this outline of conceptual distinctions to be an essential starting point for comprehending the field of environment and behavior.

Adaptation

1. The model is homeostasis, the focus is the individual.

2. The adaptation framework is concerned with the mechanisms whereby individuals maintain behavioral continuity in the face of environmental change. The physical environment is viewed as a collage of physically or socially valenced stimulus patterns that are organized with varying spatio–temporal densities and intensities. Behavior is seen as a response to these spatio–temporal gradients in which the cumulative adjustment to available stimulation is biased by the individual's prior experience. Each individual's frame of reference for accommodating new environmental stimulation is, in turn, reestablished by the attributes of that stimulation.

3. Much of this work draws upon either adaptation level theory (Helson, 1964) or the independently formulated general adaptation syndrome

(Selye, 1956). Its relevance to an understanding of environment and behavior has been elaborated by Wohlwill (1972).

Coding

1. The model is language, the focus is culture.
2. The coding model elaborates the mechanisms whereby the participants in a given social unit synchronize or otherwise coordinate appropriate activities among individuals in time and space. The physical environment is treated as meaningful juxtapositions of objects, distances, sequences, individuals, and events. Behavior is the process of symbolic communication which involves encoding one's intentions, status, or affiliations through verbal, postural, gestural, and spatial displays that others can decode without loss of meaning. Shared patterns of spatial behavior will produce mutually consistent interpretations among the members of a social unit. The display of these symbolic patterns establishes the appropriateness of specific environment-behavior relationships in specific situations.
3. While some of this work draws upon the accounts of normal appearances offered by Goffman (1971), the position is more often formalized in the models of personal space (Sommer, 1969), and proxemics (Hall, 1966). The conceptual underpinnings of the framework have been reviewed by De Long (1972) (see also Chapter 2 in this volume).

Congruence

1. The model is the niche, the focus is the social system.
2. The congruence position follows from the notion that environment and behavior are aspects of the same thing. The physical environment is a pool of bounded sets of props of varying qualities. Behavior is a prevailing and recurring display of activities, attributes, or affiliations that are distributed in time and space. This distribution of prevailing activity patterns coincides with patterns of environmental boundaries to form natural units of social organization. By identifying the linkages between units defined by this pattern of covariance, it becomes possible to determine the organization of environments across individuals or the organization of behavior across environments.
3. Although the framework is anticipated in the work on social area analysis (Shevky & Bell, 1955), it is more commonly formulated in terms of undermanning theory (Barker, 1960) or behavior setting theory (Barker, 1968). The use of the K-21 Scale and the behavior setting survey as design research techniques has been developed by Bechtel (1977). The use of the framework in research on environment and behavior has been reviewed by Willems (1973).

Contingency

1. The model is natural selection, the focus is the individual.
2. The contingency framework associates the elaboration and differentiation of individual behavioral repertoires with the consequences of prior actions. The physical environment is regarded as the locus of the elicitors and the consequences of particular human actions. Behavior is seen as the progressive discrimination between those actions that are most appropriate to the attainment of desired consequences and those that are not. Any approximation of intended consequences will lead to a replication and an elaboration of the antecedent actions in associated environmental situations.
3. This work draws quite heavily upon the techniques of operant conditioning (Skinner, 1953), and it is well-illustrated by the institutional case studies of Cohen (1974).

Diffusion

1. The model is the circuit, the focus is the spatial system.
2. The diffusion model holds that acquaintance with an artifact, process, idea, or event must precede its use in individual or collective repertoires. The environment is treated as a set of spatio–temporal networks consisting of channels and nodes of varying capacities that govern the distribution of commodities, information, energy, and prototypes in physical space. Behavior is treated either as the set of opportunities that are created by one's position in or access to these networks or as a strategy for gaining favorable position. The possibilities for selecting, utilizing, revealing, or adopting behaviors are seen as functions of spatial locations, orientations, or routines.
3. Although the position is suggested in the work on functional distance (Festinger, Schachter, & Back, 1950), it has been much more fully developed at the geographical scale as central place theory (Christaller, 1966) and in Hagerstrand's (1967) model of mean information fields. The analysis of behavior at the building scale is developed from this perspective in the model of visual access and exposure (Archea, 1977).

Dispositions

1. The model is personality, the focus is the individual.
2. The dispositional framework holds that the evaluation and use of a particular type of environment will predictably vary in accord with a constellation of personal and situational factors prevailing upon the user. The physical environment is regarded as a nominal arrangement of artifacts that exhibit shape, size, relationship, and other attributes of form and type. Behavior is treated as a process of affective assessment in which environ-

mental patterns are differentiated as a function of individual interests, capabilities, motivation, values, and circumstance. An individual's affective response toward any series of events or issues can serve as an index of that person's predisposition toward specific environments under specific extenuating circumstances.

3. Much of this work draws upon either the hierarchy of human needs (Maslow, 1954) or the independently-formulated personal construct theory (Kelly, 1955). The Environmental Response Inventory (McKechnie, 1974) is typical of the various techniques for assessing environments from a dispositional viewpoint which have recently been reviewed by Craik (1976) (see also Chapter 4 by Windley in this volume).

Performance

1. The model is the machine, the focus is the resource system.

2. The performance concept is keyed to the fact that the spatial arrangement of environmental resources mediates the amounts of time, energy, dollars, or other expendibles required to perform an activity or the rates at which they must be expended. The environment is viewed as a distribution of tools that are extended in three-dimensional space and with which persons can exchange information or energy. Behavior is equated with purposeful activity which occurs in a spatio–temporal field at some cost. It also includes strategies for conserving time, energy, or money through the efficient use of space.

3. The position has been variously formulated as a pattern language (Alexander, Ishikawa, & Silverstein, 1977), the study of human activity systems (Chapin, 1974), and the performance concept (Eberhard, 1969).

Prosthetics

1. The model is entropy, the focus is the individual.

2. The prosthetic framework is keyed to the notion that there are normative levels of human functioning that are required for the successful conduct of one's affairs in typical environments. The physical environment is treated as a medium that serves as either an amplifier that sustains or augments human capabilities or as an obstacle that confounds human performance. Behavior is seen as the level of competence that a person exhibits in a given situation. Competence is a function of a person's own psychomotor or social capabilities interacting with the facilitating or inhibitory characteristics of their environment. Persons with diminished capabilities can frequently function at nearly normative levels if the physical environment provides increased support.

3. The position has been formalized as the environmental docility hypothesis (Lawton, Chapter 3, this volume) and as the loss continuum (Pastalan, Chapter 8, this volume).

Schematics

1. The model is a map, the focus is on the individual.
2. The schematic framework is concerned with the manner in which individuals create and retain an awareness of their physical surroundings for use in guiding their purposeful activities in those surroundings. The physical environment is treated as a set of objective topological relationships among spaces, objects, events, and their attributes. Behavior is the idiosyncratic internalization of images of environmental relationships as a function of experience, and the use of these images either to guide behavior in the absence of direct sensory stimulation or to provide closure between sensory inputs and previously internalized models. Individual behaviors will differ in a given setting as a function of different images of that setting which result from different experiential histories.
3. The position had originally been independently formulated in terms of socio-spatial schemata (Lee, 1968) and as imageability (Lynch, 1960). An example of the framework's current application to environmental analysis has been synthesized as a psychology of place by Canter (1977). An extensive review of recent research and of the framework's conceptual underpinnings has been published (Moore & Golledge, 1976) (see also Weisman, Chapter 5, this volume).

Sensation

1. The model is a camera, the focus is on the species.
2. The sensation model is concerned with the physiological processes involved as an organism attends to and detects both the prevailing characteristics of its environment and the magnitude of its own actions within that environment. The physical environment is seen as an array of radiant, mechanical, chemical, and other stimulus energies, the mutual interactions of which provide information about the physical realities in which they originate. Behavior is the process of selectively or reflexively attending to portions of the stimulus array in order to detect the prevailing conditions of one's physical surroundings. The availability of accurate environmental information is a prerequisite for the adequate regulation of one's own performance.
3. A notation system developed by Thiel (1970) is an example of the work that builds upon the model of perceptual systems (Gibson, 1966).

Summary of Conceptual Frameworks

What we see here are ten different conceptions of the physical environment and ten different conceptions of individual or collective behavior, prearranged in pairs, each of which affords the committed researcher with a working frame of reference for comprehending the mutual interrelationships between the conduct of human affairs and the organization of their physical surroundings.

From the vantage point of its own advocates, each conceptual framework appears to be a complete, consistent, and correct presumptive model of reality. Each enables researchers to conveniently structure their own work. Each also provides them with the only available frame of reference for interpreting the research of others working in the same content area. Unfortunately, however, a conceptual commitment provides no basis for the translation or accumulation of research findings across frameworks. Herein lies the dilemma — all research is framework-specific. That is, knowledge has form and meaning only within a given conceptual context. Any attempt to interpret that knowledge in light of the presumptions of another framework runs the risk of violating the unstated assumptions that incorporate that knowledge into an internally consistent model of reality.

It should be noted that perception is not listed as a conceptual framework. Rather it must be treated as an event, process, or phenomenon which, like stress, migration, privacy, or satisfaction, forms a part of the content of research on environment and behavior that is subject to different formulation within different frameworks. For example, perception is central to the model of environment and behavior posited in the sensation framework, but it is only incidental to the concerns of those committed to the diffusion framework. Perceiving is treated as passive and deterministic within the sensation framework but as active and creative from the schematic point of view. From the sensation perspective, that which is perceived is a direct function of the organization of the environment or object of perception, whereas the adaptation framework attributes perceptual organization to the perceptual history of the perceiver. Such fundamental distinctions are typical.

For example, advocates of the coding framework have elaborated a model of environment and behavior in which the magnitude of person-to-person or person-to-object spacing appropriate to a given situation is regarded as an integral part of a given subculture's symbolic communication system. To interpret this, using the very individualistic dispositional presumption that behavior is evaluative, could lead us to the highly inconsistent conclusion that certain spatial relationships are preferred by certain people in certain situations — a clear violation of the coding presumption that appropriateness is not specific to individuals but is shared across members of a functioning social unit.

In short, what we have come to characterize as a vital and promising venture into interdisciplinary collaboration may be, in fact, a subtly disguised cross-disciplinary competition. Perhaps the comprehensive theories of environment and behavior that some of us seek have already been anticipated and preempted by the several distinct clusters of implicit presumptions that we have inherited from our various parent disciplines. Even without the theories themselves, our research is clearly prestructured by our diverse commitments to these fundamental concepts. Yet this picture is incomplete. Neither theories nor conceptual frameworks provide sufficient guides for research activity. They tell us what to expect and how expectations should be related to outcomes, but they do not give us a procedure for advancing these presumptive notions to the status of substantiated knowledge. To do that we need a methodological program.

METHODOLOGICAL PROGRAMS

Whereas conceptual frameworks provide us with models of reality, methodological programs provide us with models of knowledge. Each program embodies its own set of explicit and detailed rules for the conduct of inquiry and the justification of assertions. Accordingly, their contribution to research activity is epistemological rather than ontological.

Although it is commonly assumed that science is a relatively monolithic methodological program, Radnitzky (1970) has shown that there are clearly opposing schools. I sense that there are at least four distinct models of knowledge acquisition and use current in the field of environment and behavior. Each of these includes: a criterion for granting notions the status of knowledge; a scientific procedure for improving the precision of expectations; a technological procedure for increasing the control of outcomes; and specific doctrines that systematize that program's model of knowledge and certify the techniques by which it is implemented. I have, once again, attempted to abstract each of these positions in a manner that is minimally biased toward the routine methods or research designs that have followed from them.

Rationalism

1. Knowledge is logical; it is embodied in precedents. The exemplary discipline is jurisprudence.

2. The scientific procedure involves the justification of plausible arguments through appeals to logical precedents. It attributes truth to those deductive inferences that, having survived all reasonable challenges, follow from an acceptable premise.

3. The technological procedure can be characterized as the pursuit of consensus through negotiation. It proceeds on the basis of the implications of self-evident truths.

4. The program draws heavily upon the syllogisms of Aristotelian logic

and has been elaborated under the label "grounded theory" (Glaser & Strauss, 1967).

Empiricism

1. Knowledge is provable; it is embodied in theories. The exemplary discipline is physics.

2. The scientific procedure relies upon unbiased observations to confirm hypothetically predicted events that have been isolated through the use of experimental or statistical controls. Techniques of demonstrative inductive inference permit the instant assessment of thresholds for hypothesis rejection. The results are facts or probabilities assertable within known confidence limits and constrained by procedural assumptions.

3. The technological procedure is the neutral prescription of established facts in support of non-empirically derived objectives. This non-experimental, applied science procedure holds that all evidence must be entered into the confirmation process prior to the use of facts in applied situations.

4. The program has been rigidly formalized in the doctrines of logical positivism, operationalism, and the hypothetico-deductive method developed by members of the Vienna Circle (Neurath, Carnap, & Morris, 1955). These provide the basis for most current research tactics, including quasi-experimental designs (Campbell & Stanley, 1966) and unobtrusive measures (Webb, Campbell, Schwartz, & Sechrest, 1966).

Structuralism

1. Knowledge is generic; it is embodied in taxonomies. The exemplary discipline is linguistics.

2. The scientific procedure is the successive approximation of categories that interact to exhaust the naturally occurring events identifiable in a given problem area. The imposition of dichotomies, hierarchies, matrices, or other techniques of pattern analysis serve to define the invariant underlying factors that interact to produce situational variance. From an interrelated system of generic units it is possible, through deduction, to account for the position of any observable event within a given set of circumstances.

3. The technological procedure is the conservative technique of constraining intervention through deterministic proscription. A full understanding of an internally consistent pattern that generates molar events defines the situational limits within which those events can occur.

4. This predominantly European program has been partially formulated for the Anglo-American community as a genetic epistemology (Piaget, 1971). Its use in the study of environment and behavior has been elaborated by Hillier and Leaman (1973).

Instrumentalism

1. Knowledge is useful; it is embodied in models. The exemplary discipline is economics.

2. The scientific procedure involves the continual corroboration of analogs against observable states of affairs in order to improve the correspondence of the analog with emerging events. These analogs are merely conventional abstractions that have no reality status. They are used to produce tentatively substantiated representations of observable events for the purpose of making further approximations of unobservable events.

3. The technological procedure involves the use of corroborated models to govern intervention in actual situations. The application of knowledge is experimental insofar as the accumulation of evidence is concurrent with the use of the models and contributes to their continual revision.

4. The formal position is anticipated in the notions of synechism and fallibilism offered by Peirce (1955) and is further outlined in the work on critical fallibilism by Popper (1962) and Lakatos (1970). An instrumental approach to problems involving environment and behavior has been detailed by Studer (1969).

Summary of Models

Once again we have four different models of science paired with four different models of technology, all operating in the same interdisciplinary context. The development or application of knowledge as it is specified by any of these methodological programs is largely a function of professional education or training. However, unlike the rather casual manner in which conceptual commitments are passed from master to apprentice, our methodological commitments are very deliberately inculcated. The trained professional is quite aware of the rules for doing good work and is extremely suspect of work that doesn't appear to follow those rules. The dilemma here, of course, is that there is more than one set of rules for gaining or applying knowledge about environment and behavior, and it is just as impossible to assess that knowledge from a methodological position that one does not advocate as it is to comprehend reality through someone else's conceptual framework.

It is noteworthy that while scientists and technologists often freely borrow across concepts, they seldom run the risk of misinterpreting across methodologies. Rather, they assign separate and unequal status to all notions that fail to meet the standards for knowledge acquisition and use to which they are committed. For every designer who is suspicious of statistics and control groups, there is an experimentalist who is amused by intuition and juried awards. This is more than a two-cultures gap in which we tolerate each other's methodological excesses so long as we stay out of each other's way (Snow, 1964). It is a four-way epistemological crevasse located precisely at the point that our interdisciplinary commitments suggest we should open a working dialogue between behavioral scientists and environmental designers.

In spite of the fact that each methodological program explicates both a scientific and a technological procedure, most of our knowledge about environment and behavior has been acquired by researchers committed to the empiricist or structuralist programs, while most of the designers and planners charged with using this knowledge tend to advocate rationalist or instrumentalist positions. Consequently, whatever is advanced as a true or complete characterization of processes or events by the researcher is often subject to rejection by the designer who finds it illogical or useless. Conversely, to the empiricist who is schooled to treat technology as applied science in which confirmed facts are generalized only within confirmed limits, it comes as an outrageous transgression of scientific integrity when the instrumentalist invites him to use his best hunches as representations of things that can be evaluated and corrected only in subsequent applications.

Unfortunately for the field of environment and behavior, the Anglo-American research community tends to enshrine empiricism as the ideal model of science. Even those who are not fully committed to the empiricist program are led to regard assertions that do not follow from controlled observations as non-science or nonsense, to assume that confirmation must precede application, and to treat theory as an indispensible guide to scientific conduct. Yet, it would be uncharacteristic of our interdisciplinary heritage to endorse these proscriptions. Rather, we must grant scientific status to the formulations of proxemics or behavior settings which have been substantiated within the continental tradition of structuralism. We must treat the rationalist traditions of architecture and the design professions as legitimate programs for knowledge acquisition and use, not as accumulated serendipity. Finally, we must accept empiricism for what it is—one of several methodological programs current in the field of environment and behavior with no prior claim to scientific credibility.

ENVIRONMENT AND BEHAVIOR

Our interdisciplinary focus might best be characterized as the convergence of at least ten distinct models of reality and at least four distinct models of knowledge on the highly generalized notion that environments and behaviors are somehow related. The breadth of our heritage is not only unprecedented, its consequences are completely unanticipated by the content or the conduct of normal science and technology. The major departure lies in the increased heterogeneity of our interdisciplinary research and design community (see Figure 10.1). While individuals can continue to expect their conceptual and methodological commitments to effectively structure

FIGURE 10.1.

	RATIONALISM syllogism	EMPIRICISM theory	STRUCTURALISM taxonomy	INSTRUMENTALISM model
ADAPTATION		(Helson)	(Selye)	
CODING	(Goffman)	(Sommer)	(Hall)	
CONGRUENCE		(Bechtel)	(Barker)	
CONTINGENCY		(Skinner)		(Cohen)
DIFFUSION		(Festinger)	(Archea)	(Hagerstrand)
DISPOSITIONS	(Maslow)	(McKechnie)	(Kelly)	
PERFORMANCE	(Alexander)	(Chapin)		(Eberhard)
PROSTHETICS		(Lawton)		(Pastalan)
SCHEMATICS		(Canter)	(Lynch)	
SENSATION	(Thiel)	(Gibson)		

162

and guide their own work, they can no longer rely on the normal presumption that the same commitments are shared by their colleagues.

When we conceive of the notion network, we cannot be sure that our various co-workers won't infer the notion-bounded set of props, nominal arrangements, or the locus of consequences. When we identify competence, we can anticipate interpretations of opportunity, efficiency, or discrimination. Finally, when we offer tentative approximations that we find useful, we can usually expect someone to question our lack of proof. Issues that would have traditionally been definitively joined and resolved within the intercept of a single framework and a single program are now frequently diffused across half a dozen conceptual positions and two or more methodologies. It is this multiplicity of substantive and procedural options that confounds the process by which our individual contributions coalesce as internally consistent bodies of knowledge or technique.

The high probability of misinterpretation and misapplication in the field of environment and behavior should concern us, but it should not divert us. Our individual commitments to presumptive concepts and formal methodologies are absolutely essential to the successful conduct of inquiry or intervention. Rather than encourage attempts at cross-disciplinary translation, reconciliation, or generalization, we must begin to recognize that our mutual concerns are inherently inconvenient to integrate. But more important, as our work becomes increasingly interdisciplinary, we must begin to acknowledge that our conceptual commitments have led us to presume too much while our methodological commitments have led us to assume too much. With regard to our own work, we must begin to explicate the obvious. With regard to the work of others, we must begin to tolerate apparent nonsense. Furthermore, we must begin to distinguish between nonsense that appears incomprehensible — an indication of conceptual disparities — and that which appears erroneous — a clear signal of methodological differences.

THEORIES: A METHODOLOGICAL DILEMMA

It is hoped that this prolonged discourse on the conceptual and methodological pigeonholes created by the diversity of our disciplinary heritage provides a basis for considering the types of prior commitment that are necessary or sufficient for the effective guidance of applied interdisciplinary research on environment and aging. In addressing this crucial issue Pastalan (Chapter 8, this volume) has made the provocative suggestion that "missions" are an effective alternative to theoretical guidance for applied research. After a brief argument that theory per se has not proven an effective guide for his own work, he outlines his research on the "loss continuum," "forced relocation," and the "empathic model" and concludes that the commitment which has shaped this work has taken the form of a mission. He further suggests that a mission is, in general, more effective than a theory in guiding applied research.

That a theory might not be necessary in order for an effective research program to be carried out, is perfectly acceptable. That something called a mission might be a sufficient guide for research activities in applied areas is similarly acceptable. What is not clear from Pastalan's presentation, however, is precisely how theory can fail to guide certain research activities effectively, or precisely how a mission can succeed where a theory has failed. It is also not clear whether a theory, mission, or something else has guided the specific research that Pastalan discusses in Chapter 8. Using Pastalan's arguments as illustrations, I will explore these issues in considerable detail.

From the preceding review we note that theories are explicit formulations of assumptions, definitions, and relationships that are expected or found to exist among the events, processes, or other phenomena that constitute a specific area of inquiry. We also note that theories are largely anticipated by the implicit models of reality imbedded in conceptual frameworks. Aside from behavior setting theory which follows from the congruence framework, few theories have been fully elaborated that account for specific relationships between environment and behavior (Stokols, 1978). Consequently, we are left with a situation in which research is often prestructured by presumptive, rather than theoretical commitments. Certainly one reason that Pastalan can legitimately reject theoretical guidance for his applied research is the absence of formal theories that posit direct linkages between physical environments and age-related behavior. His remaining option is to develop his own theory of the relationships at issue and to establish a factual data base prior to attempting any application. This is the applied science model by which the empiricist insists that application must be preceded by confirmation.

Theory stands at the apex of the empiricist program. Its elevated status is necessitated by an elemental model of absolute knowledge whereby discrete notions or hypotheses are proven or assigned probabilities only in the isolation afforded by experimental or statistical control. Within this program, the theory serves to independently orchestrate certified facts by defining their relative positions within coherent bodies of knowledge. To do this, the theory provides an explicit basis for deriving testable hypotheses that limit the domain of inquiry to those potential truths that correspond with what is already known to be true, and that attribute any unexpected findings to procedural errors. The advantage of this system is the confidence that one can have in the truthfulness and coherence of facts that have withstood such rigorous scrutiny. The disadvantage lies in the extremely protracted effort required to assemble a comprehensive model of reality that meets the empiricist's criteria for the instant assessment of truth or probability. For the applied researcher, the disadvantages of the empiricist program appear to outweigh its advantages since it is seldom feasible to wait for theory development and knowledge acquisition to run its promised course before an intervention strategy has to be adopted. Consequently, I believe that we must concur with Pastalan's rejection of theoretical guidance on the grounds that formal theories make demands upon the quality of knowledge that are inappropriate to the applied researcher's mandate, particularly in an area as complex and underdeveloped as environment and behavior.

By endorsing Pastalan's view we not only find theory development in this field too premature for effective guidance, but we also question the merits of the very methodological program within which theory is held to be essential to the conduct of formal inquiry. Since the model of knowledge we question is empiricism, and since empiricism stands as the hallmark of our scientific tradition, we find ourselves in need of an alternative program for methodological guidance that will be minimally disruptive to our scientific credibility. In contemplating a shift in methodological commitment it is fortunate that, unlike our conceptual presumptions, our models of knowledge acquisition and use are formally schooled and are, it is hoped, subject to reschooling. My own review of methodological programs suggests at least three alternatives to theoretical guidance: (1) the logical arguments or appeals to precedent of the rationalists; (2) the systematic taxonomies of the structuralists; and (3) the utilitarian models or analogs of the instrumentalists.

We may tentatively dismiss the rationalist form of guidance by appeals to precedent on the grounds that its susceptibility to idealistic and authoritarian influence runs afoul of our scientific aspiration for impartiality. In so doing, however, we must recognize that the selected implications of selected precedents are traditionally offered as the rationale behind environmental design or management decisions. The difficulty here is clear; rational inquiry is not, in fact, governed by the precedent itself, but is governed by the selection and sequencing of those precedents that give vested intentions the appearance of logical necessities. It matters little whether these precedents are established empirically, structurally, or instrumentally. When they are selectively introduced into negotiations for the purpose of influencing the development of a consensus, they become part of the rationalist technological procedure, thus vulnerable to influence apart from evidence.

The taxonomies of the structuralists require a bit more scrutiny. First, there are more structuralists among us than our empiricist tradition permits us to acknowledge. Second, the structuralist criterion for knowledge is that it must be generically complete, that is, capable of accounting for all observable phenomena in a given field of inquiry. Within this program, a framework for knowledge is first constructed and then continuously refined to accommodate newly observed relationships. Truth is established through the successive approximation of universals, rather than by precedent, or by the instant assessment of particulars. There is no error term. The status of knowledge is conferred upon an evolving system of relationships that collectively anticipate how all possible facts must fit together. Instead of theories in which events are shown to be related, structuralism develops an understanding in which relationships interact to account for events. This generative capability permits the structuralist to accept as knowledge the kinds of complexity that the empiricist must painstakingly dissect, isolate, verify, and reassemble.

To the applied researcher charged with fitting environments to behavior, this capability for comprehending complex phenomena with a high degree of scientific authority appears quite attractive. Yet, it presents two related problems. The first is that by relying on units that are relational rather than discrete, it becomes extremely difficult to disentangle a potential course of action from its expected consequences. The second is that, where everything is seen to be intricately interrelated, it becomes almost impossible to effect a change in one situation without disrupting the prevailing status of all related situations. On the one hand, we have a Gordian knot of apparent tautologies, while, on the other hand, we have an infinite progression of potentially counterproductive consequences. Therefore, in spite of the fact that structuralist understanding is quite thorough, it comes too tightly packaged to permit convenient application and once it is untangled, the guidance is negative rather than positive.

MISSIONS: A METHODOLOGICAL SOLUTION?

By raising questions about the rationalist's susceptibility to bias, the discrete or molecular quality of knowledge demanded by the empiricist, and the intricacy of the understanding offered by the structuralist, I may appear to be dismissing the legitimacy of scientific conduct altogether. However, my real quarrel is not with science, but rather with those programs of inquiry that confound knowledge with the evasive ideal of an absolute and enduring truth that is independent of the process of knowing, yet is somehow attainable only through the use of that process.

Our concern is to identify programs of knowledge acquisition and use that will assist us in bringing expectations and outcomes into alignment. To equate this with the establishment of ultimate truths that are unrelated to the conceptual and situational context in which they are known has become the hobgoblin of modern applied science. It has led to the proliferation of educational programs and professional standards that emphasize methods at the expense of concepts. The resulting confusion is particularly evident in interdisciplinary areas like environment and behavior, fields in which necessities for action often fall victim to a multitude of independently established, partially formulated, irreconcilable truths. Accordingly, I think we must begin to recognize that most of the situations that concern us change much more quickly than our ability to substantiate logical, factual, or generic truths that are sufficiently current to justify systematic intervention.

Instrumentalism and the Mission

This brings us to the instrumentalist program — the only program in which knowledge is not ultimately equated with truth or some approximation thereof. Instead, the quality of what is known is judged by its effectiveness in developing new knowledge or in achieving preferred states of affairs. The criterion is entirely utilitarian. Knowledge is assessed according to its heuristic value alone. The only demand that the instrumentalist places on his knowledge base is that it help to increase his understanding or control of the events that concern him. This means that the instrumentalist's knowledge is relative to his intentions with regard to specific situations, rather than being relative to a substantiated theoretical or taxonomic explanation of interrelated portions of reality. Ideally, the instrumentalist program promises a guide to action that should be most effective under the conditions of maximal uncertainty common to complex and rapidly changing situations. In practice, the instrumentalist proposes to govern his inquiry through the systematic interplay of models, missions, and techniques for resolving conflicts between either of these and between more extensive bodies of evidence. The instrumentalist regards knowledge as a convention that has no inherent truth-like status. These conventions take the form of models in which poorly understood relationships in a problem area of concern to the researcher or designer are treated as if they are functional or organizational equivalents of much more fully understood relationships drawn from another content area. The two content areas may be as dissimilar as juvenile delinquency and hydraulics. The only purpose of the model is to provide an analogous or homologous abstraction of a complex or poorly understood situation in order to facilitate understanding or control.

While models hold the same position in the instrumentalist program that theories and taxonomies hold, respectively, in the empiricist and structuralist programs, two fundamental differences exist. First, models are intentionally impoverished. They only account for those portions of a situation that are of immediate concern to the researcher or designer. A model is valued, not for how truly it represents reality, but for how successful it is in isolating those factors which effect desired or expected outcomes from those which do not. Second, models are expendable. If a model works — that is, if spontaneous or intentional changes in the model predict or account for corresponding changes in a real situation — then the model is assumed to be an appropriate representation of that situation. Once a particular model fails to adequately account for the essential characteristics of the situation at issue, it becomes subject to replacement by other models drawn from entirely different content areas. A situation that is best represented as a hydraulic system on one occasion might conceivably be more adequately portrayed as an electric circuit as the research advances. Although a faltering model can be modified or embellished to accommodate unexpected outcomes, it endows no absolute or enduring truths that might preclude its total abandonment.

Short of total abandonment, however, the same logic can be used to corroborate a model for the purposes of revision or refinement. Corroboration is the instrumentalist's technique for coping with rapid change and the emergence of unanticipated phenomena. By modeling past events, it should be possible to predict a current state of affairs. The degree of correspondence between the observable present and that anticipated by the model is assumed to indicate the areas in which the model requires further elaboration or modification if it is to provide adequate forecasts of similar events in the future. As time goes on, this continual check for correspondence serves to realign the model with emerging realities. Although the instrumentalist does not believe that evidence of past events can provide guidance to what ought to occur in the future, the conventional status of his model does permit an analog that is successfully corroborated by past and present events to guide his activities until observable events outstrip its predictive capability. Rigorous modifications of the model to accommodate unanticipated circumstances are expected to produce a more precise tool for pinpointing the course of future events. Any model that cannot account for the present on its own terms cannot be expected to offer much of a prognosis for the future. In this regard, the instrumentalist is a fallibilist. He uses evidence of emerging realities to corroborate and retune the assumptions imbedded in his models.

Given this programmatic commitment to refine, revise and, failing that, to replace one's models, instrumentalism takes on the appearance of a methodology devoid of continuity. What remains constant throughout the upgrading of a model or the shift from one model to another is the purpose behind a particular course of inquiry or intervention. This corresponds to the notion of a mission that Pastalan (Chapter 8) has offered as an alternative to theory in the guidance of applied research. However, the larger question is, how to identify and defend the sense of purpose or mission that underlies a particular research or design activity. The rationalists do so by negotiation. The empiricists insist that the justification of intention is a moral or ethical issue that lies beyond the scope of scientific authority. Consequently, they negotiate their missions much as do the rationalists. The structuralists derive a sense of mission in accord with inviolable constraints defined by the known limits of all the relationships at issue. Yet each of these programs can fall back on a cushion of self-evident, proven, or generic truths that appear to preserve scientific credibility in spite of the imposition of these extra-scientific authorities. Each program assumes that no consensual, ethical, or deterministic directive can prevail if it flies in the face of true representations of a pervasive and continuous reality. By adopting the notion that the only pervasive continuum is the imperfect process of knowing and acting, the instrumentalist rejects the absolute and enduring notions of truth, and he thereby loses the cushion that established truths afford the extra-scientific ploys of the other programs. This places an added burden on the manner in which instrumentalist missions are defined. Unfortunately, the instrumentalist procedures in this regard are not as well formulated as their ideals. They believe that the phenomenal world is too complex and that our knowledge of it is too imperfect to warrant the justification of any course of action on the basis of established evidence alone. What ought to be cannot be derived from what is known to be or known to have been. Consequently, the initial assertion of a mission must be accepted on nonevidential, presumptive grounds alone. In essence, a mission is the normative form of a conceptual framework. Rather than a presumptive sense of the way in which environments and behaviors are related, a mission is a presumption of the way in which they ought to be related. Although the conventionalist status of instrumentalist knowledge does permit relevant precedents, facts, and constraints to contribute to the identification of research or design intentions, there is no delusion that such inputs endow a mission with any reality status, apart from its role in the guidance of inquiry or intervention. The key to the whole program is that one cannot justify a mission on methodological grounds alone. No properly established argument, proof, or rule can justify the assertion of research or design intentions.

In spite of this recognition that missions are necessarily presumptive, there are certain criteria that they must meet if they are to provide instrumentalism with a respectable degree of coherence, consistency, and continuity. A mission must be explicit. It has to include a definitive interpretation of prevailing and preferred states of affairs, together with some specification of the events or situations that are presumed to lie in between. In effect, a mission must provide explicit criteria against which the appropriateness of specific models can be assessed. Although they are quite general and somewhat vague, these simple criteria give the instrumentalist the greatest possible latitude to embark on a positive course of action equipped with little more than the presumptive model of reality and disciplinary conventions already at his disposal. This also means that our various senses of mission and the ranges of models applicable thereto are largely predetermined by our conceptual and disciplinary commitments. For example, we would expect advocates of the performance framework to pursue missions related to efficiency and to select models in which rates of time, energy, or capital expenditure could be readily plotted against physical parameters and behavioral outcomes. Furthermore, a commitment to this position virtually obligates a researcher or designer to attempt to alleviate any counterproductive inefficiencies that he identifies or anticipates. On the other hand, advocates of the prosthetic framework probably could not concur that inefficiencies ought to be corrected unless a detrimental impact on specific human needs could be shown to result. In fact, in most cases a prosthetic model will not even reveal dysfunctional relationships in the form of inefficiencies.

Obviously, the instrumentalist believes that it is the way that we look at a situation that determines the way that we can most effectively deal with it. For example, he would permit those inclined to address inefficiencies or human needs through improved staff training and testing programs to seek guidance in different kinds of models than those who pursue similar missions through improved building design. Rather than develop critical replications to determine which of several competing approaches is the right one, the instrumentalist encourages the proliferation and pursuit of workable alternatives. Once again, the instrumentalist program boils down to objectives and initiatives that derive their authority not from evidence of an ongoing reality, but from an open acknowledgement of the continuity and pervasiveness of diverse conceptual and disciplinary commitments within the research and design communities.

To those schooled in the more traditional scientific traditions, the presumptive assertion of missions and their use as criteria for the selection of appropriate models will appear quite arbitrary. Yet the instrumentalist holds that, just as corroboration can lead to the refinement and revision of models, so similar techniques can contribute to the systematic reformulation of the normative commitments imbedded in a particular mission. For want of a better term, I will call this strategy subsumption — the process of subsuming. Much as the cumulative retrodictions associated with corroboration realign a model with emerging events, subsumption realigns a mission with its phenomenal and temporal surroundings. Essentially, the approach begins with a hypothetical assumption that the mission in question is successfully fulfilled. The events specified as the desired state of affairs are thereby treated as fait accompli, and the model is then further projected over time or circumstance to ascertain whether or not any unwanted consequences might ultimately result. The method can be used to either subsume a particular mission in a larger temporal or situational context, or to subsume alternative missions advanced as responses to the same situation in order to establish their degree of compatibility. Subsumption will not decide whether a mission is right or wrong, but it can assess its appropriateness within a larger context and suggest a basis for reconsideration. The technique depends on the availability of well corroborated predictive models and on the availability of a pool of alternative approaches from which more inclusive formulations of similar situations can be drawn.

Both the scientific and technological procedures of the instrumentalist program begin with the overriding notion that presumptive initiatives and their subsequent refinements remain subject to further revision at all stages of a formal research or design program. In practice, the success of the instrumentalist's commitment to refinement and revision rests with the systematic interplay between corroboration and subsumption. Both are concerned with minimizing the counterintuitive and counterproductive consequences that our presumptive initiatives might otherwise produce in complex and rapidly changing situations. Given the uncertainties introduced by complexity and rapid change, no researcher or designer can avoid making mistakes. The objective of instrumentalism is to capitalize on the heuristic power of interacting missions and models within the research and design communities as a whole in order to avoid repetitions of mistakes already made and to minimize the risks associated with making new ones.

This program has certain disadvantages, including the lack of a definitive statement of its own procedural doctrine. More serious, however, is the fact that instrumentalism does not produce a cumulative body of substantiated knowledge. Its most inclusive missions and best corroborated models are neither absolute nor enduring. Rather, their life expectancies are limited by the duration of the situations to which they are addressed. As a result, instrumentalism cannot lead to the establishment of new models except for situations of intrinsically long duration or for mathematical functions that are devoid of situational content. This means that the instrumentalist must rely on those models offered by the advocates of other methodological programs. Even then, relatively few relationships are sufficiently well understood to permit their unqualified use as models. The greatest problem, however, stems from the presumptive manner in which missions or goals are initiated. The only technique available to refine or revise one of these normative presumptions must, itself, utilize a derivative of that presumption. This means that, in practice, the program is clearly tautological. However, this is also a problem for the rationalist, empiricist, and structuralist. The only difference lies in the instrumentalist's reluctance to accept the notion of absolute and enduring truth, while these other programs use this notion to conceal their inability to systematize their normative commitments.

Interestingly, what appears to be a disadvantage to a critic is often considered to be an advantage to the committed instrumentalist. By shedding the excess baggage of truth, the instrumentalist is free to dismiss many of those questions that are of minimal consequence to the issues at hand, but which often draw advocates of the other programs into pursuit. He is able to separate critical predictive relationships from the complications presented by surrounding events; he is able to define and measure his progress toward explicitly stated objectives; and he is able to revise his course of action as new manifestations of the situation at issue become apparent. To the charge that all of this is tautological, the instrumentalist can argue that, more than any other program, instrumentalism disentangles its own positive feedback cycle to provide unambiguous points for entry and exit. Its programmatic emphasis on explicitly specified intentions opens its successes and failures to additional feedback from the research and design communities as a whole. Perhaps instrumentalism's strongest point is its recognition that the greatest potential for understanding lies in the interplay between the initiatives taken by the various scientists and technologists commited to diverse missions and models, rather than in foolproof methods promising decisive assessments of pervasive and enduring truths.

The ideals of all programs of knowledge acquisition and use remain unfulfilled in practice, but for the purposes of guidance amid maximal uncertainty, instrumentalism demands the least compromise of the basic methodological commitments. It avoids the inflated methodological claims by which empiricism sanctifies factual knowledge; it is conceptually less cumbersome than is structuralism; and, unlike rationalism, it offers a systematic procedure for the resolution of biases. Although the instrumentalists may hang onto and breathe life into their successful models just as the empiricists and structuralists cling to their partially substantiated theories and taxonomies, the instrumentalists' strength remains an ability to focus on essentials — concise abstractions which permit positive action amid otherwise bewildering complexity and change. This is precisely what the other programs cannot provide. Such a program seems uniquely capable of capitalizing on the heuristic power of a research and design community with an interdisciplinary base as broad as environment and behavior. It also seems particularly well suited to applied research since the analysis of all relevant data need not be concluded prior to intervention. Rather, the introduction of much of the supporting evidence must coincide with the actual use of the model in a practical situation. In fact, in practice the scientific and methodological procedures of instrumentalism almost merge.

Although we could argue the pros and cons of the various methodological programs forever, I believe we can accept Pastalan's instrumental missions as viable alternatives to empirical theories on pragmatic rather than epistemological grounds. Most of the environmental situations that confront the aged are too complex and too unstable to permit the rigorous procedures demanded by the other programs to guide our attempts to understand and assist them. Instrumentalism allows us to proceed toward our objectives from where we are, rather than from where an idealized knowledge base would have us be. Its technological guidance is immediate, explicit, and responsive to emergent events and circumstantial complexity. That there will always be some question as to whether or not he has pursued the proper objective or mission is the price the instrumentalist must be willing to pay for the opportunity to act in situations which the rationalists, empiricists, and structuralists lack the means to understand in the time available.

In accepting guidance from missions rather than from theories, I have glossed over one critical inconsistency in Pastalan's presentation. If we are concerned with conceptual symmetry, we must note that it is the model, not the mission, that is the methodological counterpart of a theory. Yet a theory has continuity that a model does not have. In the instrumentalist program it is the mission that remains constant throughout the course of inquiry or intervention. However, a mission is presumptive and a theory is not. As a resolution to this conundrum, I suggest that we consider that the distinction that concerns us is that between empiricism and instrumentalism, and that we recognize that the formal components of the two programs are not directly comparable. This is not simply a matter of replacing descriptive or explanatory formulations with intentions or goals. As some have suggested in other contexts (Marney & Smith, 1972), I believe that Pastalan is asking us to restructure the epistemological commitments that underlie our whole approach to the problems that concern us. It is in this light that I endorse his position.

Fortunately, most of us have already fallen back on the instrumentalist procedures at one time or another for heuristic reasons. It has probably helped all of us get past some of the rough spots created by inconsistencies in whatever program we were schooled to abide by. It is the basis for inserting intervening variables or hypothetical constructs into testable hypotheses. These are among the things we all do when our concern for developing new knowledge or achieving preferred states of affairs surpasses our commitment to methodological elegance. As the result of these precedents, I see little difficulty in adopting instrumentalism as the normal program for scientific conduct in the area of environment and behavior. Perhaps I have read my own views between Pastalan's lines, but if I have added too much to his remarks, I can only say that I endorse the basic provisions of a program of knowledge acquisition and use that provides for its own reformulation in the light of emerging evidence and acknowledges that our best knowledge will be forever tentative.

To those who find this somewhat bizarre, if not completely absurd, I offer this note concerning the delusions that have been created by the emulation of physics by the social sciences. From the instrumentalist's viewpoint, it is clear that one of the reasons that nineteenth century physics is upheld as a paragon of science is that it was generally concerned with extremely stable relationships. This meant that its findings had maximum survival value which, in turn, gave them the appearance of absolute and enduring truths. This is one of the reasons that nineteenth century physics provides the instrumentalist with so many of his models — hydraulics, gravity, thermodynamics, and so forth. To those familiar with this history, I suggest further consideration of two branches of physics that do not conform to this scientistic dogma, namely meteorology and climatology. Neither lends itself to precedented explanations, isolated experimentation, or generic analysis. I suggest that if we need precedents from the hard sciences, we ought to choose these, rather than physical optics or fluid mechanics, because their encounters with uncertainty are perhaps more analogous to our own (Kellogg & Schneider, 1974). If we are ever going to provide service to the aged, we must be willing to adopt a methodological position that is responsive to their rapidly changing environmental circumstances, rather than to our own stature within the scientific community.

While Pastalan has presumed too much coherence in our interdisciplinary enterprise, he is certainly not alone in doing so. It is the responsibility of all of us to consider the consequences of our conceptual and methodological diversity. Ever since we inherited Pruitt-Igoe (the immense St. Louis public housing project whose social problems finally had to be solved by demolition) as an exemplar of maximally dysfunctional relationships between environment and behavior, we have been groping for the handle by which we could pick up the pieces and reassemble a more supportive environment. In a sense, this is our collective mission, and in pursuing it we have legitimized among ourselves the field known variously as environmental psychology, architectural psychology, man-environment relations, or ecological psychology. We no longer bury our findings in the discussion section of personality inventories or the introductions of design programs. We all believe that it is perfectly reasonable to study and design the fit between individuals or groups and their physical environments — but we all hold onto different handles. As a result, our collective activities do not have the appearance of a self-conscious, internally consistent discipline to those looking in from the outside — to legislators, regulators, designers, programmers, and others. So long as we force our audiences to infer our meanings by reading between the lines, we will fail to attract enthusiastic external support for what we do. Until what we can do to prevent another Pruitt-Igoe from appearing on the streets of our own hometowns becomes clear, we will continue to be seen as interesting curiosities by those who might otherwise embrace our cause. We are too thinly spread to synthesize our diverse capabilities. We must be willing to stake much stronger claims upon our several commitments than Pastalan, or any of us, thus far seem willing or able to do.

With regard to Pastalan's applied orientation, I see great possibilities in looking to the instrumentalist program for systematic guidance. Traditionally, researchers have dealt with knowledge as empiricists or structuralists, and designers have dealt with it as rationalists. Altman (1973) has portrayed this as a conflict between the researcher's concern for behavioral processes and the designer's concern for environmental products. Such differences have created much of our difficulty in reconciling intuitions with evidence. However, by adopting the instrumentalist's notion that knowledge is conventional and has no authority rooted in reality, we create the potential for reconciling this dilemma (see Simon, 1969). We can even regard the designer's creations as the bases for corroborating models that would have the net effect of a two-way exchange between the research and design communities, rather than the applied science model that still prevails. Yet, this methodological shift does not reconcile our conceptual differences and I do not think any attempts to do so will prove successful. However, it might be possible to do precisely what the instrumentalist does when he sets criteria for his presumptive missions — set explicit criteria for the expression of our presumptions of reality. To this end, I propose that those who perceive their missions in terms of the physical environment's impact on behavior attempt to formulate their positions in terms of explicit, self-conscious, and internally consistent relationships in which the architect can recognize the environmental component as something he manipulates when he designs, and the psychologist can recognize the behavioral component as something he can come to deal with as behavior. This is, presumably, no more than our various conceptual frameworks already set out to do. The only change needed is the forced explication of what has heretofore been implicit.

While I see this as an obligation for all of us, in Pastalan's case I see unique ramifications that relate to both what he is looking at and to what others might plan to do with what they think he sees. His forced relocation study has shown that certain patterns of using built environments can kill people. His empathic model begins to show how. This adds a great deal of weight to his work because, unlike much of our research, he has touched upon values which our society holds sacrosanct. Death, injury, and crime need not be explained in order to attract our collective attentions. The fact that Pastalan's work begins to implicate the physical environment in two of these areas creates the possibility for attracting the external mandate that our field has thus far been denied. Studies of satisfaction, isolation, and sense of community are interesting. Studies of mortality demand a response. It is for this reason that I feel that Pastalan must clarify his conceptual position. He has offered us something that we do not have to evaluate on moral or ethical grounds — our culture has done that for us. His work, like Newman's (1972), demands an immediate and active response. In order to avoid catastrophic misapplication, it must be made far more explicit than his presentation shows it to be.

CONCLUSION

Although some may argue that environment-behavior studies represent a new concern that simply has not had enough time to mature beyond its pre-scientific beginnings, I see no justification for the expectation that our collective efforts will ultimately coalesce into a normal science (Archea, 1975). As a field we are abnormal in almost every sense of the word. The abnormal breadth of our disciplinary heritage seems to generate abnormal conflicts that none of our scientific or professional predecessors had need to resolve. Accordingly, we find ourselves with an unfamiliar challenge to innovate methodologically as well as conceptually. If we are to meet this challenge, we must be willing to ask the kinds of procedural questions that we have been trained not to ask and to take the kinds of intellectual risks that we have been accustomed not to take. And we must do both within a self-imposed discipline that we never expected to have to apply to ourselves.

REFERENCES

Alexander, C., Ishikawa, S., and Silverstein, M. *A pattern language: Towns, buildings, construction.* New York: Oxford University Press, 1977.

Altman, I. Some perspectives on the study of man-environment phenomena. *Representative Research in Social Psychology,* 1973, 4, 109–126.

Archea, J. Establishing an interdisciplinary commitment. In B. Honikman (Ed.), *Responding to social change.* Stroudsburg, PA.: Dowden, Hutchinson & Ross, 1975.

Archea, J. The place of architectural factors in behavioral theories of privacy. *Journal of Social Issues,* 1977, 33, 116–137.

Barker, R. Ecology and motivation. In M. Jones (Ed.), *Nebraska symposium on motivation.* Lincoln: University of Nebraska Press, 1960.

Barker, R. *Ecological psychology: Concepts and methods for studying the environment of human behavior.* Stanford, CA.: Stanford University Press, 1968.

Bechtel, R. B. *Enclosing behavior.* Stroudsburg, PA.: Dowden, Hutchinson & Ross, 1977.

Campbell, D. T. and Stanley, J. C. *Experimental and quasi-experimental designs for research.* Chicago: Rand McNally, 1966.

Canter, D. *The psychology of place.* New York: St. Martin's Press, 1977.

Chapin, F. S., Jr. *Human activity patterns in the city: Things people do in time and in space.* New York: Wiley Interscience, 1974.

Christaller, W. *Central places in southern Germany.* C. W. Baskin (Trans.). Englewood Cliffs, NJ.: Prentice-Hall, 1966.

Cohen, H. L. Designs for learning: Case/space studies in a university, a prison, a laboratory, and a public school. In D. H. Carson (Ed.), *Man-environment interactions: Evaluations and applications,* Vol. 7, R. A. Chase (Vol. Ed.). Washington, D.C.: Environmental Design Research Association, 1974.

Craik, K. H. The personality research paradigm in environmental psychology. In S. Wapner, S. B. Cohen, and B. Kaplan (Eds.), *Experiencing the environment.* New York: Plenum Press, 1976.

De Long, A. J. The communication process: A generic model for man-environment relations. *Man-Environment Systems,* 1972, 2, 263–313.

Eberhard, J. *The performance concept: A study of its applications to housing.* Washington, D.C.: National Bureau of Standards, 1969.

Festinger, L., Schachter, S., and Back, K. *Social pressures in informal groups.* Stanford, CA.: Stanford University Press, 1950.

Gibson, J. J. *The senses considered as perceptual systems.* New York: Houghton Mifflin, 1966.

Glaser, B. and Strauss, A. L. *The discovery of grounded theory: Strategies for qualitative research.* Chicago: Aldine, 1967.

Goffman, E. *Relations in public: Microstudies of the public order.* New York: Basic Books, 1971.

Hagerstrand, T. *Innovation diffusion as a spatial process.* A. R. Pred (Trans.). Chicago: University of Chicago Press, 1967.

Hall, E. T. *The hidden dimension.* Garden City, NY.: Doubleday, 1966.

Helson, H. *Adaptation level theory.* New York: Harper & Row, 1964.

Hillier, B. and Leaman, A. Structure, system, transformation: Sciences of organization and sciences of the artificial. *Transactions of the Bartlett Society,* 1973, 9, 36–77.

Kellogg, W. W. and Schneider, S. H. Climate stabilization: For better or for worse? *Science*, 1974, *186*, 1163–1172.

Kelly, G. A. *The psychology of personal constructs*. New York: Norton, 1955.

Kuhn, T. S. The structure of scientific revolutions. In O. Neurath, R. Carnap, and C. Morris (Eds.), *International encyclopedia of unified science*, Vol. II. Chicago: University of Chicago Press, 1962.

Lakatos, I. Falsification and the methodology of scientific research programs. In I. Lakatos and A. Musgrave (Eds.), *Criticism and the growth of knowledge*. London: Cambridge University Press, 1970.

Lee, T. Urban neighborhood as a socio–spatial schema. *Human Relations*, 1968, *21*, 241–267.

Lynch, K. *The image of the city*. Cambridge, MA.: M.I.T. Press, 1960.

Marney, M. and Smith, N. Interdisciplinary synthesis. *Policy Sciences*, 1972, *3*, 299–323.

Maslow, A. H. *Motivation and personality*. New York: Harper, 1954.

McKechnie, G. E. *Manual for the Environmental Response Inventory*. Palo Alto, CA.: Consulting Psychologists Press, 1974.

Moore, G. T. and Golledge, R. G. *Environmental knowing*. Stroudsburg, PA.: Dowden, Hutchinson & Ross, 1976.

Neurath, O., Carnap, R., and Morris, C. *International encyclopedia of unified science*. Chicago: University of Chicago Press, 1955.

Newman, O. *Defensible space*. New York: Macmillan, 1972.

Peirce, C. S. Synechism, fallibilism, and evolution. In J. Buchler (Ed.), *Philosophical writings of Peirce*. New York: Dover, 1955.

Piaget, J. *Genetic epistemology*. E. Duckworth (Trans.). New York: Norton, 1971.

Popper, K. R. *Conjectures and refutations: The growth of scientific knowledge*. New York: Basic Books, 1962.

Radnitzky, G. *Contemporary schools of metascience*. Lund: Scandinavian University Books, 1970.

Rapoport, A. An approach to the construction of man-environment theory. In W. F. E. Preiser (Ed.), *Environmental design research*, Vol. 2. Stroudsburg, PA.: Dowden, Hutchinson & Ross, 1973.

Selye, H. *The stress of life*. New York: McGraw-Hill, 1956.

Shevky, E. and Bell, W. *Social area analysis*. Stanford, CA.: Stanford University Press, 1955.

Simon, H. A. *The sciences of the artificial*. Cambridge, MA.: M.I.T. Press, 1969.

Skinner, B. F. *Science and human behavior*. New York: Macmillan, 1953.

Snow, C. P. *The two cultures: And a second look*. London: Cambridge University Press, 1964.

Sommer, R. *Personal space: The behavioral basis of design*. Englewood Cliffs, NJ.: Prentice-Hall, 1969.

Stokols, D. Environmental psychology. *Annual Review of Psychology*, 1978, *29*, 253–295.

Studer, R. G. The dynamics of behavior-contingent physical systems. In G. Broadbent and A. Ward (Eds.), *Design methods in architecture*. New York: Wittenborn, 1969.

Thiel, P. Notes on the description, scaling, notation, and scoring of some perceptual and cognitive attributes of the physical environment. In H. Proshansky, W. H. Ittelson, and L. G. Rivlin (Eds.), *Environmental psychology: Man and his physical setting*. New York: Holt, Rinehart & Winston, 1970.

Webb, E. J., Campbell, D. T., Schwartz, R. D., and Sechrest, L. *Unobtrusive measures: Nonreactive research in the social sciences*. Chicago: Rand McNally, 1966.

Willems, E. P. Behavioral ecology as a perspective for man-environment research. In W. F. E. Preiser (Ed.), *Environmental design research*, Vol. 2. Stroudsburg, PA.: Dowden, Hutchinson & Ross, 1973.

Wohlwill, J. F. *Behavioral response and adaptation to environmental stimulation*. Man-Environment Relations Working Paper 72. Pennsylvania State University, 1972.

INDEX